100 WINNING RESUMES
FOR $100,000+ JOBS

100 WINNING RESUMES FOR $100,000+ JOBS

Resumes That Can Change Your Life!

Wendy S. Enelow

IMPACT PUBLICATIONS
Manassas Park, VA

100 WINNING RESUMES FOR $100,000+ JOBS

Library of Congress Cataloging-in-Publication Data

Enelow, Wendy S.
    100 winning resumes for $100,000+ jobs: resumes that can change your life / Wendy S. Enelow.
        p. cm.
    ISBN 1-57023-070-6
    1. Resumes (Employment) I. Title. II. Title: One-hundred winning resumes for one-hundred thousand dollar plus jobs
HF5383.E476 1997
808'.06665--dc21   97-7914
                                                                                CIP

For information on distribution or quantity discount rates, call (703/361-7300), FAX (703/335-9486), or write to: Sales Department, IMPACT PUBLICATIONS, 9104-N Manassas Drive, Manassas Park, VA 20111. Distributed to the trade by National Book Network, 4720 Boston Way, Suite A, Lanham, MD 20706, Tel. 301/459-8696.

CONTENTS

v

ACKNOWLEDGEMENTS

This book is ...

... Dedicated to everyone who has struggled with resume writing and job search. Here are practical tools, techniques, styles, formats and language that WILL accelerate your search.

... Dedicated to the thousands of executives with whom I have worked to plan and direct their job search campaigns. Thank you for all you have taught me — about different industries, technologies, markets, management disciplines and more.

... Dedicated to all of my clients who have said "Thanks. You got me a job!" I appreciate this, but can't take the credit. A resume has one purpose and only one purpose — to get an interview. Thanks for the thanks, but it was you and only you who got the job. Congratulations!

... Dedicated to Rebecca Stokes without whose untiring efforts and editorial assistance this book would not have been possible.

And a special thank you to my husband and my son who have given so freely for years and years, allowing me the time to devote to my business, my clients and my writing. You guys are great!

100 WINNING RESUMES
FOR $100,000+ JOBS

CHAPTER ONE

WRITING WINNING RESUMES

Is This You?

✓ **AN ACCOMPLISHED CEO**, successful in virtually every endeavor you have ever attempted. You're respected by your colleagues and known throughout your industry. Now you're faced with a simple task — just write your resume. How difficult can that be? Weeks later, you're nowhere. The strategies, words and concepts just won't come.

✓ **A TALENTED MARKETING PROFESSIONAL** with years of experience writing brochures, press releases, direct mail communications and more. You sit down to write your resume and nothing happens. Nothing. Hours, days and sometimes even weeks later, you finally have your resume complete. You hate it. It's the same as everyone else's. Nothing is sharp. Nothing is competitive.

✓ **A TOP-PERFORMING SALES EXECUTIVE** who can sell anything to anybody. No matter the challenge, the product or the market, you have always produced. You figure that writing a resume is nothing more than selling your qualifications. And, you're right. You sit at your PC for the next two days trying to determine the best selling strategy. Finally you quit. You just don't know how to sell the product when you are the product!

✓ **A SOPHISTICATED FINANCIAL EXECUTIVE** with more than 20 years experience as CFO of a Fortune 500 corporation. You're known throughout the market for your expertise in deal making, negotiating, capital financing and corporate treasury. You are a pro. When you've finished your resume, you're appalled. Your resume looks like that of every other senior finance executive. Nothing is different. Nothing is distinctive.

If any of these sound familiar, then this book is for you. If you don't fall into any of these categories, but have struggled to prepare a resume, then this book is also for you. In it, you will find the SOLUTIONS for successful resume writing and job search management.

COMPETITIVE RESUME WRITING

A New Marketing Discipline & Art

Over the past decade, as the U.S. employment market has undergone dramatic and long-lasting changes, resume writing has evolved into a much more complex and more sophisticated process. No longer is it sufficient to type a brief listing of your work history and academic credentials. Remember the days when you did this, mailed a handful of resumes to recruiters and a handful in response to advertisements? Within a week you were interviewing and within 2-3 weeks you were working.

If you remember this, forget it! The times have changed and the market has changed. Today, resume writing is a competition among often very well-qualified professionals vying for a limited number of opportunities. There's more competition than ever before. And the competition is more qualified than ever in the history of our job market. What strategies and tactics can you deploy that will differentiate you from the crowd?

Resume writing has evolved into an art. Your challenge is to consolidate the highlights of your professional career, creating a resume that is dynamic, distinctive, hard-hitting and competitive. You must determine what experiences, qualifications and accomplishments you have to "sell" that will distinguish you from the crowd and position you for job interviews and offers. You must be aggressive and focused in conveying your message. And you must fit your resume onto 1-2 pages.

Yes, that's right. Your resume should never be longer than 2 pages (unless an unusual circumstance). You're creating a "snapshot" of your career, not an autobiographical essay of your entire past. The writing and presentation must be crisp and "top-of-the-line." We've all heard the cliche that "you have just one chance to make a first impression." This is essential in resume writing, cover letter writing and job search management.

Are there any circumstances when a 3+ page resume IS appropriate?

YES. Consider this. You're the CEO of a Fortune 50 company applying for a position as CEO of another Fortune 50 company. Although your professional work experience is the most critical, so are your professional affiliations, civic affiliations, non-profit affiliations, public speaking engagements, Board of Director appointments, teaching experience and other professional activities. In a circumstance such as this, where the candidates are the top in the country, the search is quite selective and the stakes are high, often a longer resume is a more appropriate tool. The company is not just hiring the professional, they are hiring the person, his/her network of contacts and his/her reputation. Longer resumes are quite acceptable in this situation.

For any of you in academia, scientific or medical research, or health care, you know that your curriculum vitae (not resume) can be longer than two pages. For those of you not familiar with CVs, they are vastly different than resumes. The purpose of a resume is to "sell". The purpose of a CV is to highlight professional credentials, distinctions, research projects, technological skills, teaching and educational experiences, publications, symposia, etc. CVs are often lengthy documents, and are appropriate tools for professionals in education, medicine, research and science.

> **Keep your message strong, succinct and dynamic!**

RULES FOR RESUME WRITING

The best part of resume writing is that there are no rules!

On the one hand, this is great. You have lots of room for creativity and flair in presenting your qualifications. On the other hand, it often makes the task more difficult. If there are no rules, no specific formats and no definitive strategy, how are you supposed to know what to do? It can be a complicated and confusing process.

But, it can also be fun, challenging and tremendously worthwhile when you are finished. There is little else that is as personally and professionally rewarding than to view your own resume, your accomplishments, your contributions and your overall career success. It is energizing and a key component to your successful job search campaign!

Of course, you'll want to include your work history and educational credentials in your resume. Other than that, what information you include, how and where you include it, and why you include it, are up to you. There no are limits; there are no restrictions.

The single most critical element in determining what information to include in your resume is your current objective(s). Your resume must support your current goals, highlight your experiences and qualifications most related to those goals, and favorably position you for the position you are seeking.

Here's a quick example. Let's say that from 1984 to 1994 you were General Manager of a large manufacturer. Then, from 1994 to the present, you were Vice President of Sales & Marketing. Your goal today is to get back into General Management. What types of achievements, responsibilities and skills will you highlight in your resume? General management of course, with sales and marketing as a secondary skill, even though it has been the most recent experience. If your goal is sales and marketing management, the strategy would be exactly the opposite.

I often refer to this as "painting the right picture". In other words, you appropriately weight your skills and experience, shifting the focus to the areas most in line with your current objectives. Items on your resume do not have to be weighted according to actual responsibility, but rather in the manner that will alert your audience to what is most important in your job search today.

BUILDING YOUR RESUME

The Structure & The Process

OBJECTIVE

Should you use an objective on your resume? This can often be a tough call. Objectives are often quite limiting in terms of type of position and industry: **"Seeking a position in Pharmaceutical Sales & Marketing."**or, so broad that they say nothing: **"Seeking a senior-level management position where I can lead a company to improved revenues and profitability."**

If you are certain of your career goal, and are not going to look at any opportunities that do not fall into that category, then an Objective is appropriate. However, if you want to be able to use your resume in a number of different situations, then do not include an Objective, and certainly not one that is so broad that it tells your reader nothing.

Do not feel as though you must change your Objective each time to match the position to which you are applying. You want the resume process is to be easy and fast. In the vast majority of situations, you want to use the same resume over and over, modifying only your cover letter for each specific opportunity.

In situations where you do not use an Objective, let your cover letter speak of what your Objective is to each prospective employer. This gives you the opportunity to customize your Objective to that specific organization and their specific needs.

> ### REMEMBER:
> *The single most critical element in your job search is to get your resumes out -- as many and as quickly as possible. Let the process be easy!*

CAREER SUMMARY

(AKA Executive Profile, Career Profile, Core Competencies or Qualifications Summary)

When you write an Objective, you are telling your reader what you want from them. When you start your resume with a Career Summary, you are telling your reader what you can do for them and what value you bring to their organization.

A Career Summary is a brief section that highlights your skills, qualifications, knowledge and achievements, and is designed to give a quick overview of your career history. The Career Summary can be written in a paragraph, as a bulleted list of items, or any combination thereof. In essence, you take your entire professional career and consolidate it into a 1-2 page resume. Now, take the resume and consolidate into an inch or two at the top — your Summary.

Career Summaries are the single most effective tool for establishing the reader's perception of "who you are" based upon your current objectives. It is this section that allows you to "paint the picture" you want someone to see as they review your experience and your "fit" within their organization.

PROFESSIONAL EXPERIENCE

This is **THE SECTION** — your opportunity to highlight your professional experience, qualifications and achievements. Give careful thought and consideration to what you include under each job description. **EACH WORD COUNTS**!

Your challenge here is to briefly, yet aggressively describe your professional experience. For each position, you want to highlight four important things:

- **What did the company do** (A manufacturer? A distributor? A worldwide technology leader? A multi-site service organization?)

- **Your challenge** (Was it a start-up venture, a turnaround or a high-growth organization? Why did they hire you? Was it to manage the "status-quo" or did you have a special mission?)

- **Your accountability** (Overall, what is it that you were responsible for in terms of type and size of organization, number of employees, budgets, facilities, countries, regions, technologies, functions and operations?)

- **Your achievements** (What did you produce and contribute?)

Achievements are great things!

Achievements allow you to distinguish yourself from the crowd of other qualified candidates who have been responsible for the same types of functions, but who have perhaps not performed as successfully as you. For example, each CEO, CFO or Sales Director is basically responsible for the same functions. What then do you use to distinguish one from the other? The answer is quite simple —**ACHIEVEMENTS**.

To get you started in highlighting your achievements and your contributions, consider the following sample achievements. Do any of these items sound familiar?

- Increased sales by 48% across six major market segments and despite emerging competition.
- Accelerated annual profit contributions by more than 28% over previous year.
- Led the development of emerging client/server technology, from concept through R&D and manufacturing to nationwide market launch. Created what is now a $16 million revenue center for the XYZ Corporation.
- Drove market share from 10% to 22% within first six months through transition to customer-focused selling and account management strategies.
- Reengineered all critical production planning, scheduling and manufacturing processes for a 12% reduction in annual operating costs.

- Realigned field sales organization, consolidated similar markets and reduced staffing expense by 27%.
- Conceived and implemented a team-based project design and management process, increasing on-time project delivery and significantly enhancing customer retention.
- Spearheaded acquisition and implementation of advanced robotics technologies, virtually eliminated competition and won a $15 million, 5-year contract.
- Honored as 1995 "Sales Director of the Year" (out of 25 candidates).
- Won 6 sales recognition awards, 3 over-quota sales awards and the corporation's most prestigious leadership commendation.
- Revitalized customer service organization, recruited qualified management team, and increased customer satisfaction ratings from 76% to 98%.
- Identified opportunity and negotiated a strategic alliance with Uniroyal for development of on-site manufacturing and distribution operations in China.
- Orchestrated the company's successful and profitable expansion throughout emerging international markets (e.g., Africa, India, Middle East, Far East).
- Recruited and developed 10 sales representatives subsequently promoted to district and regional management positions.
- Architected the corporation's 5-year strategic business plan that positioned XYZ for 25%+ annual revenue and market growth.
- Directed start-up of new manufacturing venture that grew to more than $22 million in first year sales.
- Surpassed all turnaround objectives with 25% revenue and 37% profit gain.
- Structured and negotiated 12 mergers and acquisitions as part of the corporation's aggressive growth and corporate development initiative.
- Introduced quality circles, implemented TQM principles and led organization to ISO 9000 certification.
- Personally negotiated $2 million capital financing transaction.

NOTE: *These achievements are merely representative and given to you as "food for thought" in identifying and highlighting your own career achievements. Place your focus on the value you have delivered to your previous employers and the value you bring to a new organization.*

Position Descriptions

Start each position description with a brief introductory paragraph detailing your challenges and overall responsibilities. Then follow with a bulleted listing of your achievements and contributions. In essence, you're telling your reader —*"This is what I did and this is how well I did it."* The concept is simple; the impact significant.

Follow this same format all the way through your resume, becoming more and more brief as you get further back in time. Focus on achievements in earlier positions, not necessarily on your responsibilities unless than were unusual and/or vast.

How far back in time do you go when listing your employment experience? You certainly do not want to disqualify yourself because of your age. Unfortunately, there is no hard and fast rule. I like a "clean" picture. If you graduated from college anytime after 1968, include the date of graduation and all employment that follows. You don't have to include much detail about the early positions (you can list them or summarize in a paragraph), but show your career path and progression.

If you graduated from college prior to 1968, it is recommended to "cut" your employment history at some point (usually early to mid 1970's) and then summarize key items from past experiences. These key items might include:

- Well-known or well-respected companies.
- Fast-track promotion.
- Something you accomplished that was GREAT.
- Emerging products and technology experience.
- International experience.

EDUCATION

Include all college degrees, major courses of study and colleges/universities. DATE them all, unless they were received 30+ years ago. There is virtually no reason that you would ever show a date in the 1950's. Why give someone a reason to immediately exclude you with no thought to your achievements and your value?

It is not necessary to include colleges you attended, but from which you did not receive a degree. However, if you do not have a degree, you would, of course, include attendance with major course of study, name of college/university and dates (as appropriate).

Be sure to include all relevant professional certifications and licenses. In relation to continuing professional education, give a good sampling of course titles, universities, sponsoring organizations and dates. It is not necessary to include them all — just the highlights (particularly those most relevant to your current career objectives).

PROFESSIONAL & COMMUNITY AFFILIATIONS

Include a listing of professional and community organizations to which you belong and any specific leadership roles, committee memberships or accomplishments. You may also include any volunteer experience in this category that you feel is appropriate to your career objective. Don't overdo it — people will wonder how you have the time to work!

TECHNOLOGY SKILLS

Include your knowledge and proficiency with mainframe, PC, client/server, telecommunications, internet and other technologies. If you are not in the Information Technology industry, a brief mention in your Career Summary may be appropriate. If you are in the industry, and depending upon your specific expertise, this section may be much more detailed and include your specific technical qualifications — hardware, software, operating systems, programming languages, network protocols, etc.

HONORS & AWARDS

Include your honors, awards, commendations and recognition. This information can be integrated into your job descriptions, included under Education (if appropriate) or put into a separate category at the end of your resume. If any are of significant note (e.g., national awards, advertising awards, #1 industry ranking), you may even want to include them in your Career Summary. Use a subheading titled "Distinguished Credentials" or "Industry Honors & Awards" or "Professional Recognition".

PUBLICATIONS

Being published validates your expertise. Be sure to include your publications either in a separate category at the end of your resume or in a subheading in your Career Summary titled "Publications".

PUBLIC SPEAKING

List your public speaking engagements including title of presentation, audience, location and date. If the list is extensive, give a brief overview and only include the highlights (and, of course, those most related to your current career objectives).

TEACHING EXPERIENCE

If you are a teacher or trainer, this experience will be included in PROFESSIONAL EXPERIENCE. If, however, you are a business professional who has also taught, be sure to include this information. Just like publications, it immediately validates your qualifications. List course, school, undergraduate/graduate and dates.

FOREIGN LANGUAGE AND TRAVEL

We are all becoming global — in our businesses and often in our private lives. Be sure to include your foreign language skills and travel experience either in your Career Summary or at the end of your resume.

PERSONAL INFORMATION

I do not recommend the inclusion of personal information such as birth date, marital status, health, children, etc. Nor am I keen on hobbies and interests. I only recommend that you include this information if:

- Required by the employer.
- Important because of a unique situation (e.g., you want someone to know that you are an American citizen; you want someone to realize that you are not as old or as young as they might think).
- You have unusual interests that will grab someone's attention. I know executives who were past Olympians, have ascended mountains on all seven continents, have trekked through "untrekkable" places, are competitive triathletes and more. This type of information really sells. Include it.

NOTE: Consolidate all of the "extras" — Affiliations, Publications, Languages, etc. is under one heading titled "Professional Profile." Try this format:

PROFESSIONAL PROFILE

Affiliations	Chairman, National Industries Association
	Chairman, Industry Oversight National Association
Publications	"Database Management," PC World, May 1992
	"Cybernetics," Digital Design, January 1991
	"Netscape," Digital & Electronics Design, April 1987
Languages	Fluent in German, Dutch and French.
PC Software	Microsoft Word, Excel, Lotus, PageMaker, WordPerfect

THE RESUME WRITING PROCESS

Everything in life has a process. Resume writing is no different. If you use the following structured process, you will find the task much easier and much faster.

1. Open a file in your PC.
2. Type your name, address and contact numbers.
3. Type in all major headings (e.g., Career Summary, Professional Experience, Education, Professional Profile).
4. Fill in Professional Profile. It's easy. It's only a list of information.
5. Fill in Education. It's easy. It's only a list of information.
6. Type in job titles, company names and dates.
7. Write your job descriptions. Start from your oldest job and work forward. The older jobs are easy to write. They're short and to the point, and only highlight the most significant responsibilities and achievements. As you work forward, each position requires a bit more text and a bit more thought. Before you know it, you'll be writing your most recent job. It takes the longest, but then you're almost finished in no time at all.
8. Write your Career Summary. It will be easy now that you've just written all of your job descriptions and everything is fresh in your mind. Remember to highlight the skills, qualifications and achievements most supportive of your

current career objectives.

NOTE: *If you try to write the Summary first, it will do you in! How can you write the Summary when you have't written the text. It can take hours instead of just a few minutes.*

TWO RULES TO LIVE BY

Rule #1 - PERFECTION IS MANDATORY

Visual presentation and perfection are critical! The quality of your resume presentation is almost as important as the content. Quality attracts attention and will instantly give you a competitive edge.

Remember, people do not meet you. They meet a piece of paper. Be sure that your resume reflects your style and quality. If it's poorly prepared and presented, it doesn't matter what it says — no one will read it.

Rule #2 - NO TWO RESUMES ARE IDENTICAL

Each and every resume is different. Your challenge is to develop a resume that will effectively market your qualifications and distinguish you from the crowd. There are no set rules for writing style, format, typing or printing. People are different, employment histories are different, career goals are different and resumes are different.

Each of the next 100 resume samples that follow are "real-life" examples (specifics have been changed to protect each executive's confidentiality). What's more important, each of these resumes has worked in opening doors, getting interviews and helping to close top-level management opportunities. Use the sample words, formats, strategies and concepts as your solution and your foundation for a high-profile, high-performing resume and job search campaign.

Position yourself as the #1 candidate.
Let the competition work to keep pace with you!

CHAPTER TWO

RESUME SAMPLES

Following are 100 resume samples, categorized by job function, for professional, management and executive job search candidates. Use them to get ideas, concepts, strategies, structures, formats and words to develop your own resume.

Look carefully at each sample. There is a strategy in every instance for why a format and presentation style was selected, based upon each individual's career history and current professional goals. Find a format that most closely matches your career track and then modify the text as appropriate.

Feel free to duplicate specific content, phrases, formats and styles as they relate to your experience. That's why you bought this book!

CAREER PROFILE

QUALIFICATIONS SUMMARY

PROFESSIONAL EXPERIENCE

CORE COMPETENCIES

EDUCATION & PROFESSIONAL DEVELOPMENT

TECHNOLOGY EXPERTISE

PROFESSIONAL AFFILIATIONS

FOREIGN LANGUAGE COMPETENCIES

PUBLICATIONS & PRESENTATIONS

JOHN P. SMITH

5555 North Avenue
Los Angeles, California 92009
(619) 222-3333

CORPORATE ACCOUNTING & FINANCE PROFESSIONAL
Start-Up, Turnaround & High-Growth Corporations

Eighteen years experience in the design, development and management of comprehensive corporate accounting, budgeting, financial reporting, financial modeling, tax and MIS systems. Consistently successful in linking accounting with general operations to provide hands-on financial leadership for strategic planning, technology R&D, sales/marketing, purchasing, inventory, production and distribution.

Delivered strong and sustainable revenue and income gains. Equally effective in capturing cost reductions through process redesign and performance management.

PROFESSIONAL EXPERIENCE:

Controller   1994 to Present
NEWS, INC., Los Angeles, California
(Acquired by International Publishing in December 1995)

Recruited as an Inventory Accountant in 1994 following the acquisition of News, Inc., a $50 million multi-media and CD-ROM software publisher. Promoted to Controller with full responsibility for accounts payable, accounts receivable, general ledger, royalty and contract management, departmental budgeting, and all related MIS operations. Direct a 3-person management team and 10+ support personnel.

- Reengineered royalty and licensing agreements in cooperation with the Legal and Licensing Departments. Incorporated sophisticated financial analysis into intellectual property negotiations, designed financial models and saved over $800,000.

- Designed an Excel relational database daily revenue flash report which graphically depicted gross shipments and returns by product line. Provided senior executives with accurate data to evaluate actual sales performance versus plan in this rapidly changing commercial market.

- Launched a process-by-process redesign of key accounting functions, consolidated workflow, streamlined staffing requirements and captured over $190,000 in annual savings.

- Accelerated internal automation and full use of existing system applications. Brought inventory control module on-line, resulting in annual physical adjustment of less than 1%. Currently transitioning (via electronic transmission conversion) from AccPac to J.D. Edwards software.

- Modified amortization schedules for capitalized software development costs for the R&D Department, linked with actual units sold and integrated payroll costs to more accurately record profit margins and recapture development expenses.

    NOTE: *Instrumental in positioning division for sale at twice the acquisition cost after only two years. Assisted Price Waterhouse in preparation of 8K filings for the SEC.*

Accounting & Financial Systems Consultant   1992 to 1994
MOVERS & SHAKERS, Boston, Massachusetts

Recruited to design, implement and manage a PC-based accounting system for this sporting events management company and producer of the annual Boston Marathon. As the only accounting and finance professional in the organization, provided daily accounting, budgeting and cash management support in addition to long-range strategic, business, market and finance planning.

MOVERS & SHAKERS *(Continued)*:

- Created a comprehensive accounting and financial reporting system:
  — Prepared financial statements for fiscal years 1992, 1993 and 1994.
  — Redesigned chart of accounts to track sponsorship fees, entry fees and concession fees by multiple product classes and specific events.
  — Developed detailed job cost and profitability analysis reports as the foundation for budgeting and event planning to facilitate future growth and improved earnings.

Accounting Manager   1991 to 1992
SIERRA, Carlsbad, California

Managed accounts payable, accounts receivable, payroll, billing, credit and collections, sales and use tax filings, and financial statements for this $12 million electronics manufacturer.

- Restructured and tightened the company's cash management policy to ensure prompt recovery of all receivables to meet cash requirements of payroll and vendor commitments.

- Renegotiated payment schedule to recover $2 million from an Italian company. Personally collected first $500,000 payment and established framework for subsequent collection of all outstanding funds.

- Redesigned Bill of Materials for all products (in cooperation with Engineering Department) to facilitate development/refinement of standard cost system.

- Managed annual physical inventory in cooperation with Price Waterhouse auditors.

Director of Operations   1983 to 1991
COLORADO VIDEO, Mountain View, Colorado

Recruited as Controller for a start-up video production company servicing cable television, corporate training and expanding consumer video markets. Created all general accounting, cost accounting, budgeting, financial analysis/reporting, tax, payroll and long-range business planning systems.

Promoted to Director of Operations in 1985 with full P&L responsibility for the entire business unit. Directed sales/marketing, studio and location production, post production, technology, human resources, purchasing, and all corporate finance and administrative affairs.

- Built company from start-up to over $2 million in annual revenues.

- Evaluated emerging technology, sourced vendors and directed over $200,000 in annual technology acquisitions to develop a state-of-the-art production facility.

- Successfully marketed, negotiated and closed sales contracts with IBM, Apple, Pepsi, Department of Defense and numerous other corporate and government clients.

Previous Professional Experience:

Cost Accounting Manager, Katy Windows, Irvine, California	1981 to 1983
Cost Accountant, Anderson, Santa Monica, California	1980 to 1981
Cost & Budget Administrator, Continental Group, Boston, Massachusetts	1977 to 1980

EDUCATION:

B.S., Business Administration Management, Honors Graduate, 1979
NORTHEASTERN UNIVERSITY, Boston, Massachusetts

Certified Tax Practitioner (CTP), State of California, 1992

STEPHEN P. MITCHELL

232 South Street   Phone   (203) 232-5353
Greenwich, Connecticut 06430   Fax   (203) 232-6784

CORPORATE ACCOUNTING & FINANCE EXECUTIVE
Start-Up, Turnaround & High-Growth Corporations

Dynamic professional career in strategic planning, development and leadership of complex accounting, budgeting, cash management, payroll, financial analysis and reporting. Successful in linking accounting and finance to business operations to drive forward organizational development, control costs and improve earnings. Strong project management, team building and leadership skills. Expert PC qualifications with proficiency in Real World, Excel, Lotus 1-2-3, Microsoft Word and WordPerfect. Extensive experience in systems selection and implementation.

PROFESSIONAL EXPERIENCE:

INVESTMENT CAPITAL CORPORATION, Greenwich, Connecticut   1987 to Present

Assistant Controller (1995 to Present)
Manager - Accounting, Employee Benefits &Payroll (1990 to 1995)
Accounting Manager (1987 to 1990)

Recruited to affiliate company of Investment Group, Inc. (past employer) to direct the start-up of a complete corporate accounting function for this newly-formed syndicator. Assume additional accounting, financial and human resource responsibilities as the company has grown from 5 to 87 employees and raised over $170 million in equity sales.

Serve as the senior accounting professional in the corporation reporting directly to CFO and Controller. Scope of responsibility is diverse and includes accounts payable, accounts receivable, general ledger,   payroll, monthly sales commission, and preparation of year-end financial documentation for external audit review. Coordinate accounting systems implementation and upgrades. Direct a staff of six.

Administer the entire cash management function for both company operations and its six limited partnerships. Manage banking relationships to execute and administer escrow accounts. Coordinate fund transfers, cash receipts, disbursements and monthly reconciliations. Concurrent responsibility for the design, administration and management of all employee benefit programs and related regulatory affairs. Continue to provide cash management and accounting support to parent corporation on critical operating and long-term planning issues.

Achievements:

- Established corporate policies and procedures for general accounting, financial reporting, cash management, payroll and year-end analysis. Implemented the flexibility required to meet the dynamic needs of this high-growth corporation.

- Created a complex system of internal and external partnership accounting responsive to the needs of the corporation and compliant with all SEC regulations.

- Facilitated implementation of general accounting system and subsequent selection, development and implementation of a state-of-the-art, PC-based lease accounting system. Managed parallel system   operations through transition to new technology.

- Created the corporation's human resource policies governing recruitment, retention, payroll, commission, benefits, EEO, performance reviews, timekeeping, workers compensation and disability. Defined criteria for employment contracts and administration.

- Negotiated policies and premiums with six different insurance carriers to optimize coverage and continue fixed costs to the corporation.

STEPHEN P. MITCHELL - *Page Two*

INVESTMENT GROUP, INC., New York, New York 1983 to 1987

Accounting Supervisor (1986)
Senior Staff Accountant (1983 to 1986)

Joined this investment management firm specializing in equipment leasing, limited partnerships, real estate investments and other tax shelters. Maintained accounting and financial records for Investment Group, 7 affiliated companies, 38 limited partnerships and 3 real estate ventures. Managed staff of four.

• Acquired expertise in inventory leased equipment, wrap leases, cash distributions, cash management, investor negotiations and letter of credit transactions for non-resource loans.

SKYLINE CORPORATION, Stamford, Connecticut 1982 to 1983

Senior Financial Analyst

Senior Financial Analyst, assisting the Director of Retail Finance for this $500 million manufacturing and marketing company. Scope of responsibility was diverse and included budgeting, variance analysis, trend analysis and business unit analysis/rationalization. Worked closely with senior financial and operating executives to interpret financial data and improve business operations.

• Instrumental in the design and implementation of a computerized budget model.

INDUSTRIAL CREDIT CORPORATION, Stamford, Connecticut 1972 to 1982

Assistant Accounting Manager (1976 to 1982)
Personnel & Payroll Supervisor (1974 to 1976)
General Ledger Supervisor (1972 to 1974)

Promoted rapidly through a series of increasingly responsible accounting and personnel management positions for this $550 million diversified leasing and finance company. Managed monthly and annual financial statements, general ledger, loan reporting and management of a 15,000 account lease receivable system. Administered pension, health insurance, stock purchase and credit union plans. Filed payroll tax returns in 21 states and to the Federal Government.

• Designed and implemented daily accounting system to control $150 million of commercial paper and $91 million of long-term debt.

• Championed implementation of on-line cash application system.

OLMER CORPORATION, New Haven, Connecticut 1969 to 1972

Promoted through several positions in Accounts Payable and Payroll.

EDUCATION:

B.A., Accounting
Quinnipiac College, Hamden, Connecticut, 1969

PERSONAL PROFILE:

Native of Cuba. U.S. Citizen since 1983. Fluent Spanish.

LAURA M. HALSEY
5555 North Avenue
Los Angeles, California 92009
(619) 592-3653

CAREER PROFILE

Accounting Professional / Accounting Department Supervisor with 13 years of progressively responsible experience with high-growth, turnaround and mature corporations. Qualifications include:

- Accounts Receivable
- Accounts Payable
- Account Reconciliation
- General Ledger

- Credit & Collection
- Customer Service
- Cash Application
- Staff Training/Development

- Billing/Invoicing
- Financial Analysis/Reporting
- Chargeback/Adjustments
- Team Building/Leadership

Delivered strong and sustainable operating, financial and service gains through expertise in systems design/implementation, standardization, workflow optimization and long-range planning. Excellent analytical, problem-solving and negotiating skills. PC proficient with IBM System 38, HP 918 Image Data, Lotus and Word.

PROFESSIONAL EXPERIENCE:

INVESTOR'S, INC., Los Angeles, CA   March 1990 to December 1996

Accounts Receivable Supervisor

Recruited as Assistant Supervisor for the Accounts Receivable Department of this rapid growth national daily newspaper. Challenged to design and implement the systems, policies, procedures and technologies to regain control of the A/R function and establish a professional business unit. Promoted to Supervisor within six months. Assumed increased responsibilities for accounting, financial planning/reporting and MIS operations.

Scope of responsibility was diverse and included all billing, credit and collection activity for 1500 active accounts. Prepared monthly financial schedules, graphs, journal entries, sales commissions, and account analyses. Reviewed and approved credit applications, advertising agency discounts and advertising contracts. Monitored cash receipts application, contract adjustments and account reconciliations.

Worked in collaboration with Advertising Sales Department to provide data relevant to account history and credit status. Personally communicated with customers nationwide to resolve billing discrepancies and expedite collections. Consulted with executive management to establish corporate policy impacting A/R and credit operations.

Achievements:

- Built an Accounts Receivable organization successful in meeting the demands of the company as it grew from $7 million to $30 million in annual advertising revenues over a five year period. Met all production requirements with no additional staff.

- Redesigned procedures to collect on past due accounts and increased cash flow by 37%.

- Consistently surpassed all credit and collection targets. Maintained DSO of 35 days or less.

- Captured a $250,000 annual cost savings through development/implementation of an Advertising Management System to integrate and consolidate billing, credit and collection information from three autonomous business units.

- Designed a series of internal reporting mechanisms to measure sales, credit and collection performance.

SANFAX, Los Angeles, CA   May 1986 to March 1990

    Accounts Receivable Supervisor (1989 to 1990)
    Lead Coordinator - MIS Systems (1988)
    Lead Cash Processor (1987 to 1988)
    Cash Processor (1986)

Fast-track promotion through a series of increasingly responsible accounting, MIS and management positions with this $150 million fax machine manufacturer and wholesaler. Advanced to a final position training and supervising a staff of 10, where we provided accounting, credit and collections support for a 75-person customer service department.

Prepared monthly sales and cash receipts reports, account analyses and journal entries. Authorized customer credit adjustments and bad debt write-offs. Acquired extensive experience in customer communications and collection negotiations.

Achievements:

- Instrumental in transitioning A/R from in-house software to a fully-integrated accounting and financial reporting system. Resulted in a significant improvement in the quality, accuracy and usefulness of financial data for daily operating management and long-range business planning.

- Realigned key accounting positions, consolidated similar functions, avoided need for increased staffing, and improved information processing and reporting.

- Designed and implemented a series of standards, policies and systems to more efficiently manage accounting/financial data collection, analysis and reporting.

PUBLISHERS INC., New York, NY   April 1984 to May 1986

    Staff Accountant

Diversified accounting and financial reporting responsibilities with this nationwide book publisher and distributor. Analyzed and reconciled accounts, prepared journal entries, calculated monthly sales summary for 35 field sales representatives, and participated in month-end closing. Computed and reported monthly commission, bonus and royalties. Conducted quarterly audit of consigned products with 20 book depositories nationwide.

CAPITAL JEWELERS, INC., New York, NY   March 1983 to April 1984

    Bookkeeper

Managed accounts payable, accounts receivable and billing for this NYC-based jewelry wholesaler. Prepared cash deposits, bank reconciliations and journal entries. Worked with Assistant Controller on month-end closings and month-end reporting.

EDUCATION:

B.S., Business / Major in Accounting, San Sebastian College, Manila, Philippines, 1982

Continuing Professional Development:

Graduate of numerous professional training programs, seminars and workshops on topics including management, organizational development, credit, collections and related legal affairs. Several courses were sponsored by Dun and Bradstreet.

PAUL E. COLLINS
1000 Mistletoe Lane
Baltimore, Maryland 21121
(410) 599-2285

QUALIFICATIONS PROFILE:

ADMINISTRATIVE DIRECTOR with over 10 years experience managing cross-functional business affairs for large service organizations. Expertise includes:

- PC, MIS & Network Technology
- Administrative Policies & Procedures
- Front & Back Office Operations
- Purchasing & Vendor Negotiations
- Marketing & New Business Development

- Human Resource Affairs
- Finance, Budgeting & Banking
- Client & Public Relations
- Joint Ventures & Partnerships
- Facilities Management

Delivered strong operating results in productivity and efficiency improvement, technological advancement, cost reduction, and revenue and profit performance. Excellent training, supervisory and leadership skills. Organized and skillful project manager.

PROFESSIONAL EXPERIENCE:

Administrator   1992 to Present
MEDICAL ASSOCIATES, INC., York, Pennsylvania

Senior Administrative Director responsible for the strategic planning, staffing, budgeting and management of all administrative and business affairs for a specialized medical practice. Design and implement systems, processes and procedures for budgeting and financial affairs, office services, billing, records management, facilities management, purchasing, inventory control, and the complete human resource function (e.g., recruitment, training, scheduling, performance appraisal, benefits, compensation). Supervise a staff of 18.

- Instrumental in building revenues 50% within three years through contributions in marketing, print advertising, public relations and community relations.

- Redesigned and expanded capabilities of internal PC network through implementation of LAN client/server technology and a fully-integrated medical practice management program (ELCOMP). Resulted in tremendous improvements in operating efficiency and a $150,000 reduction in annual payroll costs.

- Managed the selection, negotiation and acquisition of over $350,000 in capital technology investment.

- Negotiated vendor contracts and maintained stable pricing for four consecutive years.

- Designed and led in-house training programs on topics including PC technology, credit and collections, administration and OSHA regulations.

- Authored business proposals to build partnerships and strategic alliances with health care provider organizations throughout the region. Structured and negotiated contracts with providers, vendors and business partners.

PAUL E. COLLINS - *Page Two*

Director of Administration   1990 to 1992
BROWN, GRANT, JACKSON & LEE, Lancaster, Pennsylvania

Planned, staffed, budgeted and directed all administrative functions for a law firm with three offices in Pennsylvania and a staff of 200+. Scope of responsibility was diverse and included human resources, employee relations, MIS and communications technology, accounting and financial reporting, purchasing, office services/administration, marketing and client relations.

- Managed a $1.1 million contract for the architectural design, layout and construction of a new law firm. Brought project in two weeks ahead of schedule and 10% under budget.

- Directed the selection and implementation of a VINES network system on PC server and numerous other software, applications and technology development projects. Total capital investment exceeded $200,000.

- Designed and produced marketing and direct mail communications in conjunction with several business/client development programs.

- Worked cooperatively with the firm's partners to plan long-term operating, administrative, financial and marketing strategies.

Director of Administration   1984 to 1990
DUKE & TAYLOR, Baltimore, Maryland

Joined a 55-employee law firm to restructure all administrative functions, introduce computer technology and improve operating efficiency/productivity. Held administrative, financial and general management responsibilities similar to those at Brown, Grant, Jackson & Lee.

- Transitioned from manual operations to complete automation with the introduction of IBM mainframe technology. Significantly improved the ability to efficiently manage and catalog volumes of legal documentation while reducing staffing requirements by more than 10%.

- Designed flexible administrative systems and processes to meet growth and expansion demands as the firm more than doubled its legal staff and client base.

Risk Manager   1978 to 1984
CITY OF ST. AUGUSTINE, St. Augustine, Florida

Directed a sophisticated internal risk management audit program of all City facilities and operations. Evaluated regulatory and safety compliance, coordinated on-site inspections with external agencies, and worked with City Attorney on pending lawsuits and litigation.

- Earned a 1979 "Certificate of Appreciation" for service to the municipality.

EDUCATION:

MBA, University of South Florida, 1983
BS, Eastern Kentucky University, 1978

Completed numerous continuing professional education programs, workshops and seminars on topics including Communications, Negotiations, Information Systems Technology, LAN & Communications Technology, Business Management and Profitability.

PROFESSIONAL AFFILIATIONS:

American Management Assn	American Academy of Procedural Coders
American Bar Assn	American Computer Systems & Technology Professionals
American Marketing Assn	American Academy of Medical Administrators
Medical Group Management Assn	American Institute of Professional Bookkeepers

HELEN P. GARRETT

200 Hillside Lane
Silver Spring, Maryland 20660
Home (301) 858-2278   Office (301) 595-6487

CAREER PROFILE

Over 15 years experience planning and directing executive-level administrative affairs and support to Chairmen, Boards of Directors and Senior Management. Combines strong planning, organizational and communications skills with the ability to independently plan and direct high-level business affairs. Qualifications include:

- *Shareholder Meetings & Communications*
- *Regulatory Reporting & Communications*
- *Corporate Political & Legislative Affairs*
- *Customer Communications & Liaison Affairs*
- *Confidential Correspondence & Data*
- *Executive Office Management*
- *Staff Training & Development*
- *Budgeting & General Accounting*
- *Special Events Planning*
- *Special Project Management*

Proficient in the use of WordPerfect for Windows 5.2. Experienced with Lotus 1-2-3.

PROFESSIONAL EXPERIENCE

INTERSTATE SAVINGS BANK, Silver Spring, Maryland   1989 to Present

Corporate Secretary
Executive Assistant to the Chairman and Board of Directors

High-profile, executive-level administrative position supporting the Chairman, Board of Directors and other top management personnel throughout the organization. Scope of responsibility is diverse and includes Board affairs, customer and stockholder communications, employee stock options, special events, regulatory reporting and executive administration.

- Executive Liaison between Chairman and Senior Management Committee, Business Departments, and employees to plan, schedule and facilitate a broad range of corporate initiatives, company operations and large-scale business functions.

- Handle confidential operating and financial information, maintain corporate records and minutes, and execute corporate contracts and agreements.

- Project Supervisor for annual shareholders report. Coordinate annual shareholders meetings, manage liaison affairs with outside counsel regarding proxy statements, and facilitate print production of shareholder communications.

- Maintain/update files for regulatory review, oversight and approval.

- Provide training and supervision to Executive Department's support staff.

HELEN P. GARRETT   Page Two

CONSTITUTION PAPER COMPANY, Washington, D.C.   1977 to 1989
Federal Corporate Affairs Division

> **Secretary to Vice President & Director / Office Manager** (1983 to 1989)
> **Assistant Administrator for Voluntary Contributors / Office Manager** (1981 to 1983)
> **Secretary to the Vice President** (1977 to 1981)

Fast-track promotion through a series of increasingly responsible administrative management positions in Constitution's government affairs and lobbying division. Worked directly with the Director to provide executive-level administrative and operating management support.

- Planned, staffed and directed all office management functions for the Department. Scope of responsibility was diverse and included A/P, A/R, budgeting, petty cash and corporate checking accounts. Recruited, trained and supervised administrative staff. Developed procedural and documentation manuals.

- Managed confidential correspondence, appointments, meetings and schedule for the Director. Personally planned and coordinated industry and inter-company meetings involving the Corporate Affairs Department.

- Independently researched, responded to and followed up on requests from Congress and company management.

- Worked cooperatively with Corporate Secretary to direct the planning/execution of the 1986 and 1988 annual shareholders meetings.

- Administered the Voluntary Contributors for a Better Government Program, nation-wide employee fundraising effort to increase support for corporate lobbying and legislative initiatives. Directed all Federal Election Commission filings and State Election Committee filings for the corporation's Political Action Committee.

PREVIOUS PROFESSIONAL EXPERIENCE included several responsible administrative and customer service management positions. Completed a three-year position with Engravers of Europe, managing sales and service relationships with foreign embassy personnel, government officials and corporate VIPs.

EDUCATION

University College/University of Maryland, College Park, Maryland
Business Courses (1989 to Present)

ITT Business Institute, Bethesda, Maryland
Secretarial & Administrative Training Program (1977)

Montgomery College, Rockville, Maryland
Music Major (1969 to 1970)

References Provided Upon Request

DONALD P. TORRENCE

1834 Wooden Court   Home   (405) 366-8965
Wichita, Kansas 32559   Office   (405) 360-0924

NON-PROFIT ORGANIZATION & ASSOCIATION EXECUTIVE

Well-qualified Leadership Executive with 15+ years experience in association management. Qualifications include:

- Financial & Budgetary Affairs
- Strategic & Mission Planning
- Policy & Procedure Development
- Fundraising & Corporate Giving
- Special Events Management
- Political & Legislative Affairs

- Member Development
- Volunteer Recruitment
- Community Outreach
- Educational Programming
- Public Speaking
- Committee Leadership

NON-PROFIT ORGANIZATION & ASSOCIATION LEADERSHIP EXPERIENCE:

AMERICAN RED CROSS

- **Finance Committee Member**, Kansas State Affiliate Chapter (1994 to Present)
  Appointed to 17-member committee responsible for oversight of a $2.3 million budget allocated for ARC-sponsored research, educational programs, fundraising, and community outreach/service programs.

- **Board of Directors**, Kansas State Affiliate Chapter (1994 to Present)
  Appointed to ARC's State Board responsible for establishing strategy, administering financial affairs, and directing all statewide operations for the organization. Consult with local chapters to expand programming, fundraising, education and service initiatives targeted to 373,000 Kansans annually.

- **Joint Fundraising Program Committee Member** (1994 to Present)
  Member of a national joint ARC and Disaster Relief Fundraising Project launched in March 1994. Completed leadership development program to train others in corporate fundraising strategies.

- **President**, Cleveland County Division (1992 to 1994)
  Elected as the senior management executive leading the entire ARC affiliate organization and all related fundraising, corporate sponsorship, special events, educational and community outreach programs. Significantly expanded the visibility of the organization and increased donations by more than 10%.

KANSAS ASSOCIATION OF LIFE UNDERWRITERS

- **Regional Vice President** (1994 to Present)
  Currently leading a multi-chapter leadership initiative to increase membership, expand marketing communications and improve professional education opportunities.

- **Board of Directors, Political Action Committee** (1988 to 1991)
  Led a 10-member committee responsible for identifying and supporting favorable legislative actions.

- **State Multiline Committee Chairman** (1987 to 1988)
  Directed statewide member development and networking programs for this 1500-member organization.

CENTRAL KANSAS ASSOCIATION OF LIFE UNDERWRITERS

- **President** (1988 to 1989)
  Elected President of a 63-member region-wide professional organization. Established policy and mission statement, designed member recruitment programs, launched high-profile fundraising and corporate giving campaigns, established volunteer network, and managed professional education and training programs. Previously served as Secretary/Treasurer and Vice President. Active member since 1985.

  - Received 1988 Public Service Award for leadership expertise in fundraising and community outreach.

DONALD P. TORRENCE   *Page Two*

WICHITA, KANSAS ROTARY CLUB

- **Foundation Committee Chairperson** (1994 to Present)
  Elected Chairperson responsible for planning and directing a club fundraising program targeted to 150-member organization. Appointed committee members, developed fundraising strategy and goals, and spearheaded all promotional and advertising programs.

- **Paul Harris Fellow & Benefactor** (1992, 1994)
  Distinguished designation for personal fundraising contributions.

- **Membership Development Chairman** (1988, 1991)
  Appointed to launch a massive marketing initiative to increase Club membership through targeted solicitation of business and civic leaders.

WASHINGTON FRANKLIN FOUNDATION

- **Staff**, Wildlife Museum & Park (1972 to 1973)
  Assisted with special events planning and site logistics, coordinated property management activities and assisted with historical tours for 3500-acre Wildlife Preserve, Western-Indian Museum and Historic Lodge.

Actively involved with several other non-profit organizations to provide support for fundraising, educational and marketing programs.

- Wichita, Kansas Chamber of Commerce (Leadership Graduate & Past Membership Chairman)
- Kansas State University O Club (Life Member)
- Kansas State University Alumni Association (Life Member)

PROFESSIONAL EXPERIENCE:

President   1994 to Present
Torrence Asset Management, Wichita, Kansas

Executive Consultant providing expertise in financial planning, estate and retirement planning, complex financial negotiations and investment management.

District Manager / Agent   1983 to 1994
Farmers Insurance Group, Wichita, Kansas

Fast-track promotion to district management position controlling an $8.8 million portfolio. Transitioned district from loss to profitability with 10% annual increase in customer base through innovative marketing strategies and campaigns. Created and led a 2 1/2 year sales, management and leadership training program. Recipient of numerous prestigious performance and management awards.

Managing Partner   1979 to 1983
Torrence Oil and Gas Operators, Topeka, Kansas

Founded and profitably operated a consulting exploration and drilling company that grew to over $1 million in managed operations. Negotiated complex land acquisition, leasing and mineral rights contracts with private owners, municipalities, government agencies and institutions. As Chief Operating Officer, directed the entire business planning, financial, human resource, contracts and administrative organization.

EDUCATION: **BS / Advertising & Public Relations**, Kansas State University, 1979
                        Management Training & Development, University of Kansas
                        National Association of Security Dealers Series 7 & 63 Licenses
                        Life Underwriting Training Council Fellow (LUTCF)

PATRICK WILLIAMSON

31654 South 27th Street West
Las Cruces, New Mexico 78551
(502) 685-4873

ASSOCIATION EXECUTIVE

Public Policy Development / Legislative Advocacy / Member Development & Retention
Budgeting & Financial Affairs / Member Services / Marketing Communications / Board Relations
Human Resource Affairs / Training & Development / Strategic Planning / Media Relations

Over 10 years executive-level experience in the development, growth and leadership of member-driven, not-for-profit organizations. Consistently successful in increasing revenues and funding, expanding membership and winning legislative support. Pioneered innovative products, programs and services to drive revenue growth and enhance member services. Law Degree from Chicago-Kent Law School.

PROFESSIONAL EXPERIENCE:

Director of Marketing   1995 to Present
ELDERS OF AMERICA, INC., Las Cruces, New Mexico

Senior Marketing Executive leading the strategic planning, design and implementation of all marketing, advertising, public relations and community outreach programs for a 450-resident senior life care community. Introduce programs, models and strategies to reengineer and reposition existing business development campaigns and accelerate growth within target markets. Conduct extensive market research to obtain baseline data for long-term strategy development and tactical plan deployment. Manage planning, budgeting, staffing, training, public relations and press relations. Coordinate regulatory affairs. Advise Executive Director on key marketing strategies.

- Increased occupancy from 96% to 99% within first six weeks.
- Revitalized resident marketing campaign with in-house training/mentoring programs.
- Spearheaded development of community outreach, special event programs and event sponsorship to build market presence and capitalize upon public/private partnerships.

Executive Director / CEO   1991 to 1995
NEW MEXICO ASSOCIATION OF HOMES & HOUSING FOR THE AGING, Las Cruces, New Mexico

Recruited as Executive Director / CEO with full operational and P&L responsibility for a not-for-profit trade association representing the senior retirement housing industry. Held complete accountability for policy, financial affairs, human resources, member development and retention, member services and legislative/political affairs.

Created a proactive, member-driven organization that developed effective public policy programs at both the state and federal levels that won support to maximize reimbursement and reduce burdensome regulatory controls. Established a visible and impactful presence throughout the legislature.

- Built Association from 92 to 205 members and affiliates (100% growth). Launched a series of high-profile advertising, marketing and member communications programs to increase member base and voice of the Association.
- Increased operating budget by more than 100% through combined efforts in expanding membership development, restructuring member dues and increasing member services (e.g., training programs, regulatory review assistance, salary and benefit models, group buying consortium, below market rate loan financing, communication services).

PATRICK WILLIAMSON - *Page Two*

- Created and marketed a unique professional staffing program that reduced member payroll costs and improved stability and quality of workforce. Program created a new and viable long-term revenue source for the Association.
- Revitalized the member communications program with a biweekly newsletter, member brochure and complete marketing/advertising portfolio.
- Pioneered a unique industry accreditation program.
- Led start-up of educational and research foundation and Political Action Committee.

Director of Public Policy   1985 to 1991
INDIANA ASSOCIATION OF HOMES FOR THE AGING, Indianapolis, Indiana

Served as **Assistant Director** of state association working to advance legislative support, funding and services to state-wide, not-for-profit senior retirement housing communities. Responsible for member development and recruitment, member services and technical assistance, and regulatory issues. Assisted Executive Director with public policy initiatives.

Promoted in 1988 to **Director of Public Policy**, a newly-created position established to meet the growing demand of increasing membership (200+). Held full responsibility for the strategic planning, policy development and management of the complete public policy program.

- Spearheaded a state-wide grassroots advocacy network and Political Action Committee (PAC) that supported successful efforts in increasing state-funded reimbursement and decreasing regulatory burden. Program served as the model for other states nationwide.
- Appointed key spokesperson to the Indiana General Assembly, Congressional delegates, state agencies, local politicians, media representatives and key business leaders.
- Authored memoranda and public statements, developed data tracking and analysis protocols, and advocated for the passage of favorable legislation and amendments. Consulted with national policy affiliate on major legislative initiatives impacting the industry.
- Consulted with members state-wide to provide expertise in third party reimbursement, public policy, legislative analysis and tax regulations.

Senior Research Director   1984 to 1985
CITIZENS FOR BRONSON, Chicago, Illinois

One-year contract assignment directing all opposition research, data collection and analysis programs for the candidate's campaign for State's Attorney.

EDUCATION:

Juris Doctor Degree, 1984
CHICAGO-KENT LAW SCHOOL, Chicago, Illinois

Bachelor of Arts Degree in Economics & Political Science, 1980
NORTHWESTERN UNIVERSITY, Chicago, Illinois

PROFESSIONAL AFFILIATIONS:

American Association of Homes & Services for the Aging
— National Purchasing Committee Member (1996)
— National Public Policy Committee Member (1994)
American Society of Association Executives
New Mexico Society of Association Executives
National Health Lawyers Association

DENISE L. HARRIS

222 West Broadway
New York, New York 10011
Business   (212) 555-3131
Residence   (718) 633-1212

CAREER PROFILE:

Distinguished management career with Bank of America leading operating divisions, technology divisions, global marketing and sales organizations, and the division strategic planning function. Expert in turnaround management, process reengineering and crisis management. Equally successful spearheading start-up banking and technology ventures and accelerating profit growth within established markets worldwide.

Distinguished Professional Activities:

- Published Author, Correspondent Banking Journal, Global Finance and Euro Money.
- Guest Speaker on correspondent banking and regulatory issues at conferences worldwide.
- Appointed Representative to the Federal Reserve Advisory Group on Payment System Risk.
- Appointed Representative on Financial Services Advisory Group to Bulgarian Government.

PROFESSIONAL EXPERIENCE:

BANK OF AMERICA, New York, New York   **1970 to Present**
(Global merchant banking institution with $100 billion in assets)

President - Financial Services Information Systems Corporation (1993 to Present)

Senior Operating Executive with P&L responsibility for the full-scale launch and growth of this technology subsidiary. "Hands-on" management of all sales, marketing and business development programs to introduce eight sophisticated financial system products.

Built organization to 60 employees (including three managers and a controller). Established all operating policies and procedures, implemented MIS technology, designed budgets and financial reporting systems, created distribution strategies and launched nationwide introduction.

- Transitioned business from revenues of less than $2 million to $10+ million in two years.
- Orchestrated asset sale and partnership divestiture, both with significant financial return.
- Currently spearheading a number of market expansion programs to position the company for long-term market growth and profitability.

Managing Director - Global Assets Department (1992 to 1993)

Staff position leading the development of the Bank's strategic business plans for the Global Assets Department. Focused efforts on identifying offshore business development opportunities to drive growth within the funds management business.

- Recommended integration of domestic and international operations to capitalize upon the strengths and core competencies of each organization.
- Worked cooperatively with General Manager in Spain to identify business opportunity and negotiate joint venture with local multinational company to start-up a subsidiary.
- Evaluated market expansion opportunities in Latin America, Asia and Europe.

Senior Vice President - Global Sales (1991 to 1992)

Led 110-person global sales, marketing and business development team challenged to transition U.S. operations from loss to profitability while accelerating international growth.

- Exceeded all turnaround objectives and returned U.S. to profitability.
- Increased international sales by 15% despite emerging competition.

Senior Vice President - International Correspondent Banking (1987 to 1991)

Senior Operating Executive leading this Division through a period of rapid growth and expansion. Scope of responsibility included Investment, Depository, Cash Management, Collection and Letter of Credit operations. Managed an international team of seven direct reports responsible for 900 operations, sales, marketing, credit and MIS personnel.

- Built profits from $27 million to $64 million within three years to become the 4th largest profit center in the Bank.

Senior Vice President - Group Head (1981 to 1987)

Full operating management responsibility for MIS, Letter of Credit Processing, Foreign Exchange, Collection, Money Transfer and Check Processing Departments. Managed a direct reporting staff of seven and more than 1200 employees.

- Led organizations through complex corporate change and re-designed to operate as an independent profit center supporting global business.
- Introduced productivity, efficiency and service improvement initiatives.
- Directed the acquisition and integration of numerous MIS technologies to refine existing systems, introduce new applications and increase processing capabilities.

Vice President (1976 to 1981)

Managed large-scale Lockbox Processing, General Ledger and Customer Account Reconciliation departments for both wholesale and retail operations. Directed a staff of up to 400 with full budgetary responsibility for all operations.

- Spearheaded a series of technology acquisitions and integrations to enhance internal management reporting and customer transaction processing capabilities.
- Delivered significant improvements in data quality. Restored customer credibility.

Early career positions as **Assistant Treasurer** and **Assistant Vice President**. Managed accounting and securities processing operations. Two year special assignment developing and implementing Bank-wide Affirmative Action plan.

EDUCATION:

HARVARD UNIVERSITY
Graduate, Professional Management Development Program (abbreviated MBA)

PROFESSIONAL & CIVIC AFFILIATIONS:

Board of Directors, Executive Leadership Council
President, Executive Leadership Council Foundation
Co-Founder, Urban Bankers Coalition
Board of Directors, Greater New Jersey YMCA

DANIEL R. POWELL
4466 Oakwood Court
Cleveland, Ohio 44323
(216) 883-9922

BANKING, LENDING & FINANCIAL SERVICES EXECUTIVE

Twenty-year management career as a Senior Operating Executive leading successful start-up, turnaround and high-growth organizations. Expert in building consensus and leading cross-functional teams to action and achievement. Combines strong P&L, general management, strategic planning, sales and marketing expertise with the ability to capitalize upon market trends and emerging market opportunities. Comprehensive knowledge of lending, underwriting and loan processing procedures, systems and technologies. MBA Degree.

Built production volumes to unprecedented levels and delivered fee income 55% over projection.

PROFESSIONAL EXPERIENCE:

U.S. BANK, Cleveland, Ohio   1994 to Present

Senior Vice President

Recruited to this $13 billion mortgage oriented consumer bank by Korn/Ferry International. Challenged to lead the turnaround and return to profitability of the Residential Lending Division. Concurrently, integrated one merger and one acquisition to now control a Residential Lending portfolio twice original size. Given full strategic planning and operating management responsibility for a complete revitalization of sales, marketing, customer service, product development, loan underwriting, loan processing, quality control, pricing and investor sales. Manage an $8 million annual operating budget and a direct staff of 105.

- Developed strong and sustainable financial gains:
  - 242% increase in production volume over 1994 1Q.
  - 101% increase in production volume over previous year.
  - 11% reduction in staffing requirements in largest operating division.
  - 56% improvement in service performance (28.8 to 12.8 days for loan approval).
- Transitioned bank from a price-sensitive competitor to a quality-based service organization. Introduced production/performance measurement tools, recruited talented sales management, and implemented incentives to increase service levels and improve customer retention.
- Championed and successfully launched new Wholesale/Correspondent Lending Department in 1994. Increased first-year funding from $6 million to over $100 million in 1995, with 1996 production in excess of $200 million.
- Directed residential lending due diligence activities in support of U.S. Bank's aggressive M&A program. Actively involved in structuring and negotiating the 1995 acquisition of two Household International operating locations and the 1995 merger with First Fed of Michigan.
- Spearheaded design and implementation of sophisticated lending systems and technologies.
- Voting member of the Commercial Real Estate and Corporate Loan Committees.

BANKER'S MORTGAGE CORPORATION, Chicago, Illinois   1987 to 1994
(Subsidiary of Banker's Corp)

Senior Vice President (1992 to 1994)
Regional Vice President (1988 to 1992)
District Loan Manager (1987 to 1988)

Joined this $45 billion institution as a Vice President/District Loan Manager in Southport Connecticut. As the only Banker's employee in New England at that time, challenged to build market presence and create a strong profit center.

DANIEL R. POWELL   *Page Two*

BANKER'S MORTGAGE CORPORATION *(Continued)*:

- Finished as number two office in first year and achieved profitability within seven months.
- Promoted in 1988 to Regional Vice President, the youngest manager in the company's history.
- Led the New England region through a period of unprecedented growth to six branches, 92 people and loan production of more than $350 million in 1992.

Promoted to Senior Vice President of Midwest Area of National District Lending Department in 1992. Given full P&L responsibility for three regions, 15 district lending offices, 240 employees and a $9.5 million annual operating budget. Granted loan approval authority to $750,000.

- Delivered a $200 million increase in production volume within first year to over $1 billion. Generated net fee income of $17 million.
- Led National District Lending in average net fee income per office, service performance and delinquencies.
- Created an innovative performance/productivity analysis and reporting method subsequently integrated throughout the entire corporation.

DELOITTE & TOUCHE, New York, New York   1987

Independent Consultant

Recruited to manage a complete redesign of all user documentation for the firm's Partner Accounting System (compensation and benefits for all Deloitte & Touche partners worldwide). Promoted to Team Leader within two months of engagement. Led a 6-person cross-functional business systems and management team.

FIRST FEDERAL SAVINGS BANK, White Plains, New York   1986 to 1987

Assistant Vice President - Underwriting (1987)
Supervisor - Loan Counseling & Processing (1986 to 1987)

Recruited as Supervisor of Loan Processing and Counseling for this $4.5 billion thrift. Reduced backlog of loans in process from 140 days to less than 30 days within three months and immediately promoted to Assistant Vice President. Led three-person Underwriting Department and chaired Loan Committee. Introduced improved quality processes to ensure that loans were properly documented for secondary market sale.

MORRISON REALTY, INC., Houston, Texas   1979 to 1986

Sales Manager directing agent recruitment and training, lender relations, print advertising, budgeting and financial reporting. Spearheaded successful and profitable entry into the insurance services industry, building new business to more than 80% of total company revenues.

KNOX, INC., Houston, Texas   1976 to 1978

Account Representative selling U.S. Government debt securities to thrift and banking institutions for this regional investment banking firm. Led training class in first year revenue booked.

UNITED STATES AIR FORCE - Aeromedical Technician, Tyndall AFB, Florida   1973 to 1975

EDUCATION: **MBA**, University of Chicago - Graduate School of Business, 1995
                    BA, University of the State of New York - Albany, 1993

JOHN WARNER

700 Lincoln Place
Baltimore, Maryland 21212

Home (410) 632-5544   Office (410) 442-4567

SENIOR BANKING & FINANCIAL SERVICES EXECUTIVE

Global Marketing & Business Development / Portfolio Development & Management
Transaction & Relationship Banking Services / Strategic Planning & Organization Development
New Venture Start-Up & High Growth / Risk & Asset Management / Product & Service Pricing

MBA in Finance. CPA Certification.

PROFESSIONAL EXPERIENCE:

BANK ONE, Baltimore, Maryland   1973 to Present

Distinguished management career with one of the highest rated financial institutions in the U.S. (Standard & Poors, Moody's). Spearheaded high-profile and financially successful business development programs which successfully expanded Bank One's presence throughout emerging business and international markets. Career highlights include:

Senior Vice President, Transportation & Leasing Group (1989 to Present)

Promoted from Senior Vice President of Maritime Division to develop and direct the entire Transportation and Leasing Group. Given complete responsibility for building a portfolio of four independent operating divisions (Marine, Air, Rail, General Leasing) targeted to distinct business markets worldwide.

Scope of responsibility includes a professional staff of 20 and a $600 million risk asset portfolio (loans, leases, lines of credit and letters of credit for secured transportation equipment financings). In addition, build and direct fee-generating banking relationships with customers worldwide (e.g., cash management, foreign exchange, depository, investment management, trust).

- **Delivered 6% of the bank's total earnings in 1994** ($7 million in net income with ROA of 1.6% and ROE of 15%. Achieved net interest margin of 2.4% and efficiency ratio of 37%. Continue to maintain portfolio with no non-performing assets.

- Further expanded the global market penetration and financial success of the Marine Transportation Division. Continued to build loan portfolio from $100 million to $225 million, DDA portfolio to $20 million and annual fee income to an average of $700,000.

- Built Rail Transportation Division from 1988 concept into a $120 million loan portfolio, $2 million deposit base and $200,000 in annual fee income. Established business infrastructure, sales/marketing organization, lending and credit administration policies and internal administration.

- Appointed President of Bank One Leasecorp in 1992, responsible for the management of a general leasing division (e.g., FFE, computer technologies, medical and manufacturing equipment, robotics). Built portfolio to $170 million.

- Expanded links with and support to other Bank One business centers' customer-based relationships.

JOHN WARNER - *Page Two*

Senior Vice President, Maritime Division (1981 to 1988)

Senior Manager with full responsibility for the strategic planning, development, staffing and management of a newly-created global banking division. Launched worldwide marketing programs targeted to major shipping centers and vessel owners throughout the U.S., U.K., Latin America, Greece and Hong Kong. Built an integrated portfolio of transaction banking and relationship banking services to provide a single point of contact to key account base.

- Built loan portfolio from $15 million to $100 million, deposits to $10+ million and fee income to more than $300,000.

- Established long-term and profitable relationships with major shipping lines worldwide (e.g., Maersk, Sealand, International Shipholding).

- Captured Port of Baltimore's maritime community (e.g., stevedoring companies, steamship agencies, freight forwarders, customhouse brokers). Outplaced all previous competition.

- Led the design of a series of industry-specific banking, cash management and service programs for the U.S. maritime industry.

NOTE: Retain full operating control of the Maritime Division in current position.

Vice President & Manager, London Branch (1979 to 1980)

Accepted one-year reassignment to direct the business development effort of Bank One's U.K. operation. Built relationships with corporate and industrial accounts for lending, depository and financial management services. Worked cooperatively with another vice president responsible for internal branch operations, staffing, transaction processing, accounting, lending, credit and headquarters reporting.

- Assisted in building loan portfolio from start-up to over $100 million within first year.

- Established key account relationships with major European corporations including Unilever, Phillips and ESAB.

Vice President, Latin American Division (1973 to 1978)

Marketed Bank One's relationship and transaction banking services to U.S. headquartered multinational corporations with operating divisions, subsidiaries, joint ventures and other business interests throughout Latin America.

- Established a critical business relationship with DuPont to manage 50% of their U.S. documentary collection service. Processed tens of millions of dollars in annual transactions at a substantial profit return to the bank.

- Captured Latin American corporate accounts (e.g., IBM, Sears, Xerox, Continental Can, ITT, American Can) within a highly-competitive international banking market.

EDUCATION: **MBA / Finance Major**, University of North Carolina, 1973
BS in Economics / Finance Major, University of Pennsylvania (Wharton School), 1968
CPA, State of Maryland, 1980

PROFESSIONAL ACTIVITIES:

Affiliations	Member, Finance Committee & Board of Directors, Quikee Food, Inc. *($1 billion gross revenue, 530-site retail convenience chain)*
Publications	Published Author, <u>Euromoney</u> (1993, 1994) *(Articles on ship and rail equipment financing)*
Languages	Fluent in Spanish.

PERSONAL PROFILE: First Lieutenant, U.S. Army (Vietnam Veteran). Licensed Private Pilot.

JOHN T. BROWN

385 Cherry Hill Road
Moorestwon, New Jersey 08235
(609) 238-5511

CONSTRUCTION INDUSTRY EXECUTIVE

*Senior-Level Management / Claims Avoidance & Mitigation / Expert Testimony / CPM Scheduling
Law & Litigation / Contract Negotiations & Administration / Resource & Asset Management*

Industry Expert with 20+ years of direct profit and loss management. Experienced Counsel and Professional Engineer. Career highlights include:

- Directed sophisticated, multi-million dollar construction projects.
- Managed hundreds of millions of dollars in construction claims, disputes and litigation.
- Provided expert witness testimony before local, state and federal courts.
- Created turnkey construction service programs that drove millions in new revenues.
- Established successful and profitable construction consulting practices.

PROFESSIONAL EXPERIENCE:

President & Chief Executive Officer   1987 to Present
INTERNATIONAL CONSTRUCTION CONSULTANTS, Philadelphia, Pennsylvania

Promoted from affiliate company (Fleet Massey Company) to President & CEO of this professional consulting group specializing in claims avoidance and mitigation, contract dispute resolution, project scheduling (CPM) and construction management. As Senior Operating Executive, responsible for strategic business planning, legal affairs, finance and accounting, sales/marketing, new business development, professional staffing and P&L management.

Manage the entire consulting practice and all client relationships. Personally handle complex projects, claims and negotiations. Travel nationwide to provide expert testimony and litigation support at local, state and federal court proceedings on behalf of client companies.

Management Achievements

- Improved annual profit contribution by 10%-20%.

- Reduced overhead operating costs by more than 35%, streamlined workflow, reallocated personnel and optimized existing resources.

- Directed company-sponsored seminars and training programs for government agencies, construction companies, professional associations and private organizations.

Claims Avoidance & Mitigation

- Built a consulting group recognized nationally for expertise in claims management. Facilitated cross-functional teams responsible for comprehensive analysis of construction management, scheduling delays, time impact, productivity, contracts, plans, specifications and field operations.

- Directed complex claims analysis, avoidance and mitigation for projects totalling over $350 million in construction value. Worked cooperatively with in-house and external counsel to facilitate claims resolution and settlement.

JOHN T. BROWN - *Page Two*

Litigation Support & Expert Witness Testimony

- Provided expert testimony for major claims actions in local, state and federal court. Testified on construction delays and damages, wrongful termination, environmental issues, contract interpretation, defective specifications and other matters.

- Appeared before the Corps of Engineers Board of Contract Appeals, New Jersey Superior Court, Pennsylvania State Supreme Court, U.S. District Court and the Delaware Court of Common Pleas.

Construction Management

- Built a comprehensive Construction Management (CM) / Project Management Oversight (PMO) organization providing fully-integrated, turnkey services — cost estimating, design review, CPM scheduling, change order review, on-site inspection, shop drawing review, tenant relations, permitting and on-site construction supervision.

- Directed approximately $300 million in construction projects for institutional, office and warehousing facilities, public utilities and commercial/corporate revitalization.

CPM Scheduling

- Built scheduling services from small venture into highly-profitable revenue center. Personally directed entire scheduling function for $235+ million in heavy, highway and railway construction. Directed development of scheduling specifications for federal, state and public agencies.

- Created a comprehensive services program providing initial master project schedules, pre-bid CPM schedules, construction contract schedules, monthly schedule updates, and both time impact and delay analysis.

Vice President / Board of Directors   1986 to 1987
FLEET MASSEY COMPANY, Camden, New Jersey

Member of a 6-person senior management team responsible for the strategic planning, development, financial affairs and operations of this marine, heavy and highway construction company. Personally managed complex legal and claims related matters.

President / General Counsel / Vice President   1969 to 1986
ERICKSON, INC., Philadelphia, Pennsylvania

Fast-track promotion through a series of increasingly responsible positions, from Engineer/ Estimator to President of this heavy and highway construction company (founded in 1916). Company was recognized as one of *Engineering News Record's* 400 largest contractors in 1980.

Scope of responsibility was diverse and included P&L, general management, administrative, legal, human resource and business development functions. Concurrently, directed claims management and expert witness testimony. Oversaw field operations and managed affiliate electrical contracting business.

- Built annual revenues to $20+ million and delivered consistent improvements in profitability and net earnings.

- Competitively bid, won and managed over $125 million in construction projects. Personally structured and negotiated all major transactions.

- Established long-term and profitable business relationships with several major clients including the Pennsylvania Department of Transportation and the City of Philadelphia.

Design Liaison Engineer   1968 to 1969
PENNSYLVANIA DEPARTMENT OF TRANSPORTATION, Philadelphia, Pennsylvania

Liaison with engineers and architects for design reviews and scheduling of large highway and bridge construction projects. Coordinated efforts of technical support departments.

Test Operations Engineer   1966 to 1968
THE BOEING COMPANY, Federal Way, Washington

Directed sophisticated test programs for the development of prototype research aircraft and systems (Chinook Helicopter). Managed projects from initial planning through final reporting to the U.S. Department of the Army. Facilitated cross-functional project teams.

EDUCATION:

UNIVERSITY OF PENNSYLVANIA LAW SCHOOL, Philadelphia, Pennsylvania
Juris Doctor Degree, 1983

DREXEL UNIVERSITY, Philadelphia, Pennsylvania
Master of Civil Engineering, 1973
Bachelor of Civil Engineering, 1966

TEACHING EXPERIENCE:

Adjunct Assistant Professor in Civil Engineering at Villanova University, 1985 to 1986

Highlights of Seminar Presentations:

- "Claims Avoidance - What Can You Do?," American Society of Civil Engineers, New Jersey Construction & Engineering Expo, and Contractors Association of Delaware
- "The Claims Consultant's Role," Building Contractors Association
- "Running Construction Projects Effectively," Building Contractors Association and Northeast Construction Expo
- "How to Avoid Construction Disputes & Increase Profits," Pennsylvania Engineering Conference
- "Architect/Engineer Liability," New York Engineering Conference

PROFESSIONAL PROFILE:

Certification:	**Registered Professional Engineer**, Pennsylvania, New Jersey, Delaware
Bar Admissions:	U.S. Supreme Court, U.S. Court of Appeals for the Third District, U.S. District Courts for the District and State Courts in Pennsylvania and and New Jersey.
Publication:	*"Claims Avoidance - What Can You Do?,"* Construction Today, Spring 1990.
Affiliations:	National Society of Professional Engineers, American Arbitration Association, American Society of Highway Engineers, American Bar Association, and other state and local associations.
Committees:	• American Bar Association - Forum Committee on the Construction Industry; Public Contract Forum; Dispute Resolution Committee • Philadelphia Bar Association - Construction Law Committee; Chairman, Land Development Committee • General Building Contractors Association - Education Committee, Cost Effective Construction Committee

MICHAEL B. SMITH

6894 West Chester Pike
Charlottesville, Virginia 23551
(804) 235-6271

FACILITIES & PROPERTY MANAGEMENT PROFESSIONAL

Over 15 years experience in the construction, renovation, maintenance and management of multi-use commercial properties and large facilities complexes. Committed to quality customer service and satisfaction. Experience includes:

- Project Planning & Design
- Project Scheduling & Site Management
- Project Estimating & Budgeting
- Regulatory Compliance

- Purchasing & Materials Management
- Subcontractor Negotiations
- Workflow Planning & Coordination
- Capital Improvements & Expansions

Excellent qualifications in managing general building trades and technical elements of architectural maintenance and construction. Thorough working knowledge of building codes and regulations including ADA, JCAHO, NFPA-LIFE SAFETY, OSHA and BOCA.

PROFESSIONAL EXPERIENCE:

JEFFERSON ESTATES, Charlottesville, Virginia   1974 to Present

300-acre site with 11 primary buildings totalling over 3 million square feet. Properties include a 1 million square foot multi-specialty children's hospital, 12 satellite medical clinics/offices throughout Virginia, and a 42,000 square foot mansion (open for public tours).

Promoted rapidly through a series of increasingly responsible facilities maintenance and management positions to current promotion as:

Supervisor - Facilities Engineering & Planning

More than 10 years direct management responsibility for the facilities operation, including building and grounds management, new construction and facilities renovation. Direct a staff of 30. Manage an $850,000 annual operating budget and an average of $150,000+ in annual capital improvement projects.

Scope of responsibility is diverse and includes the complete project management cycle, from initial design and estimating through planning, scheduling, and site supervision. In addition, responsible for materials planning, purchasing, vendor contract negotiations and inventory control. Coordinate project scheduling to minimize impact upon daily business and medical operations.

MICHAEL B. SMITH
Page Two

Operating & Management Achievements:

- Changed the perception of the Maintenance Department from "blue collar" into a responsive customer-service organization. Implemented systems, processes and schedules to improve service delivery and customer satisfaction.

- Designed and implemented an inventory control system that reduced annual materials expenditures by 10%.

- Restructured staff, workflow and projects to accommodate 25% reduction in workforce. Maintained all production schedules and workflow despite downsizing.

- Developed and implemented improved preventive maintenance programs.

- Appointed to Performance Appraisal Committee working with Human Resource Director to design a new performance-based staff assessment tool for use throughout the entire organization. Selected by HR Director to participate in the first training group for group/meeting facilitation.

- Planned and managed on-site special events for up to 20,000 people.

Project Highlights:

- Directed the renovation of a 9000 square foot area in a 50-year-old building to house an Early Learning Center. Delivered $65,000 project on time and within budget. Managed asbestos and lead paint abatement and all regulatory inspections/approvals.

- Consulted with Superintendent to develop a 5-year renovation and restoration plan for the Jefferson Estate Property. Currently managing completion of this $1.3 million project.

- Worked with Project Design Team for the development of a 4500 square foot hematology/oncology suite. Personally managed all layout and construction for this $120,000 project.

- Directed conversion of an 8400 square foot storage area into "Class A" administrative departments. Controlled $90,000 project budget.

EDUCATION:

B.A., Psychology, College of William & Mary, Williamsburg, Virginia, 1974

Continuing Professional Studies:

- Facilities Compliance Under ADA
- National Fire Prevention Association Life Safety Codes
- OSHA Confined Space Standards
- Fire Brigade Training I & II
- Management Training Seminars
- Facilitation Skills Seminar (Meeting Facilitator)

SAMUEL L. JACKSON
856 Seaside Drive
Providence, Rhode Island 05235

Home (219) 310-6831   Office (219) 658-6484

SENIOR OPERATING & MANAGEMENT EXECUTIVE
Driving Organizational Change, Process Redesign, Quality & Continuous Improvement

---

Hands-on Operating Manager with 10 years professional experience. Expert in analyzing existing operations and implementing the strategies, processes and technologies to improve organizational performance. Leader in the design of Activity Based Management concepts to facilitate process improvement.

Delivered multi-million dollar improvements in productivity and operating efficiency, cost reduction and earnings. Strong P&L management, project management, information technology, human resources and benchmarking experience. Sharp presentation, negotiation and team building qualifications. MBA Degree.

PROFESSIONAL EXPERIENCE:

KPMG PEAT MARWICK LLP, Providence, Rhode Island   1992 to Present

Manager - Strategic Service Consulting

- Promoted from Senior Consultant to Operating Manager of an exclusive business group specializing in the design, development, implementation and leadership of Activity Based Management, Total Quality Management, Process Analysis & Redesign and Manufacturing Systems to achieve Continuous Improvement objectives.

- Manage cross-functional project teams providing expertise in operating, costing, staffing, technical, design, performance management, productivity, quality and efficiency processes to manufacturing corporations throughout the U.S., Mexico and Canada.

- Work in cooperation with operating management teams to facilitate broad-ranging organizational and process improvement programs impacting manufacturing and production, distribution, materials, human resources, MIS and industrial automation, budgeting, costing and product lines.

- Pioneer in Activity Based Management strategies for the identification of the true cost and value of each business process and product. Utilize ABM to drive organizational change and improvement, process redesign, outsourcing, capital appropriation, complexity reduction, facilities redesign, technology advancement and more.

- Completed over eight projects, delivering strong and sustainable operating and financial gains to each client company.

- Drive forward new business development through direct sales, marketing presentations and proposal development.

Project Highlights - Operating, Process & Financial Achievements

- Reduced parts, material and material handling costs by $500,000 and successfully outsourced complex subassembly operation for a large automotive assembly plant.

- Rationalized product line and reduced operating costs by $2+ million annually for a spring and stamping manufacturer.

SAMUEL L. JACKSON

Page Two

KPMG PEAT MARWICK LLP *(Continued)*:

- Increased gear inspection response time by 40% for an automotive transmission and casting manufacturer. Resulted in justification for a $500,000 capital investment to accommodate production volume.

- Redesigned Activity Based Costing Process and reduced implementation cycle time by 73%.

- Reduced operating downtime on major product line by 27% and reengineered Factory Information System processes for 72% reduction in data input costs for one department of a large automotive manufacturer.

- Implemented KANBAN system at an automotive transmission plant increasing production by 2%. Justified purchase of $800,000 of material handling returnable containers.

VELOBIND MANUFACTURING, Cape Cod, Massachusetts   1988 to 1992
($1.1 billion technology manufacturing division of International Technologies)

Continuous Improvement Facilitator / Project Leader (1989 to 1992)
Senior Engineer (1988 to 1989)

One of only 14 professionals selected to spearhead the corporation's first-ever Total Quality Management program. Introduced team-based management, self-managing work teams, SPC methods and other continuous improvement initiatives. Personally trained over 5000 employees and facilitated cross-functional process improvement teams at two large operating plants.

- Led the corporation's successful Malcolm Baldrige National Quality Award application process.

- Presented Continuous Improvement and Employee Involvement educational seminars to corporations and professional business groups throughout the region.

- As Senior Engineer, initiated a series of shop floor continuous improvement processes which reduced a $12 million utility bill by $500,000.

COMBUSTION ENGINEERING, Boston, Massachusetts   1987 to 1988

Estimating Engineer - International Division

Member of a 5-person cross-functional project team responsible design, pricing and proposal development for the competitive win of multi-million dollar power plant construction projects.

EDUCATION:

MBA (Management)	New York University, New York, New York, 1994
BS (Engineering)	Western New England College, Springfield, Massachusetts, 1987
Certification	Process Communication, 1992
Certification	Myers-Briggs Type Indicator, 1991

MARGARET R. JOHNSTON

101 Wabash Avenue #682
Chicago, Illinois 60606

Home (847) 315-6784   Office   (847) 544-2587   Fax (847) 544-6498

SENIOR OPERATING & MANAGEMENT EXECUTIVE

Expert in Process Redesign, Performance Reengineering & Productivity/Performance Improvement

Over 15 years top-flight management experience consulting and directing manufacturing, production and industrial operations worldwide. Pioneer in the design and delivery of innovative change management programs that have generated millions of dollars in cost savings through redesign of internal operating, production and business processes. Expert in facilitating change in a workforce to support reengineering initiatives and meet organizational operating, financial and quality objectives.

PROFESSIONAL EXPERIENCE:

INTERNATIONAL CONSULTING, Chicago, Illinois   1985 to Present

Consultant / Project Manager / Site Implementation Manager

Recruited to join this global consulting group based upon expertise in the design and delivery of value-added process improvements for large scale manufacturers. Assigned to Value Chain Discipline, one of four distinct consulting disciplines, working with clients worldwide to provide expertise in operations, process redesign, productivity improvement and quality.

- Recognized as a subject matter expert on facilitating process change and implementation through training, mentoring and motivation of operating staff and management teams.

Project Highlights & Achievements:

- **U.S. Chemical Products Manufacturer**
  Three-year assignment to a Fortune 500 corporation to facilitate the introduction of process improvement initiatives. Led initial process change that delivered $15 million in cost savings in first year to demonstrate the operational and economic value of business process redesign.

  Long-term efforts impacted operations at 22 sites throughout the U.S. and Europe, and led to successful redesign of processes in maintenance, purchasing, transportation, capital project management, environmental safety & health, product management and other core business functions. Advocated and won the support of in-house operating and management teams to drive forward and maintain process changes.

  RESULTS: Instrumental in implementation of over 15 workstream process changes that cumulatively saved the corporation over $150 million in operating costs.

- **U.K. Pharmaceutical Products Manufacturer**
  Led 6-person consulting team in extensive internal reengineering and process redesign impacting key operating units of the corporation (e.g., quality, production, warehousing, distribution, staffing, manufacturing).

  RESULTS: Created innovative Crewing Allocation Map (manpower allocation model) that reduced staffing costs by 50% within the logistics function and subsequently served as the prototypeother projects. Led a packaging area capacity analysis and process redesign that reduced manpower/machine requirements by 60%.

- **Automobile Manufacturer**
  Launched a complete redesign of maintenance and tool engineering processes for company's Canadian-based operations.

  RESULTS: Delivered a 30% reduction in staffing requirements, reduced delivery lead times and maintained overtime at a rate less than in all previous years of operation.

- **International Information Management Project**
  Led development of prospect database for internal telemarketing and business development that drove International's revenue stream throughout mature and emerging markets.

  Transferred to corporate headquarters to lead the development/implementation of solutions-driven information technologies for a diversity of internal applications. Facilitated needs assessment, hardware/software selection, and implementation of customized technologies.

- **International Consulting Projects**
  Maintain an active leadership role in the design and delivery of process improvement initiatives for internal applications. Co-designed program management process for Leadership Learning Lab and creation of Market Focused Reengineering Methodology (MFR) to create global centers of excellence to support client field engagements.

  Currently operating and participating in a redesign of the staffing process utilized to allocate 350 professionals to 60+ ongoing client projects throughout North America.

NABISCO BRANDS INC., Chicago, Illinois   1980 to 1985

Maintenance Systems Manager (1984 to 1985)
Process Engineering Manager (1981 to 1983)
Process Engineer (1980 to 1981)

Pioneered innovative process development and improvement initiatives throughout the company. Controlled millions of dollars in operating and capital budgets. Led a staff of eight.

- Analyzed, designed and installed process layout including support utilities for a facility with $6.3 million in capital costs. Total capital expenditures exceeded $3.1 million.
- Researched, designed, and supervised installation and start-up of a new continuous production process that increased capacity, quality and material yield while reducing labor costs by 50% for a major product line.

KELLOGG COMPANY, Battle Creek, Michigan   1978 to 1980

Director of Manufacturing (1978 to 1980)
Engineering Manager (1978)

Recruited to direct the design and construction of a new manufacturing facility. Promoted to Director of Manufacturing leading operations at four production facilities.

- Researched, designed, and directed construction and installation of a continuous production operation which increased capacity 800%, reduced labor costs 66% and improved yield 8%.
- Reengineered operating and human resource processes to upgrade raw material yields. Efforts resulted in a 10% reduction in annual purchasing costs.

GENERAL FOODS CORPORATION, St. Paul, Minnesota   1974 to 1977

Senior Process Engineer (1977)
Maintenance Supervisor (1974 to 1977)

Designed and implemented process, quality and facility improvement projects. Designated as an "operations troubleshooter" for the division, travelling to facilities nationwide to direct plant start-ups, resolve long-standing process problems and increase production output.

- Spearheaded problem-solving team implementing process changes that extended the life of $3 million in capital equipment from three years to 20+ years.
- Increased production from 4100 units to 11,400 units per shift over a five-month period.

EDUCATION: **BS / Mechanical Engineering**, University of Illinois, 1974
                   Continuing Professional Education in Information Technology and Statistics.

NICOLE L. HARRIS
23225 George Washington Boulevard
Arlington, Virginia 22553
Home (703) 654-7773   Work (703) 843-4657

CUSTOMER SERVICE AND DISTRIBUTION MANAGER

Results-driven professional with 10 years experience managing high-volume business operations. Excellent problem-solving skills and a strong orientation in customer service/satisfaction. Able to work under pressure in fast-paced, time-sensitive environments. Experienced in analyzing and streamlining product delivery systems to increase productivity, quality and efficiency. Proven ability to manage projects from planning through execution and completion. PC proficient in Microsoft office applications with extensive knowledge of system capabilities.

- Customer Relations
- Policy/Procedure Development
- Distribution/Warehousing Management
- Order Management

- Freight & Transportation Operations
- Productivity Improvement
- Staff Training/Development
- Business Systems Implementation

PROFESSIONAL EXPERIENCE:

PILSEN, INC., Fairfax, Virginia   1986 to Present
(Largest importer of international beers in the U.S.)

> **Customer Service Manager** (August 1990 to Present)
> **Customer Service Coordinator** (January 1990 to August 1990)
> **Distribution Analyst** (1986 to 1990)

Rapidly promoted through several increasingly responsible assignments to current position as Customer Service Manager. Direct the strategic planning, development, staffing, management and financial performance of Pilsen's customer service organization. Scope of responsibility impacts product flow and distribution to 900 distributors nationwide with revenues of more than $350 million annually.

Manage the depletion of warehouse inventory (3 million cases per month) with a monthly asset value of $9 million. Effectively communicate with customers, sales representatives and carriers to facilitate expedient and cost-effective product delivery. Liaison between breweries, warehouses and distributors.

Train, direct and motivate a staff of six. Manage and coordinate action plans for daily operation of the Customer Service Department, establish work priorities, and assist staff with problem resolution.

Project team member for the implementation of a new inventory management system to support the business and improve customer service. The system comprises applications from American Software, runs on an IBM AS400 platform, supports remote warehouses and is linked to major vendors. Worked extensively with MIS staff as client representative to develop user requirements, work flow procedures and user documentation. Trained staff at both corporate headquarters and warehouse facilities during implementation phase. Post-implementation responsibilities involved a series of improvement projects.

NICOLE L. HARRIS

Page Two

PILSEN, INC. *(Continued)*:

- Successfully maintained exemplary customer service levels during the introduction and explosive growth of Pilsen Ice, the largest imported product launch in the industry.

- Coordinated the implementation of new packaging affecting the entire Pilsen brand family. Worked cooperatively with wholesalers and sales staff in placing orders and converting existing orders to ensure proper timing of inventory runouts at the distributor level.

- Reorganized customer service organization and improved customer service levels from 70% to over 95%.

- Created and initiated procedures and reporting to facilitate the sale of excess stock, partial pallets and over-age stock to avoid product obsolescence.

- Managed all customer service activities associated with the conversion of 300 wholesalers (30% of customer base) from Pilsen to Coors as part of the 1997 acquisition.

- Selected from among 85 employees to receive the prestigious President's Award for consistent excellence in performance, productivity and attitude in 1993 and 1995.

BENEFITS ADMINISTRATION, Centerport, New York   1984 to 1986

Account Supervisor

Processed millions of dollars in major medical and dental claims for member groups. Consulted with clients regarding coverage, claims and payment. Researched and resolved complex issues.

NATIONAL INSURANCE COMPANY, Hackensack, New Jersey   1978 to 1984

Dental Claims Supervisor

Supervised a staff of five in a dental claims unit. Audited processed claims and maintained production reports. Designed and implemented new office procedures to increase productivity and facilitate greater efficiency.

PROFESSIONAL TRAINING AND EDUCATION:

Management Training & Development
Customer Service Management
Computer Technology

Diploma, Westbury High School, New York, 1977

References Available Upon Request

KENNETH R. THOMPSON, M.Ed.

3593 Ivy League Hill   Home   (801) 336-5978
Springfield, Massachusetts 08251   Office   (801) 853-4476

HIGHER EDUCATION EXECUTIVE / SENIOR MANAGER / VICE PRESIDENT

Twenty-year collegiate and university management career with three distinguished institutions. Consistently successful in introducing strategic marketing and operational plans, athletic programs and student services to increase enrollment, enhance the student experience and strengthen competitive market position. Strong leadership, communication, and student and institutional advocacy skills. Committed to holistic student development and learning experience. Core competencies include:

- Departmental/Divisional Leadership
- Admissions & Recruitment
- Enrollment Management
- Financial Aid
- Strategic Planning
- Budgeting & Financial Planning

- Intercollegiate Athletic Operations
- Alumni Relations & Fundraising
- Career Development & Placement
- Campus & Residence Life
- Student Activities & Services
- Analytical & Statistical Methodologies

PROFESSIONAL EXPERIENCE:

MORRISON COLLEGE, Springfield, Massachusetts   1979 to Present

Recruited to this small private college in 1979 and promoted through a series of increasingly responsible management positions. Instrumental in transitioning from a regionally-based college into a nationally-recognized institution. Pioneered innovative marketing, recruitment, financial aid, student service, alumni development and technology programs. Career highlights include:

Vice President of Enrollment & Student Life / Dean of Campus Life (1989 to Present)

Senior Executive with full responsibility for the strategic planning, development, budgeting and operating leadership of Admissions, Financial Aid, Intercollegiate Athletics & Recreation, Alumni Relations and Career Development Departments. In partnership with Dean of Students, oversee Greek Affairs, Student Activities, Community Service, Social Judicial Board and Residence Life. Manage $900,000 in annual operating/administrative budgets. Teach wellness curriculum.

Admissions & Enrollment

- Innovated high-profile student recruitment and retention programs that have increased enrollment 10% and five-year graduation rates 8%.

- Created an integrated recruitment, admissions and financial aid program that delivered for five consecutive years a freshman class which exceeded enrollment targets and remained at or below budgeted financial aid. Currently award $9 million annually in financial aid to 900+ students.

- Expanded print communications to extend marketing, advertising and promotional programs.

- Directed design of application review grid methodology and implementation of LAN data management system.

Financial Aid

- Orchestrated development of a predictive methodology to project financial aid funding requirements based on historical trends.

- Facilitated introduction of leading edge software program (Micro/PowerFaids) to enhance forecasting, analysis and reporting capabilities.

KENNETH R. THOMPSON, M.Ed.   *Page Two*

Athletics

- Spearheaded the design and implementation of a student-focused program of intercollegiate and intramural athletics. Focused department's mission and reallocated resources to enhance program quality and increase student participation.

- Currently leading comprehensive capital campaign to raise $3.3 million for construction of all-weather track and renovation of athletic playing fields.

- Upgraded student employment program in athletic facilities to reduce staffing costs to the College while increasing career training and development opportunities for the student population.

- Launched complete reorganization of Athletic Department management team, restructured core processes and procedures, and produced comprehensive operations manual.

Alumni Relations

- Appointed for two-year tenure as Director of Alumni Relations, leading a number of innovative alumni development and management programs.

- Developed plan to organize 15,000 alumni by geographic regions to accelerate support for admissions, careers, volunteerism and fundraising.

- Established on-campus, lifelong learning program for alumni to increase alumni involvement and further strengthen partnerships.

- Developed leadership program targeted to recent graduates and dedicated to long-term support.

Dean of Admissions & Financial Aid (1983 to 1989)

Promoted to plan and direct the reorganization and refinement of the Admissions and Financial Aid Departments. Redesigned core processes, streamlined operations and accelerated program growth. Directed a staff of 14 and managed a $300,000 annual operating budget.

- Created and launched a multi-faceted recruitment program including high school visitations, open house visitations, targeted direct mail, guidance counselor cultivation and alumni admissions networking. Results included 185% increase in admissions inquiries, 53% increase in applications and 10% increase in matriculants.

- Appointed to senior management team which developed and implemented the College's strategic planning processes for enrollment, facilities, curriculum, personnel, finances and public relations.

Associate Dean / Assistant Dean of Admissions & Freshmen (1979 to 1983)

High-profile position building market presence nationwide to increase enrollment. Directed freshman orientation and advisement programs with a team of 30 faculty/staff advisors and 100 student volunteers. Directly supervised 10 professional and support staff in Admissions Department.

Highlights of Committee Participation & Leadership:

- Member, Middle States Accreditation Committee, Subcommittee on Campus Climate (1995 to 1996)
- Member, College Committee on Athletics, Recreation & Intramurals (1993 to Present)
- Member, Centennial Athletic Conference (1993 to Present)
- Co-Chair, Athletic Facility Task Force (1992 to 1993)
- Member, Middle States Five-Year Review Committee (1990 to 1991)
- Chair (5 years) & Member, College Retention Committee (1989 to Present)
- Member, Budget Advisory Committee (1989 to 1993)
- Chair, College Center Renovation Committee (1989 to 1990)
- Member, College Marketing Task Force (1986 to 1990)

UNIVERSITY OF TENNESSEE, Knoxville, Tennessee   1977 to 1979

Graduate Advisor to Dean of Students

Broad administrative, organizational and special projects responsibilities in the Office of the Dean of Students for this 7000-student university.

- Appointed to the University's Risk Management Committee and as Coordinator of In-State Residency Committee.

- Planned and directed a large-scale research project on competitive strategies for student retention.

BURLINGTON COLLEGE, Burlington, North Carolina   1975 to 1977

Associate Dean of Admissions

Led a team of two professional and three support staff in directing student recruitment and admissions programs for this 500-student institution.

EDUCATION:

HARVARD UNIVERSITY GRADUATE SCHOOL OF EDUCATION
Institute of Educational Management, 1995

UNIVERSITY OF TENNESSEE
M.Ed., Higher Education Administration, 1979

BURLINGTON COLLEGE
B.A., Interdisciplinary Philosophy, <u>summa cum laude</u>, 1975

PROFESSIONAL AFFILIATIONS:

Member, MA Department of Education Visiting Team, Harcum Junior College
Member, National Collegiate Athletic Association
Member, The College Board
Past Member, MA Association of School & College Admissions Counselors
Past Member, MASCAC Executive Committee
Past Member, National Association of College Admissions Counselors

COMMUNITY ACTIVITIES:

Board of Directors, Morrison College Habitat for Humanity
Co-Founder, Morrison College/Jefferson Elementary School Partnership
Member, Church Adult Christian Education Committee
Coach, South Parkland Youth Association
Past Member, Board of Directors, Springfield YMCA
Past Member, Big Brothers/Big Sisters of Springfield
Past Member, Selection Committee, Mack Truck Scholarship Program
Past Member, Selection Committee, Sponsored Scholarship Program (ETS)

ANDREW R. KENNEDY
312 Saratoga Springs Road
Allentown, Pennsylvania 19344
(610) 713-9711

NUCLEAR UTILITY / ENERGY / PROCESS INDUSTRY EXECUTIVE

Strategic & Financial Planning / Finance & Budget Analysis / Engineering & Technology
Executive Marketing / MIS / Training & Development / Project Planning & Costing
Organizational Development / Productivity & Efficiency Improvement / Cost Reduction
Regulatory Affairs / Risk Analysis / Manpower Planning / Process Reengineering

Successful industry executive with an impressive record of achievement in designing the strategies, analyses, methods, processes and operations to improve financial performance. MBA Degree.

PROFESSIONAL EXPERIENCE:

PENNSYLVANIA POWER & LIGHT COMPANY, Allentown, Pennsylvania   1981 to Present

Promoted rapidly during 14-year career through a series of increasingly responsible operating and management positions to current assignment as the **Supervisor of Operating Experience Services**. Innovated state-of-the-art processes to manage large-scale utility operations with focus on cost control, safety management, personnel development and regulatory compliance. Provided technical, finance and operating leadership in complex business divisions. Delivered significant and sustainable results:

- Pioneered an innovative maintenance work observation and analysis technique that increased labor availability and captured over $500,000 in annual operating cost savings. Introduced leading edge probabilistic risk assessment methods that saved over $5 million in power generation costs.

- Identified $5 million in cost reduction of a $117 million operating budget. Launched a series of high-profile process analysis, productivity improvement and quality initiatives that saved and additional $1 million in operating costs.

- Authored comprehensive justification for Public Utilities Commission of schedule delays on construction of a $4.25 billion, 2-unit nuclear power plant. Resulted in 100% allowance for all project costs in approved rate base.

- Pioneered innovative operating processes including the first Human Performance Enhancement Program, Master Resource Planning Protocols, Regulatory Compliance Standards and a Professional Certification Program.

- Designed and managed a multi-tiered cost improvement program which reduced operating expenses and resulted in a net decrease of 2% in the customer cost of electrical utility.

- Created a maintenance backlog reduction program that reduced open work orders by 15% and average age of backlog by 20%.

- Designed standards and models for financial planning, performance analysis, manpower planning, estimating, costing, budgeting and forecasting implemented throughout the entire corporation.

- Led a series of successful MIS and networking technologies installations and system upgrades.

ANDREW R. KENNEDY - *Page Two*

SUMMARY OF POSITIONS & KEY RESPONSIBILITIES:

Supervisor - Operating Experience Services (1995 to Present)
Supervisor - Nuclear Compliance (1994 to 1995)

Promoted to high-profile position directing all nuclear compliance programs for the entire organization. Scope of responsibility includes technical specifications compliance and interpretation, operability determination procedures and methods, reporting processes, deficiency and corrective action programs, root cause analysis and investigation programs, and daily interface with NRC resident inspectors.

Transferred to newly created position as Supervisor of Operating Experience Services in February 1995. Maintain all previous responsibilities with additional accountability for the analysis and trending of all nuclear operating experience events.

- Pioneered development of Human Performance Enhancement Program, a self-reporting system of non-consequential and "near miss" events, utilized to analyze trends and identify precursors to consequential events. Created solutions-driven strategies to enhance long-term performance factors.

- Restored cooperative relationships with on-site NRC inspectors and preempted escalation of potential regulatory issues.

- Orchestrated transition from obsolete mainframe-based deficiency management information system to newly-designed LAN technology incorporating Microsoft ACCESS, Oracle and other graphical software applications.

- Designed leading-edge root cause analysis methods, developed standards and criteria, and incorporated into existing training materials.

- Instituted 24-hour investigations for all new internal operating experience events (800+ per year). Program has subsequently been reviewed by other utilities nationwide and is currently pending issuance of "Industry Good Practice" designation by the Institute of Nuclear Power Operations.

Acting Supervisor - Nuclear Planning & Cost Services (1993 to 1994)

Directed 20 engineers and analysts responsible for all costing, budgeting, process redesign, financial planning and operating planning functions for this $4 million business unit. Coordinated strategic, annual operating and 5-year business planning. Managed organization-wide benchmarking initiatives.

- Replaced former financial budgeting and reporting system with an integrated on-line, real-time information system to network plant operations with headquarters and provide computerized decision making models and analyses.

- Provided technical and engineering expertise for a massive system retrofit and construction program. Brought $3 million project in under budget and ahead of schedule.

- Designed a professional certification program to upgrade technical and project management skills.

Senior Project Engineer - Susquehanna Planning & Cost Services (1985 to 1993)

Led a team of 4 engineers, 2 computer analysts and external consultants responsible for cost management and financial planning process development, analysis and reporting of $190 million O&M budget and a $60 million capital expenditure budget. Designed new computer technology for cost and planning functions, developed labor estimating standards and spearheaded productivity improvement programs.

Senior Project Engineer - General Office Planning & Scheduling Group (1981 to 1985)

Supervised a team of 6 engineers and analysts responsible for master resource plans and integrated schedules for facilities construction, start-up, operations and maintenance.

ANDREW R. KENNEDY - *Page Three*

OWENS-CORNING FIBERGLAS CORPORATION, Toledo, Ohio   1970 to 1981

    Project Manager (1979 to 1981)
    Schedule Manager (1978 to 1979)
    Project Engineer (1977 to 1978)
    Project Control Supervisor (1976 to 1977)
    Cost Control Engineer (1970 to 1976)

Fast-track promotion through a series of increasingly responsible capital project estimating, costing, planning and scheduling positions. Directed general and subcontractor scheduling and all manpower planning functions for the then-largest fiberglass reinforcements manufacturing facility in the U.S.

Promoted to final position as Project Manager with full responsibility for marketing and process development of state-of-the-art specialty insulation systems (primarily for the process and nuclear industries). Authored Nuclear Quality Assurance Manual for systems design and manufacture.

- Launched marketing plan for new product portfolio that delivered over $10 million in first year sales.

- Designed new thermal insulation technology for cryogenic and underground piping systems that generated over $18 million in new revenues.

- Directed on-site system installations worldwide.

EDUCATION:

MBA / Finance, Lehigh University, 1985
BS / Mechanical Engineering, University of Notre Dame, 1970

Post Graduate Studies in Industrial Engineering and Management

PROFESSIONAL PROFILE:

Licenses
- Professional Engineer (PE), Registered in Pennsylvania & Kansas
- Certified Cost Engineer (CCE), American Association of Cost Engineers
- Certified BWR Non-Licensed Operator

Publications
- Presented 12 technical papers at professional symposia and conferences, including Lehigh University, American Association of Cost Engineers, Pennsylvania Electric Association, Edison Electric Institute, American Society of Mechanical Engineers, American Nuclear Society and Institute of Industrial Engineers.

Affiliations
- Director & Past President, Eastern PA Association of Cost Engineers
- Legislative "Minuteman," National Society of Professional Engineers
- Past Fund Raising Chairperson, MATHCOUNTS, National Society of Professional Engineers
- Member, Institute of Industrial Engineers

MICHELLE JENKINS

10 Goosedown Court
Morrestown, New Jersey 08532
Home (609)732-9705   Office (609) 296-6479

ENVIRONMENTAL ENGINEER / ENVIRONMENTAL HEALTH & SAFETY MANAGER
Wastewater, Solid, Air & Site Hazard Remediation

CAREER PROFILE

Fourteen years of increasingly responsible experience in Environmental & Safety Engineering. Directed remediation of more than 100 sites nationwide, reducing corporate exposure and liability, cutting costs and achieving regulatory compliance. MS Degree in Environmental Engineering. Qualifications include:

- Environmental Technology & Engineering
- Site Assessment & Remediation
- Resource Recovery & Conservation
- Governmental Liaison Affairs
- Acquisition & Investment Analysis
- Public Speaking & Media Affairs
- Policymaking & Process Management
- Project Budgeting & Management
- Environmental Law & Litigation
- Cross-Functional Team Leadership
- Environmental & Safety Training
- Crisis Management & Emergency Response

Regulatory Affairs

Expert knowledge of Superfund requirements and methodology (including four years direct employment with the EPA), and all RCRA, TSCA, CERCLA, SARA, UST and CWA regulations. Extensive knowledge of governmental regulations, occupational safety (OSHA), industrial hygiene standards, health and safety affairs, and permitting.

Industry Experience

Broad experience in heavy manufacturing including chemicals, polymers, electronics, advanced technology, metals, oil and gas, mechanical components and consumer products.

Project Management Experience

Directed project teams of up to 25 engineers and field managers at sites nationwide. Wrote project remediation and management plans, prepared budgets, acquired technology resources and directed field operations. Managed outside liaison affairs with consultants, regulatory agency personnel, attorneys and the press.

PROFESSIONAL EXPERIENCE

Environmental Engineer , UNITED INTERNATIONAL, Princeton, New Jersey   1994 to Present

- Directed 350+ site remediation projects in less than two years.
- Saved $1 million in remediation costs on proposed site acquisitions, foreclosures and divestitures.
- Only Environmental Engineer in the entire corporation.

Environmental Engineer, AMERICAN WATER HEATER, Johnson City, Tennessee   1993 to 1994

- Spearheaded design, development and implementation of company-wide environmental health and safety program for this large manufacturer. Achieved 100% regulatory compliance.
- Delivered $650,000 cost savings on large soil remediation project.

PROFESSIONAL EXPERIENCE *(Continued)*

Project Manager, GENERAL ELECTRIC COMPANY, Fairfield, Connecticut   1991 to 1993

- Created a comprehensive hazardous materials remediation, resource recovery and conservation program for a $10 million GE facility.
- Controlled $1.4 million in remediation funds.
- Managed technical and regulatory reviews of proposed acquisitions and divestitures.

Project Manager, AMOCO OIL COMPANY, Farmington Hills, Michigan   1989 to 1991

- Led remediation teams in the design/development of soil and groundwater remediation systems, proposed technologies for subsurface investigation and other advanced environmental engineering programs.
- Managed up to 860 ongoing projects with supervisory responsibility for both in-house and consulting engineers.

Environmental Engineer, ENVIRONMENTAL PROTECTION AGENCY, Atlanta, Georgia   1985 to 1989

- Superfund Project Manager for CERCLA, RCRA and Underground Storage Tank programs throughout the U.S. Completed more than 100 projects and regulatory reviews.

Environmental Engineer, WANG LABORATORIES, Lowell, Massachusetts   1983 to 1985

- Designed and managed environmental systems for hazardous waste, hazardous materials, air emissions and wastewater discharges.

MILITARY SERVICE

Bioenvironmental Engineer/Safety Officer, U.S. AIR FORCE RESERVE, Denver, Colorado   1984 to 1991

- Directed safety and environmental programs at large base installation. Designed and led on-site training programs on hazard recognition, documentation, handling, transportation and abatement/remediation.

EDUCATION

MS (Environmental Engineering), Tufts University, Medford, Massachusetts, 1982
BS (Biology), Morgan State University, Baltimore, Maryland, 1979
Diploma (Bioenvironmental & Safety Engineering), USAF School of Aerospace Medicine, 1984

AFFILIATIONS

National Environmental Health Association
National Association of Environmental Professionals
American Conference of Government Industrial Hygienists
National Society for Black Engineers

MATTHEW R. KINARD
232 Horse Stable Road
St. Paul, Minnesota 55203
(612) 384-4652

CAREER PROFILE:

Senior R&D Professional successful in leading sophisticated product design, development and scale-up programs for diverse market and industry demands. Liaison among R&D, manufacturing and marketing to define customer demand, lead product development and facilitate cost-effective, quality-driven production. Experienced in health care, pharmacology, photo imagesetting, printing, industrial, automotive and construction products/technologies.

Excellent qualifications in cross-functional team leadership, resource management, project planning and technical documentation. Effective customer liaison with strong interpersonal and communication skills. Expertise in designed experiment and statistical analysis methodologies.

PROFESSIONAL EXPERIENCE:

3M CORPORATION, St. Paul, Minnesota   1979 to Present

Seventeen-year career leading complex R&D programs for several core 3M divisions. Recognized for outstanding research, product development and project management expertise.

- Nominated for 3M's "Technical Circle of Excellence" award in 1995.
- Finalist for 3M's "Corporate Quality Achievement" award in 1993 and 1995.

Research Specialist - Printing & Publishing Systems Division (1989 to Present)
3M, St. Paul, Minnesota / **Rochester Technical Center (RTC)**, Rochester, New York

Senior R&D Scientist for 3M's family of new Onyx™ Silver-Halide Imagesetting Products designed to increase efficiency, improve productivity and reduce the cost of commercial printing operations. Challenged to accelerate product development, introduce methods and designs to increase product functionality, and redesign and implement processes to reduce annual R&D and manufacturing costs. Function as Acting Manager of RTC in absence of manager.

Scope of responsibility includes leadership of the entire Onyx™ Program R&D function and the direct training/supervision of a cross-functional team of scientists and engineers. Guide Marketing and Technical Services teams in identifying customer/market demand and developing appropriate products, line extensions and technologies. Consult directly with key accounts nationwide.

- Technical Team Leader for scale-up and continuous improvement of Silver-Halide products. Delivered significant improvements in performance, consistency and manufacturability. **RESULTS:**

  — Directed development of new product line and line extensions that delivered $7.8 million in revenues in 1996.
  — Reduced factory unit costs by 20% ($200,000+).

- Co-Developer and Co-Team Leader for scale-up of new laser imagesetting plate (line extension). Directed a 15-person R&D, quality assurance and technical service team. **RESULTS:**

  — Increased factory emulsion productivity by 50%.
  — Reduced sensitometric speed variability by 33%.
  — Resolved key production scale-up issues using designed experiments.
  — Delivered product on time and within budget despite several critical redevelopment stages.
  — Projected volume of $6.5 million in new revenues to the corporation.

- Developer and Team Leader for delivery of reduced speed RLD/HN imagesetting plate (line extension). Redesigned core product in response to specific market/customer demands to increase product functionality, field performance and reliability.

  — Currently facilitating final product completion and field testing prior to full-scale introduction.

MATTHEW R. KINARD - *Page Two*

3M CORPORATION *(Continued)*:

Medical Service Representative (1984 to 1989)
3M Riker, St. Paul, Minnesota

Recruited to 3M's pharmaceutical and transdermal drug delivery systems business unit to identify and strengthen experience in customer/market demand. Challenged to launch the introduction of new pharmaceutical products while continuing to build volume in existing product lines.

- Successfully introduced first of a new class of antiarrhythmic agents to the University of Iowa Medical Center. Worked closely with University cardiologists over a three-year period to launch product and facilitate further drug studies.

- Won 1987 "Outstanding Sales Achievement Award" and nomination for "Top Performer's Group" in 1986 and 1987.

Post-Doctoral Fellow - Chemistry & Pharmacology (1982 to 1984)
University of Minnesota / Rochester School of Medicine & Dentistry, Rochester, New York

Two-year leave of absence from 3M to complete an NIH-funded intensive post-doctoral research training fellowship. Conducted in-vitro investigation of the mechanism of activation of cyclophosphamide, a highly-effective, but toxic anti-tumor agent, to determine if more stable, less-toxic analogues could be developed.

- Conducted preliminary laboratory investigations that led to subsequent development of new analogues for pharmacological testing.

- Recipient of the competitive and prestigious Wilson Fellowship.

Senior Chemist - Industrial Specialties Division (1979 to 1982)
3M Center, St. Paul, Minnesota

Led development, introduction and successful application of new urethane foam tapes for automotive applications. Concurrent with R&D responsibilities, provided technical service/support to major customers and to 3M's nationwide sales and marketing teams.

- Guided development through the R&D cycle including pilot plant and factory production scale-up.

Previous Professional Experience:

Industrial Chemist - Eastman Kodak Company (1974 to 1975)
Quality Control Supervisor - U.S. Gypsum Co. (1971 to 1974)

EDUCATION:

Ph.D., Organic (Heterocyclic) Chemistry, University of East Anglia, Norwich, England, 1979
M.Sc., Organic Chemistry, University of East Anglia, Norwich, England, 1976
B.A., Chemistry, State University of New York, Buffalo, New York, 1971

PROFESSIONAL AFFILIATIONS:

American Institute of Chemists (Fellow)
American Chemical Society
American Association for the Advancement of Science

ADAM F. EDMONDS
418 Alexander Street
Philadelphia, Pennsylvania 18969
(215) 721-0294

SENIOR ENGINEERING & PROJECT MANAGEMENT EXECUTIVE
Expert in the Design & Installation of Complex Technology Systems

---

Fifteen years of progressively responsible experience in engineering design and project management for clients in the US, Canada, Latin America, Far East and Australia. Combines excellent technical, analytical and engineering qualifications with demonstrated achievement in delivering multi-million dollar projects on time and within budget. Strong leadership, team building and problem solving expertise. Qualifications:

- Project Design & Management
- Engineering Management
- Estimating, Budgeting and P&L
- Field Installation Management
- Resource Planning & Management

- Client Presentations & Negotiations
- Cross-Functional Team Leadership
- Vendor Selection & Negotiation
- Material Selection & Management
- Product & Technology R&D

Excellent skills in client relationship management and cross-cultural communications. PC proficient with CADRA CAD, Lotus, Microsoft Projects, WordPerfect, and other spreadsheet, database and word processing applications. Experienced in PC FORTRAN and BASIC programming.

PROFESSIONAL EXPERIENCE:

ACCURATE SYSTEMS, Chester, Pennsylvania   1996 to Present
(Material Handling Systems Technology)

Project Manager / Project Director

Recruited to direct the design, development and installation of high-speed material handling equipment and related bar coding technology, designed specifically for the postal, mail handling and direct mail industries worldwide.

AMC CORPORATION, Berwyn, Pennsylvania   1982 to 1996
(Material Handling Systems Division)

Project Manager / Senior Design Engineer (1990 to 1996)
Design Engineer (1983 to 1990)
Engineer (1982 to 1983)

Fast-track promotion through a series of increasingly responsible engineering and project management positions in a $100 million business group. Responsible for the cost-effective design and management of "turnkey" automated material handling systems for clients worldwide. Held P&L responsibility for all assigned projects (from $4 million to $16 million).

Managed programs from initial concept and proposal preparation through design, specification, installation, commission, debug and final client acceptance. Provided technical and engineering assistance to marketing teams and participated in client presentations/contract negotiations. Led cross-functional teams of software, electrical and mechanical engineers throughout entire project cycle. Managed relationships with project managers, production managers and plant managers at client sites worldwide.

ADAM F. EDMONDS
Page Two

AMC CORPORATION *(Continued):*

Project Highlights & Achievements:

- **News Limited (Australia)**. Directed completion of 6-year, $16 million project with installation at four sites in Australia. Delivered project at 10.1% over profit projections.

- **Singapore Press Holdings (Singapore)**. Negotiated 60% of $3 million project as "up front" cash to finance project design, engineering and installation.

- **The Age (Australia)**. Led successful turnaround of technically challenging project (first time installation of new non-wire guided vehicle system). Resolved technical issues and negotiated favorable settlement at $382,000 over initial selling price.

- **World Press (US)**. Integrated all RAVEN (automated material handling systems) into one large-scale project, defined installation phases, led client presentations and returned project to "on-time, on-budget" status.

- Other major clients included **The New York Times, The Washington Post, Fruit of the Loom (US), Apotex (Canada), Reckitt & Colman (Brazil)** and **Vernon Warehouse**. Managed a mixed portfolio of projects, each with unique technical challenges and emphasis on cost-effective project delivery and customer satisfaction.

- Championed concept and spearheaded initial design of an automatic loading table (C-93) designed specifically for newspaper publishing. Revenues are projected at $15+ million.

NOTE: *Early career experience designing automatic guided vehicles and bulk handling systems.*

ALTECH INDUSTRIES, Allentown, Pennsylvania   1980 to 1982

Product Engineer

Designed, developed and facilitated manufacture of vapor recovery systems for oil storage tanks. Coordinated departmental and production scheduling, customer interface, project planning and field installations.

EDUCATION:

M.S., Mechanical Engineering, Lehigh University, Bethlehem, Pennsylvania, 1989
B.S., Mechanical Engineering, Lafayette College, Easton, Pennsylvania, 1980

GERARD MONTEGUE

1650 Avenue de la Parc, Apt. 52
Montreal, Quebec H36 2R1

Phone (514) 231-6545   Fax (514) 231-6544

FOOD & BEVERAGE / HOSPITALITY / RESTAURANT MANAGEMENT

Fifteen years experience in Food & Beverage Management for exclusive hotels, restaurants and conference centers. Excellent qualifications in planning, marketing, budgeting, expense control, staffing, training and quality management. Contributed to significant revenue gains and cost reductions.

Multinational experience. Fluent in English, French and Arabic. Worldwide travel throughout the U.S., Canada, Turkey, Cyprus, Kuwait, United Arab Emirates (Dubai), Saudi Arabia, Bahrain, Egypt, Philippines and Switzerland. Permanent Resident of Canada.

Certified Food & Beverage Executive (CFBE), 1992
U.S. Educational Institute of American Hotel & Motel Association

PROFESSIONAL EXPERIENCE:

Conference Center Manager   1994 to 1996
BAHRAIN CONFERENCE CENTER / HYATT REGENCY HOTEL - Bahrain

Recruited to plan and direct the start-up of the country's first-ever conference center at this 5-star hotel complex. Managed all pre-opening activities (e.g., operations, equipment, staff recruitment, training) and a high-profile marketing and business development effort. Responsible for F&B operations, banquet and conference management, VIP relations, contract negotiations, event planning/logistics, kitchen operations, and all customer service functions.

- Built the Center from concept into a 22-employee operation generating over US$350,000 in revenues within first three months. Concurrently, managed 70 contract staff.
- Created policies, procedures, standards and performance goals.
- Designed budgeting, expense control and month-end reporting methods.
- Trained both permanent and contract staff in quality-based service.

NOTE: Resigned position in December 1996 to relocate to Canada.

Assistant Food & Beverage Manager   1990 to 1994
HASSAN HOTELS & RESORTS MANAGEMENT COMPANY - Dubai

Joined Hassan following their acquisition of the 5-star International Hotel of Dubai (previous employer). Working in cooperation with F&B Director, managed all operations for four on-site outlets, room service, and outside catering and banquets. Managed a permanent staff of 125 and up to 70 contract personnel. Authorized expenditures for US$3 million annual purchasing budget.

Held concurrent management responsibility for all on-site catering for the Head of State at the Dubai Royal Palace (Hassan held exclusive contract). Personally planned, staffed and managed events for worldwide political leaders and visiting dignitaries.

- Increased F&B revenues to US$750,000 per month. Expanded operations and service offerings, introduced operating/quality standards, and delivered consistently superior customer service.

*NOTE: Joined Hassan in 1990 after one year as **Restaurant Manager with International Hotel of Dubai** (acquired Hilton International in 1989).*

GERARD MONTEGUE   *Page Two*

Acting Restaurant Manager   1986 to 1989
HILTON INTERNATIONAL - Abu Dabi
(5 star hotel with 406 rooms/suites, ballroom, 13 meeting rooms with 1150 guest capacity, 3 restaurants, tea lounge, 2 executive floors and complete sports/recreational facilities)

Full operating and P&L responsibility for management of La Palma Restaurant. Responsibility was diverse and included budgeting, staffing, training, kitchen operations, purchasing, inventory management, menu planning, customer service and quality control. Managed 20 employees.

- Built La Palma into the #1 restaurant in Abu Dabi with over 162,000 covers annually (approximately US$2.5 million).
- Achieved or surpassed all food, beverage and labor cost controls/budget goals.

Assistant Maitre D'Hotel   1985 to 1986
LE SOVERIEGN - Kuwait
(5 star hotel with 377 rooms/suites, 3 restaurants, tea lounge, 900 cover banquet operation, and sports facilities)

Second-in-command of all F&B operations throughout this metropolitan hotel. Focused efforts on improving service standards, designing operational and quality controls, and identifying/capturing cost reductions. Trained and supervised a staff of 24.

- Generated market's highest percentage of repeat clientele compared to similar F&B operations.

Previous Professional Experience (1979 to 1985) at exclusive, 5-star hotels including **Holiday Inn Pyramid** (Cairo), **Marriott Hotel** (Cairo) and **Massarah Intercontinental** (Saudia Arabia). Promoted rapidly through a series of increasingly responsible F&B service positions.

EDUCATION:

Graduate - Food & Beverage Management Program, 1993
Ecole Hotelier de la Societe Suisse des Hoteliers, Lausanne, Switzerland

Graduate - Hospitality Management Diploma, 1993
Educational Institute of American Hotel & Motel Association, Michigan, US

Graduate - Food & Beverage Management Specialization Program, 1989
Educational Institute of American Hotel & Motel Association, Michigan, US

CONTINUING PROFESSIONAL EDUCATION:

Completed extensive continuing professional education throughout career. Course highlights include:

- Time Management for Executives, 1994
- Sales & Marketing Promotions, 1993
- Managing Computers in the Hospitality Industry, 1992
- Hospitality Purchasing Management, 1992
- Action Centered Leadership, Kuwait Hotels Company, 1992
- Hospitality Human Resources Management, 1990
- Customer First Program, Bahrain Hotels Company, 1989
- Train the Trainers Course, Hilton International, 1989
- Organization & Administration, 1989

PROFESSIONAL AFFILIATIONS:

Associate Member, Hotel Catering & Institutional Management Association - U.K.
Chef de Table, Confrerie de la chaine des Rotisseurs - Kuwait

MARK J. RICHARDSON

5647 Roosevelt Street
Atlanta, Georgia 33854
(404) 954-6547

OBJECTIVE: Corporate Finance — Planning, Analysis, Administration & Management.

QUALIFICATIONS:

- Financial Analysis & Reporting
- Capital Budgeting & Administration
- Project Forecasting & Budgeting
- Project Staffing & Management
- Public Speaking & Presentation
- Customer Development & Management
- Economic Analysis
- Quantitative Analysis
- Resource Planning & Allocation
- Cost & Benefit Analysis
- Team Building & Leadership
- Technology Concepts & Theory

Excellent qualifications in managing large-scale projects, from concept through planning, design, development and task management. Precise, detail-oriented and analytical. Proficient in MS Project, Excel, Word and PowerPoint. Fluent in Spanish; reading knowledge of Russian. Member, Financial Management Association.

EDUCATION:

MBA (Finance)	EMORY UNIVERSITY	December 1996
MA (Linguistics)	FLORIDA STATE UNIVERSITY	May 1990
BA (Spanish & English)	MIAMI UNIVERSITY	May 1984

PROFESSIONAL EXPERIENCE:

AT&T / LUCENT TECHNOLOGIES   1992 to Present

Senior Technology Project Manager (1993 to Present)
Project Coordinator (1992 to 1993)

Senior Project Manager leading cross-functional teams of up to 50 in-house and contract personnel in the design, development and delivery of advanced language translation technology solutions to support client globalization requirements. Develop project quotations and work designs, prepare cost and revenue budgets, and control P&L to achieve/surpass company financial objectives.

Completed over 100 projects during past three years. Currently managing a portfolio of 15 projects with total revenue value of $2+ million.

MARK J. RICHARDSON

Page Two

AT&T / LUCENT TECHNOLOGIES *(Continued):*

Project Highlights & Achievements:

- Ranked as the top-producing project manager in the company, generating over $1 million in new revenues in the past 12 months. Personally generated over 80% of total revenue of facility in September 1996.

- Appointed Project Manager for $1 million contract with Hewlett Packard. Currently leading 50-person project team of programmers, software engineers, technology consultants, translators and support personnel worldwide.

- Delivered all projects on time and within budget. Brought numerous projects in under budget (up to 20% under expense goals).

- Led successful projects for Abbott Laboratories, Baxter International, AT&T and other major corporate clients nationwide.

- Won the1995 "Employee of the Year Award."

- After only one month with the company, assigned management responsibility for the largest and most challenging project (Intel). Delivered project on time and 25% under budget. Nominated for the "Employee of the Year Award."

U.S. ARMY / MILITARY INTELLIGENCE CORPS   1986 to 1991

Chinese Linguist / Military Intelligence Officer

Promoted from Chinese Linguist to Commissioned Lieutenant in the Military Intelligence Corps. Demonstrated expertise in the collection, analysis, reporting and presentation of sensitive military and operational data. Held Top Secret Security Clearance.

References Provided Upon Request

MICHAEL T. WINSTON
15 Summerhill Place
Atlanta, Georgia 30263
(770) 251-8286

SENIOR FINANCIAL EXECUTIVE
Start-Up, Turnaround, High-Growth & Multinational Corporations

Corporate Finance Executive with 15+ years of senior-level financial, operating, general management and consulting experience. Expert qualifications in financial planning and analysis, budgeting, cash management, banking, debt management, treasury, cost and general accounting, cost reduction and performance/profit improvement. CPA.

Structured and negotiated complex public and private financings, mergers, acquisitions and divestitures with aggregate value of $5+ billion throughout career. Top-flight negotiating experience.

PROFESSIONAL EXPERIENCE:

DUNHAM SERVICE CORPORATION, Atlanta, GA   1994 to Present
($200 million third party logistics contractor.)

Vice President / Chief Financial Officer
Senior Financial Executive with full responsibility for the planning, staffing, operating performance and leadership of the corporation's complete financial, accounting and administrative functions. Led an aggressive evaluation of all company operations, personnel, departments and business units to establish baseline data for performance reengineering and profit growth.

- Provided "hands-on" operating and financial leadership for successful turnaround. Transitioned company from $6.5 million loss in 1994 to $6.5 million profit cash flow in 1996.
- Pioneered the corporation's first outsourcing program (human resources), significantly improving HR capabilities while reducing annual costs to corporation by more than $100,000.
- Evaluated information technology requirements and spearheaded selection/implementation of several upgrades (including J.D. Edwards financial reporting system).

OUTBOARD MARINE CORPORATION, Waukegan, IL   1991 to 1993
(World's largest outboard motor manufacturer. $1+ billion in annual revenues.)

Vice President / Chief Financial Officer
Recruited to plan and orchestrate the financial turnaround of this global manufacturer with #1 major recognition despite several non-performing business units. Given full responsibility for redesigning all core financial processes, including annual planning and forecasting, budgeting, cash management, treasury, internal audit, banking and long-range investment planning. Led a staff of 60.

- Instrumental in transitioning company from $100 million loss to a modest profit through product line rationalization, divestiture, manufacturing operations consolidation, business process redesign and aggressive cost controls. Efforts impacted the entire organization, over 5000 employees and operations throughout North America, Europe and Latin America.
- Initiated and managed a $75 million public convertible debt issue.
- Restructured $200 million bank debt from secured to unsecured lending status.
- Reengineered all financial operations and reduced staffing requirements by 30%.
- Orchestrated implementation of PC-based financial reporting/forecasting system.
- Provided strategic leadership for critical business development and marketing programs.

JAY ALIX & ASSOCIATES, Southfield, MI   1987 to 1991
(Management consulting firm specializing in turnarounds and crisis management.)

Principal
Guided senior financial, operating and management teams of client companies through critical reengineering, turnaround and financial restructuring engagements. Worked in cooperation with cross-functional projects teams in several successful endeavors:

- $800 million business unit and product line divestiture for Wang Laboratories.
- Five separate engagements involving divestitures, asset sales and restructurings to sustain TIE Communications.
- Complex business unit divestiture for G. Heilman Brewing.
- Strategic planning and development of divestiture plan for Cardinal Industries.

CLEVITE INDUSTRIES, INC., Glenview, IL   1981 to 1987
($500 million multinational industrial manufacturer.)

Vice President / Chief Financial Officer
Led all corporate financial and administrative affairs during a period of significant reorganization and transition, from 1981 revenues of $500 million through economic downturn to 1982 revenues of $367 million to subsequent regrowth and return to $500+ million in annual sales. Created dynamic financial, analytical, budgeting, reporting, forecasting and asset management systems responsive to changing organizational needs.

- Negotiated $400 million recapitalization in 1986 as part of the corporation's IPO.
- Structured and negotiated debt refinancing package with 23 institutions, resulting in a $10 million savings in annual interest and dividend costs.
- Designed and implemented sophisticated financial reporting and forecasting system.
- Directed successful divestiture of several foreign entities and consolidation of domestic manufacturing facilities to reduce costs and improve profit return.
- Company was rated as an "outstanding LBO" by a venture capital investment group.

BENDIX CORPORATION, Southfield, MI   1976 to 1981
($4 billion multinational, multi-industry corporation.)

Vice President / Chief Financial Officer - Bendix Forest Products (1979 to 1981)
Assistant Treasurer - Bendix Headquarters (1977 to 1979)
Assistant Corporate Controller - Bendix Headquarters (1976 to 1977)
Fast-track promotion through a series of increasingly responsible corporate finance positions. Advanced to **VP/CFO** with full treasury, controllership and MIS responsibility for the $700 million Forest Products business unit.

ACME CLEVELAND CORP. / LA SALLE MACHINE TOOL, INC., Cleveland, OH   1969 to 1976
($400 million industrial manufacturer.)

Corporate Controller - Acme Cleveland (1975 to 1976)
Vice President of Finance - LaSalle Machine Tool (1972 to 1975)
Corporate Controller - LaSalle Machine Tool (1971)
Assistant to the President - LaSalle Machine Tool (1969 to 1970)

COOPERS AND LYBRAND, Detroit, MI   1965 to 1969

Staff Auditor / Senior Auditor

EDUCATION: **B.B.A.**, University of Michigan, 1967

RICHARD F. SMITH

1290 South Plains Avenue
Kansas City, Kansas 66213
(913) 421-8974

SENIOR FINANCE & ADMINISTRATION EXECUTIVE

*Strategic Business & Financial Planning / General Accounting / Corporate Banking & Lending
Merger & Acquisition Management / Investment Management / Corporate Tax / MIS Technology*

Over 15 years of senior-level Corporate Finance experience for start-up, turnaround and high-growth corporations. Combines expert strategic and tactical financial expertise with strong qualifications in general management, human resources management and transaction structuring/negotiations. Certified Public Accountant (CPA). MBA Degree with Finance Concentration.

Delivered strong and sustainable financial gains in highly-competitive business markets nationwide through expertise in cost reduction, process redesign, revenue growth and profit improvement.

PROFESSIONAL EXPERIENCE:

Senior Vice President/Treasurer   1980 to Present
MATTHEW F. BROOKSTONE COMPANY, Kansas City, Missouri
(National mortgage banking corporation)

Chief Financial Officer responsible for the strategic planning, development and leadership of two distinct accounting/finance operations: Corporate Accounting and Investor Accounting. Scope of responsibility is diverse and includes financial analysis/reporting, tax planning, cash management, corporate banking, lending, budgeting and audit management. Supervise a staff of 12 professionals and para-professionals.

Achievements:

- **Improved net profitability by $400,000** in 1996 following an aggressive redesign of bank pricing and costs.

- **Increased net interest income by 100%** through implementation of corporate cash management system and negotiation of cooperative banking relationships. Developed pricing policies for bank credit facilities to fully utilize escrow balances to reduce interest costs.

- Led the consolidation of the corporation's branch offices through a 7-state region in the Western U.S. in response to projected changes within the industry. Maintained profitability throughout tenure despite declining market conditions.

- Spearheaded design, programming and implementation of leading edge MIS technologies to automate accounting and financial reporting functions. **Reduced personnel requirements by 50%+** and significantly improved the quality, accuracy and timeliness of financial data. Currently facilitating transition from mainframe to client/server technology.

- Designed tax strategies for corporate stockholders which reduced potential tax liabilities and improved net investment yield.

- Renegotiated employee benefit programs, improved the company's ability to recruit qualified personnel, and maintained costs within an escalating health care environment. Rewrote corporate policies for the entire human resources function.

RICHARD F. SMITH - *Page Two*

PROFESSIONAL EXPERIENCE *(Continued):*

Comptroller   1978 to 1979
SURFACE TRANSPORTATION INTERNATIONAL, Kansas City, Missouri
(National maintenance and service provider to the rail transportation industry)

Recruited by previous client at Grant Thornton to create all internal accounting, auditing and financial management functions for a start-up corporation. Established corporate banking relationships, developed budgets, prepared income and expense projections, and implemented a complete corporate accounting and audit procedures program. Developed corporate HR procedures for recruitment, training, benefits administration and employee retention.

<u>Achievements:</u>

- Brought the accounting, administrative and reporting functions from start-up to full automation.

- Independently developed a complete accounting system, all human resource policies, and related administrative support functions for an affiliated start-up operation.

- Acquired extensive experience in merger and acquisition management as a member of the management team responsible for negotiating the profitable sale of the company to a publicly-owned national corporation.

In-Charge Auditor   1974 to 1977
GRANT THORNTON, CPA'S, Kansas City, Missouri
(formerly Alexander Grant & Company)

Directed financial audits for numerous industries and organizations (e.g., service, manufacturing, non-profit, financial). Supervised staff auditors assigned to specific engagements.

EDUCATION:

MBA (Finance), 1990
ROCKHURST COLLEGE, Kansas City, Missouri

BS (Accounting), Cum Laude, 1974
BRIGHAM YOUNG UNIVERSITY, Provo, Utah

PROFESSIONAL AFFILIATIONS:

American Institute of Certified Public Accountants (AICPA)
Missouri Institute of Certified Public Accountants (MSCPA)
Board of Directors, Better Business Bureau

References Provided Upon Request

DARRELL ALBERSTON
1305 West Swamp Creek Road
Troutville, Louisiana 70525

Phone (504) 633-2633

Fax (504) 627-6922

CORPORATE FINANCE EXECUTIVE
Start-Up, Turnaround, High-Growth & Multinational Organizations

Dynamic management career building and leading corporate finance and accounting organizations for a diversity of partnerships, joint ventures, subsidiaries and corporations. Combines expert strategic planning and finance qualifications with strong business development, negotiation and leadership skills.

- Financial Planning & Analysis
- General Accounting & Reporting
- Budgeting (Capital & Operating)
- Tax Planning & Compliance
- Cash Management & Optimization

- Investment Management
- Equity & Debt Financing
- Road Show Presentations
- Credit & Lending
- Asset Management & Yield

PROFESSIONAL EXPERIENCE:

COVINGTON INVESTMENT CORPORATION   1990 to Present

Principal - Financial & Management Consulting

Senior Consultant specializing in corporate finance, investment finance, capital formation and long-range corporate planning. Completed numerous engagements and special projects throughout diverse commercial and industrial markets.

Provide expertise in all core financial planning, analysis and operating issues. Consult regarding financial and investment transactions, banking, lending and credit management. Evaluate key operating units and their financial performance to guide management in process-driven reengineering programs. Advise regarding retirement planning, corporate legal affairs and corporate administration.

- Guided executive team in the start-up of a national franchise furniture business. Prepared proformas, budgets and long-range projections. Defined immediate and long-term cash requirements, established banking relationships, and structured key supplier contracts. Negotiated favorable lease transactions and created internal financial analysis/reporting systems.

- Architected a second-stage financing plan for a privately-held steel drum manufacturer. Authored PPO memorandum and raised $3.5 million. Subsequently led corporation through a sophisticated ESOP transition.

- Designed exit strategy and recruited executive candidate for privately-held corporation.

Expanded practice to include investment and/or management in a portfolio of real estate, energy and equipment leasing ventures. Designed capital structure for each new venture, raised debt and equity funding, negotiated partnerships, and directed ventures through development, start-up, management and/or divestiture.

- Directed acquisition of several failed real estate properties, marketed and leased up, and subsequently divested for an average 100% ROI.

- Delivered a strong 20% ROI to investor group in medical, electronic and office equipment leasing venture.

GRAHAM RESOURCES, INC.   1978 to 1990

> **Executive Vice President** (1986 to 1990)
> **Senior Vice President - Corporate Development** (1982 to 1986)
> **Vice President - Finance** (1980 to 1982)
> **Treasurer** (1979 to 1980)
> **Tax Director** (1978 to 1979)
>
> Fast-track promotion through a series of increasingly responsible financial management positions as Graham Resources grew from just under $1 million to $50+ million in value. Created a dynamic financial infrastructure, flexible in meeting the rapid growth and expansion of the corporation. Introduced systems, controls and processes to provide accurate and appropriate financial leadership for long-term growth and improved profitability.
>
> As Senior Finance Executive, directed the entire corporate finance function. Achievements included:
>
> - Created all corporate accounting, budgeting, cash management, asset management, lending, tax, legal, credit, corporate development and administrative affairs.
>
> - Designed sophisticated financial planning, analysis and modeling processes to guide the corporation and its investment portfolio.
>
> - Structured and negotiated complex financial transactions (e.g., credit, lending, investment, limited partnerships, convertible debt, common/preferred equity, capital raising).
>
> - Acted as an internal financial and management consultant to guide operating teams in achieving profit and performance goals.
>
> - Appointed to the Board of Directors and Senior Management Committee in 1986.
>
> - Created the corporate and investment finance systems to manage growth from $3 million of assets under management to $1.5 billion. Structured, negotiated, registered, marketed and invested all capital from public, private and institutional sectors.
>
> - Optimized cash yields for 35 different partnerships. Delivered up to 18% annual ROI.

ARTHUR ANDERSEN & CO.   1972 to 1978

> **Tax Manager**
>
> Tax Staff, Senior and Manager for international CPA firm. Specialized in individual, partnership and corporate income taxes and individual estate taxes with heavy emphasis on long-range tax and financial planning. Managed client engagements in the oil and gas, real estate, banking and maritime industries.

EDUCATION: **BS (Business Administration)**, Louisiana State University, 1972
                  Certified Public Accountant, 1974

AFFILIATIONS: American Institute of Certified Public Accountants
                    Louisiana Society of Certified Public Accountants

PAUL B. FINNEGAN
200 Peaks View Place
Los Angeles, California 91000

Residence (805) 400-1000   Business (805) 400-7000

SENIOR OPERATING & MANAGEMENT EXECUTIVE
Start-Up, Turnaround & High-Growth Corporations

Demonstrated record of leadership in building corporate value. Consistently accelerated revenues and profit growth through expertise in marketing, finance and management. Qualifications include:

Corporate Finance

- Expert in full range of corporate financial affairs, including general and project accounting, cash flow management, banking, tax, budgeting, forecasting, financial analysis and financial reporting. **RESULT: Created complete financial infrastructure to support venture that grew from start-up to $37 million.**

Investment Finance

- Prepared written and oral presentations for institutional and private investors to fund business start-up, expansion and project financing. Prepared all financial documents, coordinated regulatory reviews and identified alternative funding sources. **RESULT: Raised approximately $125 million throughout career for companies and clients.**

Marketing & Business Development

- Evaluated market demand and opportunity, created strategic marketing and business development plans, designed marketing communications and launched market penetration. **RESULT: Led successful expansion into new business markets and won strong market positioning against well-established competition. Generated over $6.5 million in new revenues and closed over 500 account sales.**

Sales Management

- Built and led top-producing sales and support teams that consistently delivered revenues in excess of projections and won increasing market share against strong competition. **RESULT: Negotiated and closed over $130 million in gross sales throughout career.**

Training & Development

- Expert in the design and development of customized training programs with emphasis on sales, marketing, finance, leadership development, communication skills, public speaking and general management. **RESULT: Strengthened sales and management teams as President and Sales Champion of the Dale Carnegie course. Trained 200+ professionals over a three-year period.**

Information Technology

- Introduced PC systems and applications to automate finance, accounting, sales and lease administration, marketing and general management functions. **RESULT: Replaced manual systems with state-of-the-art technology and improved productivity, efficiency and organizational capabilities with Lotus and Microsoft applications. Outsourced operating and financial functions through systems applications.**

MBA Degree in Finance & Marketing. Experienced Instructor in:
Sales, Marketing & Public Speaking for Dale Carnegie courses and University of Southern California.

PAUL B. FINNEGAN

Page Two

GENERAL PARTNERSHIPS, INC., West Los Angeles, CA   1993 to 1995
General Partner / Operating Partner

Raised initial financing and led start-up of a business venture. Held full P&L responsibility for the strategic planning, development and leadership of the entire business organization, including sales, marketing, new business development, corporate finance, accounting and investment finance. Implemented information technology and successfully outsourced majority of administrative and management functions.

- Built company from start-up to $37 million, generating $6.3 million in after tax profits.
- Led implementation of PC technology to automate all financial, asset management, accounting, reporting and administrative functions.
- Prepared financial and operating documentation for major presentations to private and institutional lenders, business partners and investors. Raised over $16.3 million from start-up monies of $360,000 partner contributions.
- Founded affiliate brokerage company, building revenues to six figures within first year.
- Managed private tax consulting services, delivering 20% tax reduction to key clients.

CENTURY 21, Sherman Oaks, CA   1981 to 1993

First Vice President (1991 to 1993)
Associate Vice President / Member of Chairman's Council (1984 to 1991)
Senior Sales Consultant (1981 to 1984)

Fast-track promotion through a series of increasing responsible sales, marketing and regional management positions. Achieved the highest position of any commissioned sales person in the organization. Consistently ranked in the top 5% nationwide. Final promotion to First Vice President with full P&L responsibility for Southern California region, managing up to 15 major sales projects valued at an average $10+ million each.

- Generated over $131 million in sales volume with over 500 transactions.
- Delivered gross revenues averaging in excess of $400,000 for 10+ consecutive years.

JOHN STEWART WALKER, Sherman Oaks, CA   1973 to 1981
Senior Sales Consultant

Promoted to Senior Sales Consultant in 1979, after achieving assigned quota for five consecutive years. Built territory in West Los Angeles from start-up to gross sales of $1.6 million within first year. Expanded sales throughout adjacent regions.

XEROX CORPORATION, Los Angeles, CA   1972 to 1973
Sales Representative/Sales Manager

Led six field sales and technical support personnel building market value and driving revenue growth within highly competitive Southern California. Achieved quota both years.

IBM CORPORATION, Los Angeles, CA   1968 to 1971
Account Manager

EDUCATION:

MBA (Finance & Marketing), University of Southern California
BS (Accounting), Temple University

ELIZABETH R. WERNER

21 East Washington Parkway • Detroit Michigan 48995 • (616) 232-6544

EXECUTIVE PROFILE

Senior Management Executive successful in building profitable organizations within highly competitive consumer markets. Broad-based general management and P&L management of all corporate operating, sales, marketing, product, technology and human resource management functions.

Featured in Inc. Magazine in August 1994 for expertise in market/business development.

PROFESSIONAL EXPERIENCE

PRESIDENT - Heritage - Detroit, Michigan - 1983 to Present

Founded corporation in 1983 in response to emerging market niche. Built from start-up to 24 retail stores generating over $6 million in annual revenue with 250 employees. Lead a 4-person senior management team, 48 business unit managers and all sales, support and service staff.

Sales Growth	• Delivered revenue growth averaging 18% to build volume to $6+ million in 1995.
Finance	• Negotiated $500,000 credit line with major banking institution to fund growth, expansion and working capital.
Strategic Planning	• Instituted strategic planning process for entire corporation and all operating units. Established revenue and profit goals, cost reduction initiatives, and actions plans that consistently improved earnings and strengthened customer satisfaction.
Real Estate	• Reduced annual real estate leasing costs by more than 25% through personal management of all leasing contracts.
Legal Affairs	• Directed the corporate legal function and all leasing, contract, employee law and regulatory affairs.
Marketing/Advertising	• Designed a portfolio of sales promotions, direct mail, print advertising and marketing communications to expand penetration throughout targeted markets.
PC Technology	• Directed the selection, installation and management of a PC network linking corporate headquarters with all operating locations. Implemented Electronic Bar Code Scanning to improve merchandise control and loss prevention.
Purchasing	• Established a worldwide purchasing function working with 700+ vendors and seven major NYC buying groups to reduce annual costs through volume discounting.
Distribution	• Redesigned inventory planning/management strategies, leased distribution center and improved the allocation of product between operating locations.
Human Resources	• Created a complete human resources function and directed all recruitment, training, development, benefits, compensation and performance appraisal processes.

VICE PRESIDENT/TREASURER - Shoes Unlimited - Detroit, Michigan - 1975 to 1986

Fast-track promotion from Sales Associate to Assistant Buyer to Buyer to VP/Treasurer for this $20 million, 50-site corporation. Acquired extensive qualifications in budgeting, banking, cash management, accounting, financial planning, financial reporting and profitability analysis.

EDUCATION

B.S., Marketing - Minor in Accounting - Wayne State University - Detroit, Michigan - 1975

SHEILA STEWART

594 Beach Access Road
Pensacola, Florida 32561

Home   (904) 947-6990
Office   (904) 553-6990

QUALIFICATIONS PROFILE

HUMAN RESOURCE AFFAIRS

Excellent qualifications in the recruitment, interviewing, selection and supervision of up to 40 professional and support staff. Skilled in staff training, development and performance management to meet operating and financial goals. Extensive experience in workforce diversity, team building and group leadership. **RESULT: Built work teams that consistently met/exceeded business goals for productivity, efficiency and quality of operations.**

CUSTOMER SERVICE / CLIENT RELATIONS

Independently managed relationships with major accounts (e.g., National Organization for Women, Fleet Reserve Association). Served as direct liaison to facilitate client relationships, resolve billing and operating problems, and outperform competitive organizations. Actively involved in developing new product/service lines to meet client/market demand. **RESULT: Delivered strong and sustainable improvements in client service, satisfaction and retention.**

ACCOUNTING MANAGEMENT

Expert qualifications in accounts receivable, billing, reimbursement, accounting/financial analysis, financial reporting, cost/benefit analysis, insurance and claims administration. Managed $4 million operating budget, variance analysis reporting and long-term financial planning efforts. **RESULT: Designed and implemented policies, procedures and processes that improved cash flow, reduced outstanding debt and strengthened bottom-line profitability.**

PROJECT PLANNING & MANAGEMENT

Skilled in leading cross-functional business teams in the planning and execution of special projects for Marketing, Operations, Accounting and Information Technology. Able to critically evaluate project requirements and coordinate the delivery of appropriate resources and personnel to meet operating demands. **RESULT: Built cooperative working relationships between hourly, staff and management personnel to facilitate project completion on time, within budget and as per operating requirements.**

OFFICE MANAGEMENT / BUSINESS ADMINISTRATION

Broad-based qualifications in administrative, clerical and business support functions. Organized, efficient and precise with strong planning, communication and liaison skills. Extensive PC qualifications. **RESULT: Designed/implemented administrative processes to reduce redundancy, streamline operations and improve daily operations.**

PROFESSIONAL EXPERIENCE

1996 to Present   **Supervisor, Physician Billing**   Springfield General Hospital
Recruited to this large regional medical center to manage the entire billing department for more than seven clinics and 46 hospital employed physicians. Act as direct liaison between clinics and billing department to ensure all documents are processed within a timely manner. Direct a team of 10 insurance claims specialists and support personnel.

1994 to 1996	**Accounts Receivable Manager**	Department of Surgery Associates
1991 to 1994	**Reimbursement Coordinator**	George Washington University Medical Center
1990 to 1991	**Account Coordinator**	Consumers United Insurance Company
1989 to 1990	**Policyholder Communicator**	Smith-Sternau Organization, Inc.
1987 to 1989	**Claims Reviewer/Secretary**	Blue Cross & Blue Shield
1984 to 1987	**Business Manager**	Campus Book Store

EDUCATION

M.B.A. Candidate, expected December 1997
B.S., Business Management, University of Maryland, Baltimore, Maryland, 1984

STEVEN L. JONES

500 W. Barstow #102
Fresno, California 93407

Home (209) 434-1988
Fax (209) 275-6572

CAREER PROFILE:

Experienced businessman with excellent qualifications in general management, human resources, customer relations and communications. Seeking the opportunity to transfer experience into a unique employment opportunity involving international travel, people and culture.

PERSONAL PROFILE:

- **Advisory Board Member**, Fairmont State College Elderhostel Program.
- **Founding Chairman**, Fairmont County Private Industry Council.
- **Volunteer Human Resources Consultant**, Fresno Philharmonic Orchestra.
- Sports enthusiast. Enjoy scuba diving, sailing, tennis, skiing, biking, jogging and working out.
- Extensive travel throughout Europe, the Orient and the Caribbean.
- Food and wine connoisseur. Art collector. Single. Interested in travel and/or relocation.

CAREER HISTORY:

Human Resources Director, Producers Cotton Oil Company, Fairmont, California

Twenty-three year career as the Senior Human Resources Executive for this diversified cotton producer and processor. Directed all HR programs for 500 permanent and 1200-1500 seasonal employees at 75 locations throughout California and Arizona. Member of a 7-person executive team responsible for the strategic planning, leadership and bottom-line financial performance of the corporation.

Customer Relations

- Travelled to company and customer sites to strengthen business relationships, increase production volumes and sales revenues, and maintain competitiveness in the global business market.

Human Resources & Training/Development

- Created and directed the HR organization as the company grew and diversified its operations. Scope of responsibility included recruitment, benefits and pension plan administration, wage and salary administration, employee relations, promotion of benefits and retirement, payroll processing, and union contract negotiations.

Personnel Training/Development

- Designed and implemented skills training, job training, leadership development, safety and a variety of other programs for seasonal, hourly, administrative and management personnel. Created instructional materials, educational resources, and job performance standards and incentives.

General Management

- Strong qualifications in strategic planning, budgeting, expense control, multi-site operations management, capital acquisition, marketing/new business development, facilities management, equipment management and policy/procedure development. Decisive and direct, yet flexible in responding to the constantly changing demands of staff, customers and operations throughout the company.

Public Speaking & Presentations

- Wrote and delivered hundreds of public presentations throughout career. Dynamic, articulate and humorous speaker.

EDUCATION:

B.S., Business Administration, Minors in Speech & Psychology, Fairmont State College

DAVID SWISHER

231 Snowcap Drive   (701) 873-6411   Minot, North Dakota 58071

PROFESSIONAL QUALIFICATIONS:

- Project Planning/Management
- Presentations/Public Speaking
- Purchasing/Inventory Control
- Resource/Facilities Management
- Planning/Organization/Analysis

- Personnel Training/Supervision
- Human Resource Administration
- Written/Oral Communications
- Team/Group Leadership
- Security/Investigations

Extensive hands-on experience in data entry, verification, analysis and reporting. Hardware includes PC III, AT&T 605, Zenith 648, UNISYS 386 and various peripheral devices.

EXPERIENCE:

INVESTMENT CENTERS OF AMERICA - Kansas City, Missouri   1994 to Present

Investment Representative marketing stocks, bonds, IRAs, annuities, mutual funds, and life, health and long term care insurance to individuals and small business owners throughout the region. Earned state insurance license and National Association of Security Dealers Series 7 and 63 registrations.

UNITED STATES AIR FORCE - U.S., England, Germany, Italy   1981 to 1992

Eleven-year career was highlighted by rapid promotion through a series of increasingly responsible positions. Received several distinguished awards and commendations for exemplary performance. Highlights included:

Customer Service Center Manager

- Managed large-scale personnel recordkeeping function supporting over 4900 personnel. Directed related data collection and system input/output operations. Coordinated workflow, equipment utilization, personnel assignments and information dissemination. Trained and supervised a staff of 10. Active member of Total Quality Management and Improvement team charged with streamlining/ consolidating operations, improving productivity and enhancing organizational efficiency.

Security Specialist / Security Chief

- Planned and directed large-scale security and investigations management operations to ensure the safety/security of personnel, facilities, resources, technologies and intelligence. Conducted detailed investigations of alleged security violations and criminal activity with sole responsibility for investigation planning, staffing, management and reporting. Collected/analyzed extensive documentation and wrote security reports. Directed related staffing, training and resource management functions.

Facilities Manager

- Supervised facilities management including power generation, environmental control and water treatment systems. Coordinated capital improvement projects, ensured fully operational status of all equipment, managed related purchasing and inventory control functions, and supervised facilities maintenance staff. Actively involved in implementing methods to upgrade facility safety programs.

EDUCATION: **Currently Pursuing Master of Science Degree in Administration**
Central Michigan University, Minot AFB, North Dakota

Bachelor of Science Degree, 1990
University of the State of New York, Albany, New York

Associate of Arts & Sciences (2 degrees), 1990 and 1992
Community College of the Air Force, Maxwell, Alabama

SHARON BRANSON

11 Summerwind Lane
Rockville Centre, New York 11516
(516) 588-5382

PROFESSIONAL QUALIFICATIONS:

Creative and talented professional with 10 years of progressively responsible business experience. Combines strong administrative, organizational and communication skills with expertise in:

- Project Planning, Staffing & Management
- Customer Service & Key Account Relationship Management
- Sales & Expense Forecasting & Analysis
- Special Events Planning & Management
- Order Processing & Product Distribution
- Inventory Control & Merchandise Management
- Purchasing & Vendor Negotiations
- Staff Training & Supervision
- PC-Based Administrative, Word Processing & Spreadsheet Applications

PROFESSIONAL EXPERIENCE:

1994 to Present   **Calvin Klein, Inc.**, New York, New York

Direct administrative, customer service, sales and marketing services to corporate customers in Boston, Florida and an 8-state Midwestern region. Instrumental in building revenues by 50% to $3.5 million in 1996. Consult with Order Entry and Customer Service Departments to design new sales monitoring, product forecasting and distribution management systems.

1993 to 1994   **Esprit**, New York, New York

Coordinated sales, marketing, customer service and product management for key customers throughout the New York metro region. Contributed to a $600,000 increase in annual revenue growth within a highly competitive business market. Designed and implemented a series of PC-based sales management, order processing and business trend analysis programs.

1992 to 1993   **Rivage**, New York, New York

Consulted with senior management team to deliver high-quality products and merchandising strategies to department stores nationwide. Managed the administrative and inventory control functions for New York City showroom.

1988 to 1991   **Liz Claiborne Accessories, Inc.**, New York, New York

Managed product sales, customer service, sales reporting and administrative support functions for some of the corporation's largest commercial accounts. Instrumental in building revenues by $2.2 million within two years.

1987 to 1988   **Abraham and Straus**, Huntington/Brooklyn, New York

Fast-track promotion through a series of increasingly responsible positions in administration, department management, staff training and supervision, purchasing and inventory control.

EDUCATION:

B.S., Clothing and Textiles, Dean's List, December 1987
STATE UNIVERSITY OF NEW YORK COLLEGE AT ONEONTA

A.A.S., Fashion Buying and Merchandising, December 1986
FASHION INSTITUTE OF TECHNOLOGY

RACHEL MARTINEZ   2523 45th Street North, Miami, Florida 33445   (305) 232-8421

PROFESSIONAL QUALIFICATIONS:

Talented professional with excellent academic credentials and several years professional experience in the U.S. and Latin America. Strong analytical, research and project management skills combined with expertise in building/managing international business relationships. Fluent in English and Spanish. PC proficient.

- International Business Management
- International Banking & Finance
- International Business Law
- Global Marketing & Business Development
- Economic, Political & Demographic Research

- International Trade & Import/Export
- Strategic Planning & Risk Assessment
- Marketing Distribution Channels
- Cross-Cultural Communications
- Business Case Analysis

EDUCATION:

SAINT THOMAS UNIVERSITY, Miami, Florida
MBA Degree - Cum Laude Graduate (GPA 3.59/4.00), 1991
Graduate Certificate in International Business, 1991
BA Degree - Political Science - Cum Laude Graduate (GPA 3.68/4.00), 1988

PROFESSIONAL EXPERIENCE:

Owner/General Manager   1993 to Present
CECILIA'S, Hialeah, Florida

Founded and currently operate a marketing organization selling crafts, cosmetics and gift products. Define product mix, develop pricing structures, design innovative advertising and marketing communications, and coordinate purchasing and inventory control. Research competitive market activity to determine promotional strategies and product positioning.

- Recruited, trained and currently direct a team of sales and marketing distributors.

Faculty Member - Business/Economics Division   1991 to 1993
FORT LAUDERDALE COLLEGE, Fort Lauderdale, Florida

Taught undergraduate courses in International Business Management, Import-Export, Business Ethics and Marketing Distribution Channels. Prepared class materials, directed special study and research projects, and conducted reading seminars in general International Business topics.

Full-Time Graduate Student   1988 to 1991

Assistant Accounts Receivable Representative   1988 to 1989
SAINT THOMAS UNIVERSITY, Miami, Florida

Managed, balanced and reported student and university operating accounts. Prepared daily bank deposits, administered petty cash fund and processed invoices. Trained/supervised student workers.

PROFESSIONAL AFFILIATIONS:

NATIONAL SOCIETY OF HISPANIC MBAs *(Miami Chapter)*

- **Vice President of Education.** Currently spearheading the planning, design and implementation of a series of University outreach programs to increase Hispanic student enrollment in MBA programs throughout Southern Florida. Orchestrating the establishment of Miami-based scholarship fund and career orientation workshops previously managed through national headquarters. Supervise nine volunteers. (1995 to Present)

- **Secretary & Chairperson, Events Committee.** Administered member database, recordkeeping and documentation, prepared member marketing communications, and facilitated logistics for meetings, workshops, and special events. (1993 to 1994)

NOREEN SWANSON, M.D.
239 Central Park West
New York, New York 10021
(212) 525-9878

HEALTH CARE ADMINISTRATOR / HOSPITAL DIRECTOR / BUSINESS MANAGER

Medical & Clinical Services / Finance & Budgeting / Regulatory Affairs / Training & Development
Policy Development / Physician Recruitment / Resources & Facilities Management / Public Affairs
Provider Relations / Patient Relations / Legislative Affairs / Insurance Administration

Health Care Administrator with 10+ years experience leading the development and delivery of profitable health care systems throughout the U.S., Canada and Europe. Combines strong business and financial management expertise with 16 years experience as a licensed medical doctor. PC proficient.

PROFESSIONAL EXPERIENCE:

Health Care Administrator - Policy, Quality of Care & Services Delivery   1992 to Present

Devoted the past four years to the planning, development, funding and implementation of improved health care delivery systems worldwide. Work in cooperation with hospital administrators, financial executives, government agencies, legislators, regulators, policymakers and public advocacy groups to drive forward innovative health care and managed care programs.

Care Foundation - South America (1994 to 1996)
Two-year position with an international charitable health care organization providing teams of health care administrators, primary care physicians, nurses, researchers and others throughout remote parts of the world. Held joint administrative and clinical responsibilities.

- Travelled throughout the jungles of South America introducing preventive medicine, nutrition and immunization programs.
- Conducted primary field research on medicinal properties and studied natural resistance to malaria and other tropical diseases.

Finland Ministry of Health (1994)
Twelve-month consulting assignment guiding the modernization and expansion of emergency management systems throughout all of Finland.

- Led management training programs on core health care issues (e.g., service delivery, quality of care, reimbursement, staffing, resource maximization, facilities management, technology, budgeting).
- Introduced several new management and administrative processes into existing health care operations and delivered average annual cost savings of 20%.

Nova Scotia, Canada Ministry of Health (1992 to 1993)
Thirteen-month *locum tenens* position guiding development of health care policy, establishing health care service programs and spearheading health care cost containment initiatives.

- Orchestrated preliminary planning and development for implementation of emergency medical response system throughout all of Nova Scotia.
- Introduced the "American" system of emergency room management and compensation structures into more than 150 hospitals.

Mississippi State Board of Health (1992)
Twelve-month *locum tenens* position providing policy, quality, planning and administrative leadership to the health care providers and provider organizations throughout the State of Mississippi. Focused efforts on expanding services and realigning cost structures.

- Accelerated the turnaround, service expansion and return to profitability of health clinic.

NOREEN SWANSON, M.D.   *Page Two*

Medical Director - Emergency Department   1985 to 1991
WATKINS REGIONAL MEDICAL CENTER, Atlanta, Georgia

Senior Operating Executive directing all policy, business, financial, administrative, staffing and medical care operations for the Emergency Department of this 440-bed acute care hospital. Scope of responsibility was diverse and included:

Business Management
- Introduced state-of-the-art utilization review, quality assurance and internal audit programs to facilitate ongoing improvements in the delivery and cost of care.
- Directed physician recruitment, credentialing, scheduling and contract negotiations.
- Administered all insurance billing and collection programs with Medicaid, Medicare, Champus and major insurance companies nationwide.
- Designed/taught emergency training for field and hospital-based emergency response teams.
- Testified before the General Assembly on core health care issues (e.g., cost, reimbursement, Medicare, Medicaid, emergency care, delivery systems).

Financial Management
- Guided Board of Directors and executive team in the development of annual operating and capital budgets for the $32 million Emergency Department.
- Directed all general accounting, financial planning and reporting, budgeting, billing, collections and medical coding operations.
- Improved workflow/productivity through innovative training and process reengineering.
- Spearheaded several fundraising campaigns for new emergency department and capital improvement projects. Achieved total contributions of more than $11 million.

Senior Administrative & Medical Director   1981 to 1985
U.S. ARMY MEDICAL CORPS, Bamberg, Germany

Directed all operations for a large medical clinic servicing 15,000 military personnel, dependents and civilians. Responsible for care provider organization, all financial and budgeting affairs, purchasing, staffing, reporting, facilities, regulatory affairs and administration. Managed team of 500+ physicians, nurses, medical corpsman, technicians and support staff.

- Introduced chart review, peer review, utilization review and quality assurance programs throughout all departments.
- Pioneered an innovative preventive medicine program for troops worldwide.

Medical Intern   1980 to 1981
TRIPLER ARMY MEDICAL CENTER, Honolulu, Hawaii

One-year internship rotating through all primary care areas in this 1000-bed military hospital. Appointed Chairman of Internship Class, served on Utilization Review and Quality Assurance Committee, and managed several successful fundraising campaigns. Designed and taught emergency care training programs.

EDUCATION & PROFESSIONAL CREDENTIALS:

M.D., University of Mississippi School of Medicine, 1980
B.S., Biochemistry, Mississippi State University, 1976

Diplomate of the American Board of Emergency Medicine, 1988
Fellow of the American Academy of Family Physicians, 1987
Recertification in ACLS, BCLS and ATLS, 1996

PROFESSIONAL & CIVIC MEMBERSHIPS:

American Academy of Medical Directors, American Academy of Family Physicians, American College of Emergency Physicians, American Medical Association, Center for Battered Women & Abused Children (Volunteer)

KENNETH W. CHASTE

3721 Walnut Tree Lane
San Francisco, California 94575

Home (310) 826-5252   Fax (310) 384-5721   Office (310) 385-7218

HEALTH CARE INDUSTRY EXECUTIVE

Dynamic 20+ year career as the President, CEO, CFO and Administrator of multi-site health care organizations. Expert in strategic planning, finance, MIS technology, human resources, community outreach, regulatory/legislative affairs and organizational development for turnaround and high-growth ventures. Analytical and decisive with excellent negotiation and team building skills. Creative in solutions engineering and performance/quality improvement.

PROFESSIONAL EXPERIENCE:

COLUMBIA HEALTH CARE SYSTEM
SAN FRANCISCO COMMUNITY HOSPITAL, San Francisco, CA   1984 to 1996

President/CEO - Columbia / Administrator/CEO - San Francisco (1990 to 1996)
Senior Vice President & CFO - Columbia (1987 to 1990)
Vice President & CFO - Columbia (1986 to 1987)
Assistant Administrator & CFO - San Francisco (1984 to 1986)

Fast-track promotion through a series of increasingly responsible general management and financial management positions with Columbia Health Care System (regional health care delivery system) and San Francisco Community Hospital (291-bed acute care hospital with 360 physicians and 1300 employees). Concurrent administrative and financial responsibility for 99-bed skilled nursing facility (acquisition) and 60-bed rehabilitation hospital (joint venture). Held full P&L responsibility for all business units.

- Saved the corporation from imminent bankruptcy through immediate cost reduction, divestiture of non-profitable assets, and restructure of long-term debt and lease obligations. Created critical partnerships with employees and management personnel throughout the organization to drive reengineering, process improvement and long-term stability. Currently operating at positive cash flow.

- Reduced operating losses 65% over a three-year period despite 10% volume decrease through introduction of new services and elimination of non-profitable, non-core operations. Delivered over $1.2 million in annual net profit from two new clinical programs.

- Eliminated short-term debt of $3.8 million, reduced long-term debt by $500,000+, improved current ratio from 1.55/1 to 2.00/1 and built cash reserves to $2.1 million.

- Identified opportunity, structured and negotiated a joint venture that created $2.9 million in unrestricted new cash capital.

- Won political and community support for acquisition of land and loan guarantees from the Redevelopment Agency for the construction of an $8 million medical office complex.

- Issued $39 million of tax exempt bonds to finance construction of a 5-story, 150,000 sq. ft., 126-bed patient tower.

- Reduced days in accounts receivable from 98 to 49.

- Created a MSO/IPA to allow medical staff to compete for HMO business.

KENNETH W. CHASTE

Page Two

PROFESSIONAL EXPERIENCE *(Continued)*:

JEFFERSON MEMORIAL HOSPITAL, Inglewood, CA   1981 to 1984

Vice President of Fiscal Services

Recruited as the Senior Finance Executive for this two-facility, 606-bed health care corporation. Responsible for all accounting, budgeting, forecasting, financial reporting, billing, business office, treasury, cash management, banking, purchasing and MIS operations.

- Issued $65 million of tax exempt bonds to finance acquisition, capital improvement and renovation projects.

- Resolved long-standing problems with computer system conversion and completed installation to replace obsolete systems.

- Implemented improved collection procedures and reduced DSO from 122 to 72.

KENNEDY ASSOCIATES, INC., Rancho Palos Verdes, CA   1980 to 1981

Executive Vice President & CFO

Recruited to plan and orchestrate an aggressive turnaround of this mini-conglomerate with national interests in franchising, consulting, wholesale and retail sales, and business management/ownership.

- Surpassed all turnaround objectives. Transitioned company from major loss to profitability, reconfigured operating units and product lines, introduced sound fiscal practices and built a solid organizational infrastructure to lead the company forward.

PREVIOUS PROFESSIONAL HEALTH CARE INDUSTRY EXPERIENCE (1975 to 1980):

Associate Administrator & CFO, Centennial Hospital Medical Center, Inglewood, CA

Director of Fiscal Affairs, Henry Ford Hospital, Detroit, MI

Controller, St. Joseph Hospital, Flint, MI

EDUCATION:

M.S., Health Care Administration, University of La Verne, La Verne, CA, 1989
B.S., Accounting & Finance, Indiana University, Bloomington, IN, 1975
Certified Public Accountant

LARRY M. VAN WINKEL

2587 Lumber Mill Road
Oklahoma City, Oklahoma 75347
Phone (803) 234-8647
Fax (803) 234-8623

HEALTH CARE INDUSTRY EXECUTIVE
Managed Care / Management Service Organizations / Physician Hospital Organizations
Health Care Systems Marketing / Physician Relations / Practice Management

Executive Director / Operations Manager / Marketing Director with expertise in the strategic planning, development and leadership of sophisticated health care practice organizations. Contributed to multi-million dollar revenue growth through advances in managed care concepts, contract services, market development, finance/accounting and human resources. Extensive MIS and PC technology skills. Integrated and standardized operating and administrative systems to deliver strong and sustainable cost reductions. MBA Degree.

PROFESSIONAL EXPERIENCE:

MIDWESTERN HEALTH ALLIANCE, Oklahoma City, Oklahoma   1994 to Present

EXECUTIVE DIRECTOR

Recruited as the Senior Operating Executive for this newly-created health care management company providing contract services to a 7-site, multi-hospital network. Challenged to reduce operating costs and improve market penetration through the strategic integration of management functions into one centralized organization utilizing existing staff and facilities.

Scope of responsibility is diverse and includes accounting and finance, financial reporting, payroll administration, banking, credit, budgeting, program development/implementation, marketing and community outreach. Lead a team of 20 through a matrixed organization.

Achievements:

- Created a regional integrated delivery system with centralized strategic planning, administrative, recruitment, marketing, purchasing and contracting services.

- Established operating policies and procedures for new business venture, defined immediate and long-term operating goals, and realigned financial and personnel resources to provide comprehensive management services.

- Fully integrated all purchasing, vendor sourcing, and inventory planning and control functions for hospital group. Projections forecast a 5% reduction in pharmacy costs and a 50% reduction in medical/surgical inventory carrying costs through implementation of JIT delivery system.

- Developed a regional health education network and coordinated resource allocation throughout the health care delivery system.

LARRY M. VAN WINKEL - *Page Two*

CONSOLIDATED MEDICAL CENTERS, Denver, Colorado   1989 to 1994

CORPORATE DIRECTOR / DIRECTOR OF MARKETING
ACTING OPERATIONS MANAGER

High-profile management position as one of two operating executives responsible for the dramatic growth of this ambulatory health care network (primary care, occupational medicine and rehabilitation). In cooperation with President/CEO, led the organization through a period of rapid expansion.

- Built CMC from two outpatient facilities with $3.3 million in annual revenues to six facilities with $10.4 million in annual revenues and 125 employees (including 15+ physicians and 25+ therapists).

- Delivered 214% revenue gain over five years (averaged 21% annually) and significantly improved customer service/satisfaction ratings.

- Established CMC as the largest occupational health care system in the metro Denver market.

- Linked CMC with specialty physician practices to create a pioneering managed care organization providing comprehensive administrative, sales/marketing, MIS, budgeting/financial and operating management expertise to the clinical care network.

- Negotiated "win-win" managed care contracts and joint ventures with specialty care physicians, employers, third party administrators and insurance companies.

Created strategic plans and objectives to build managed care network, drive revenue growth, integrate administrative infrastructure, and build a regional marketing and business development network. Recruited, trained and supervised marketing personnel, launched public relations initiatives and customer service programs, and designed a portfolio of marketing communications (e.g., brochures, print advertisements, satisfaction surveys).

Spearheaded computerization of the entire business organization. Automated operational forms, created computerized superbill and implemented leading edge case management system that significantly improved service levels and efficiencies. Established service delivery protocols, pricing systems and a comprehensive operating procedures manual.

Previous Professional Experience (1984 to 1989) as an Account Representative, Credit Analyst and Credit Manager. Acquired excellent experience in credit/financial analysis, commercial and consumer lending, portfolio administration ($18 million) and sales/marketing/new business development. Employers included:

US West Financial Services, Kansas City, Missouri (1987 to 1989)
The CIT Group / Equipment Financing, Inc., Overland Park, Kansas (1986 to 1987)
Norwest Financial Services, Springfield, Missouri (1984 to 1985)

EDUCATION:

Master of Business Administration, July 1988
UNIVERSITY OF MISSOURI, Kansas City, Missouri

Bachelor of Science (General Business), December 1984
SOUTHWEST MISSOURI STATE UNIVERSITY, Springfield, Missouri

DENNIS JAMISON
Route 7 Box 350
Allentown, Pennsylvania 17571

Home (717) 204-2314   Office (717) 525-8000

HUMAN RESOURCES & LABOR RELATIONS DIRECTOR
Plant, Multi-Plant, Division & Corporate Headquarters

- Union Negotiations & Mediation
- Equal Employment
- Organization Development
- Safety Management
- Preventive Labor Relations Strategies
- Grievance & Arbitration Proceedings
- Multinational Workforce Management

- Compensation & Benefits Design
- Training & Development
- Recruitment & Employment
- HR Policy Design & Administration
- Succession Planning
- Operating Unit Support
- Employee & Labor Law

Union negotiating and administration experience with the OCAW, IBT, IBEW, IUE, Boilermakers, Steamfitters, Constructions Trades Council and numerous independent unions nationwide.

Technologies: HRIS, Lotus, WordPerfect, MS Access and Word
Languages: Conversational Spanish

PROFESSIONAL EXPERIENCE:

BICC CABLES - INDUSTRIAL CABLES COMPANY, Allentown, PA   1994 to Present
$130 million, 600 employee (union & non-union), 3-site wire & cable technology components manufacturer

<u>Director of Human Resources</u>
Senior Executive with full policy, strategic planning, operating and financial responsibility for all HR affairs for Industrial Cables Company and its operations in Indiana, Pennsylvania and Canada. Direct employment, compensation, employee and labor relations, security, health and safety, employee communications and employee services. Led a 10-person HR staff and support team.

Challenged to upgrade the quality and services of the HR function to meet the corporation's emerging business demands and long-term management development requirements. Senior advisor and confidante to executive management team on all core business, strategic planning, financial and HR affairs.

- Spearheaded the selection, acquisition and integration of PC-based HRIS technology to automate employee database, benefits, salary and administrative functions.
- Designed and implemented a series of employee training programs on safety, compliance, attendance, communications and performance improvement.

PIRELLI CABLE CORPORATION   1989 to 1994
$600 million, 1700-employee (union & non-union), 8-site manufacturer

<u>Plant Human Resources Manager</u>, Abbeyville, SC (1993 to 1994)
Accepted plant-level HR management position (280 employees) following corporate-wide reorganization. Challenged to restructure HR operations and more effectively integrate combined union/non-union workforce. Managed all generalist and labor relations affairs.

- Recruited and trained a 205-person, non-union replacement workforce during union work stoppage. Thwarted all union tactics and retained workforce permanently.

DENNIS JAMISON - *Page Two*

<u>**Division Human Resources Manager**</u>, Florham Park, NJ (1989 to 1993)

Senior HR Executive for five operating sites nationwide. Established HR and labor relations policies impacting more than 350 employees. Standardized HR practices for benefit and salary administration, expanded internal training opportunities, expanded HRIS applications, and revitalized recruitment program.

- Chosen for 6-month special assignment as **General Manager** leading the successful closure of Puerto Rican affiliate.
- Designed and implemented succession planning, position task identification, employee empowerment and employee/management communications plans as part of workforce reengineering initiative. Eliminated two complete management layers and significantly reduced annual staffing costs.
- Restructured hourly benefit plans for 60/40 payment split and saved $140,000 in first year costs. Wrote policy and implemented first-ever drug screening and employee assistance programs.
- Successfully defended against aggressive union organizing attempt.

ATLAS POWER COMPANY, Quakertown, PA   1988 to 1989
$90 million, 250 employee (union) manufacturer

<u>**Manager of Human Resources**</u>

Senior HR Manager directing recruitment, training, compensation, labor relations, and other core HR and employee relations functions. Guided policy development for programs, services and actions impacting the entire workforce and all core HR functions.

- Appointed Chief Labor Spokesperson negotiating cooperative agreements for a multi-craft mechanic concept. Delivered zero wage increases on strikeable wage reopener.

YABUCOA SUN OIL COMPANY, Puerto Rico   1985 to 1988
$110 million, 185 employee (non-union) oil production company

<u>**Manager - Employee & Plant Services**</u>

Wrote policies and directed programs for employment, labor relations, wage and salary administration, training, placement, health and safety, benefits and employee services. Demonstrated proficiency in cross-cultural communications and workforce management.

SUN REFINING & MARKETING COMPANY, MI, NJ, RI, PA   1970 to 1985
$1.6 billion diversified petroleum products corporation

Fast-track promotion through a series of increasingly responsible HR management positions including Manager of **Industrial Relations, Labor Relations Manager** and **Division HR Manager**. As **Senior Labor Relations Specialist**, responsible for 2000+ union and non-union employees in five operating locations nationwide.

- Led negotiations for two-tiered wage structures with no increases for two years. Resulted in $300,000 in immediate cost savings, elimination of restrictive work practices and significant improvement in seniority provisions.

EDUCATION:

BA Degree (Liberal Arts, Business & Economics), Bloomsburg State University, 1970

Continuing Professional Education in Human Resources, Management Development, Leadership, Communications and Total Quality Management (Crosby Associates).

JEFFREY M. ANDERSON

4325 South River Road #102
Baltimore, Maryland 22012
Phone/Fax: (410) 295-6547
Internet Address: janderson@nsa.org

ORGANIZATIONAL DEVELOPMENT / BUSINESS DEVELOPMENT / TRAINING & DEVELOPMENT

Human Resources Professional with a unique expertise in the development of business systems, processes and organizational infrastructures that have improved productivity, increased efficiency, enhanced quality and strengthened financial results. Outstanding record in personnel training, development and leadership. Particularly successful in new venture start-up, international marketing and new business development. Qualifications include:

- Organizational Design & Development
- Strategic & Tactical Planning
- Needs Assessment & Analysis
- Competency & Skills Assessment
- Technology Joint Ventures & Partnerships

- Project Planning & Management
- Executive Training & Leadership
- Policy & Procedure Development
- Process Design & Benchmarking
- Cross-Cultural Business Relations

Extensive qualifications in the full range of HR generalist functions:

- Recruitment & Selection
- Labor & Employee Relations
- Grievance Policies & Proceedings

- Compensation & Benefits
- HRIS Technologies
- EEO & Diversity Management

Lived and worked in the U.S., Japan, Germany, Singapore and Indochina. Fluent Japanese (conversational and written). Extensive public speaking experience at national conferences and symposia. Published journal author. Member, American Management Association, ASTD, NSPI and SIETAR.

TECHNOLOGY SKILLS:

Proficient in the use of Microsoft Products (Word, Excel, PowerPoint, Project, Access), Visio, ABC Flowchart, SAS, dBase, UNIX, Lotus 123, WordPerfect, Framemaker, PageMaker, Persuasion and others.

PROFESSIONAL EXPERIENCE:

Director - Organizational Development   1994 to Present
NATIONAL SECURITY AGENCY, Fort Meade, Maryland

Recruited to NSA as part of corporate-wide strategic initiative to reengineer the organization, implement efficiency and cost improvements, strengthen operations/management teams, and increase competitive positioning. Responsible for process mapping, benchmarking and a comprehensive TQM initiative.

Concurrently, provided strategic oversight for development of a total benefit, health, wellness and compensation strategy, and to transition all HR operating units into one integrated business unit. Use HR project as foundation to create reengineering model for all other NSA business units.

- Authored RFP for a fully-integrated benefit data management system. Saved $300,000 through in-house proposal preparation for technology that is projected to save $3 million to $5 million in annual benefit and compensation costs.

- Joined the New Business Development Division in December 1994 to identify and develop international joint venture and partnership programs. Working to create opportunities and develop marketing, business development and organizational plans.

JEFFREY M. ANDERSON   *Page Two*

Senior Consultant   1992 to 1994
ANDERSON CONSULTING, Alexandria, Virginia

Consulted with major corporate clients nationwide to provide leadership expertise in the areas of organizational development, training and development, project management, skill and competency assessment, and development of administrative documentation for policies and procedures. Completed engagements in the health care, telecommunications, technology and automotive industries.

- Created sophisticated technology training programs, training documentation and instructional methods for Bell Atlantic, TCI Communications and U.S. West. Designed programs to strengthen operating infrastructures, improve staff capabilities and facilitate productivity/efficiency gains.

- Launched an international workforce diversity training initiative for International Healthcare as part of the corporation's global expansion program.

Senior Manager   1988 to 1990
TOSHIBA NETWORK SWITCHING - Singapore and Japan

Recruited in the U.S. for a high-profile position guiding the development of business processes for the joint venture transfer of technical R&D operations from Japan to the U.S. Created the organizational infrastructure for a fully-integrated R&D, sales and technology support business unit. Developed administrative documentation, operating policies and procedures, customer service and support program standards, and a comprehensive training and development function.

- Consulted with major U.S. corporations to evaluate their specific technology requirements and position Toshiba for successful market launch.

Manager of Organizational Development   1985 to 1988
SIEMENS - Germany

Recruited in U.S. to join Siemens' operations in Germany and develop/manage organizational process to transition R&D operations to U.S. Defined business structure, developed policies/procedures, authored RFPs for project support, and coordinated staffing requirements to building training organization.

- Spearheaded $8 million joint venture between Siemens and the University of Florida for the research and development of computer-based training and instructional systems.

Assistant Manager - Instructional Technology   1980 to 1984
AT&T CENTER FOR TECHNICAL EDUCATION, Poughkeepsie, New York

Joined the Bell System's prestigious high-tech technology training center to facilitate development of instructional programming for R&D hardware and software technical engineering teams. Facilitated cross-functional technology and organizational development teams.

- Developed and presented a series of telecommunications technology training programs for AT&T's internal technology and R&D teams. Created computer-based curricula, multi-media instructional tools and administrative training documentation.

EDUCATION:

Ed.D., Organizational Development / Training & Development, Florida State University, 1992
(Doctoral dissertation published in the U.S. and Japan in 1992)
M.S., Administration, Northern Illinois University, 1980
B.S., Education, Northern Illinois University, 1977

GAYLE M. FAYGAN

1235 Fifth Avenue South #329
New York, New York 10021
(212) 535-5086

HUMAN RESOURCES EXECUTIVE

*Expert in Corporate Culture Change and Performance Improvement
for Start-Up, Turnaround and High-Growth Organizations*

Dynamic 13-year management career creating business-driven/market-driven HR organizations worldwide. Recognized for innovation in creating first-time HR policies, programs and processes that have delivered strong and sustainable results. Excellent HR generalist and employee relations qualifications.

PROFESSIONAL EXPERIENCE:

BANK OF NEW YORK, New York, New York   1990 to Present

Human Resources Manager - Singapore (1993 to Present)

Promoted and transferred to Singapore to lead the turnaround of the HR organization which was plagued with labor charges and completely ineffective in managing HR affairs for the region. Given full responsibility for redesigning the HR infrastructure, policies, procedures and services to support 500 employees in six different operating divisions and across seven staff functions.

Scope of responsibility is diverse and includes employee and labor relations, salary and benefits administration, payroll, succession planning, organization development, professional training, recruitment and performance management. Direct a staff of five HR professionals.

- Surpassed all turnaround objectives and delivered unprecedented gains in the performance and capabilities of the HR organization. Transitioned from administrative payroll function into a comprehensive, value-added business unit responsive to customer needs.

- Achieved the highest audit rating of any HR organization in the entire corporation for 1996 (highest in Asia for the past five years).

- Won a 1995 "Excalibur Award" for outstanding management and leadership performance.

Manager - Employee Relations (1992 to 1993)

Thirteen-month assignment directing corporate-wide employee relations for the 3200-person operating facility. Responsible for AAP, EEOC cases, policy interpretation and implementation, and a series of special HR/organization development projects.

- Designed and directed a standardized reduction in force program (including four divestitures) impacting 2700 employees. Achieved workforce downsizing with minimal legal claims.

- Spearheaded the design, development and successful implementation of an Employee Relations Network concept to link corporate ER with operating units and create a proactive, employee-focused business organization.

Human Resources Division Executive - Institutional Trust (1990 to 1992)
Human Resources Manager - Institutional Trust (1990)

HR Generalist for Bank of New York's Institutional Trust subsidiary. Promoted within six months with responsibility for all HR functions for 700 employees in North America and Europe. Managed large corporate downsizing, partial business unit divestiture and re-development of new HR organization. Directed a staff of HR generalists at three operating locations.

GAYLE M. FAYGAN   *Page Two*

BANK OF NEW YORK *(Continued)*:

- Reengineered core HR processes, designed performance-based recognition system, introduced change management initiatives, developed flexible benefit programs and consolidated compensation levels.

- Piloted career mobility system that was subsequently implemented throughout Bank of New York's global business structure.

- Successfully managed strategic downsizing through divestiture and voluntary retirement.

SAVOY, INC. *(Chase Manhattan Subsidiary)*, New York, New York   1989 to 1990

Human Resources Manager

Recruited as Senior HR Executive following Savoy's acquisition of a privately-held technology company. Given responsibility for recruitment and selection, benefits, compensation, training, organization development, employee relations and HR regulatory affairs. Consulted with executive management regarding long-term manpower planning, succession design and overall strategic planning.

- Created a complete HR organization and merged the disparate cultures of well-established multinational with emerging venture.

CLAIROL, INC., Stamford, Connecticut   1988

Senior Human Resources Administrator

Twelve-month assignment as HR generalist for 300-person Information Services and Customer Service organization. Challenged to introduce improved HR policies and organization development processes to strengthen regional workforce.

- Renegotiated policies and fee structures with external recruiters and reduced annual recruitment costs by 18%.

- Designed and implemented market-focused compensation plan, new employee program and a number of employee relations initiatives.

WHIRLPOOL CORPORATION, Benton Harbor, Michigan   1983 to 1988

Human Resources Marketing Administrator - Corporate Administrative Center (1985 to 1988)
Human Resources Administrator - La Porte Distribution Center (1984 to 1985)
Management Trainee - Human Resources (1983 to 1984)

Fast-track promotion through a series of increasingly responsible HR management assignments to final position managing HR generalist affairs for Corporate Education Center, Strategic Planning Group and 35 Customer/Technical Service Centers nationwide.

- Provided HR support for mergers, acquisitions, joint ventures and corporate development initiatives.

- Designed and implemented cafeteria benefits program and facilitated HR introduction into new line of business.

- Introduced transitional career pathing with UAW local, designed network recruitment strategies for area universities, implemented targeted selection interviewing system and authored HR policy manual.

EDUCATION:

B.A., Sociology / Communications, Hanover College, Hanover, Indiana, 1983

SARAH E. GREENE

249 Bay Street	Phone (714) 939-5437
Bayside, California 92923	Fax (714) 451-1348

EXECUTIVE PROFILE:

MANAGEMENT DEVELOPMENT / ORGANIZATION DEVELOPMENT / TRAINING

- Recipient of the 1993 "Company of the Year Award" for training from the American Society of Training and Development (Orange County Chapter).
- Twice nominated for the 1993 and 1994 "Award of Excellence" from holding company (Freedom Communications).

CAREER PROFILE:

Dynamic professional career building state-of-the-art organization development, management development and training processes for large corporations with operations worldwide. Partnered human resources and development initiatives with all core business units to create proactive organizations with consistent gains in productivity, performance, quality and service. Expert in facilitating groups through complex problem-solving to action and improvement. Core competencies include:

- Self-Directed Work Teams
- Strategic & Succession Planning
- Organization Needs Assessment
- Seminar/Workshop Design
- HR Policies & Procedures

- Performance Management & Appraisal Processes
- Supervisory Training & Communications
- Private & Public Partnerships
- Train-the-Trainer Development
- Executive Training & Leadership

PROFESSIONAL EXPERIENCE:

Training & Organization Development Consultant   1995 to Present
WINDSOR-WEST & ASSOCIATES, Bayside, California

Executive Consultant providing custom-designed training and organization development programs to commercial, industrial, institutional and non-profit clients throughout the region. Introduce pioneering training and OD processes to link human resources to operations, facilitating productivity, quality and service gains. Specialize in "Train-the-Trainer" workshops.

Manager Human Resources - Training & Development   1989 to 1995
THE LOS ANGELES COUNTY REGISTER, Los Angeles, California

Senior Training & Development Executive for privately-owned newspaper with approximately 2600 employees. Challenged to create an industry-leading training process to meet the dynamic needs of the organization as it downsized, reorganized and restructured to meet competitive market demands.

THE LOS ANGELES COUNTY REGISTER *(Continued):*

- Guided executives and managers in identifying organizational needs and performed specific OD interventions as part of reengineering and process improvement plans.
- Conducted training needs assessments with managers and employees, and designed/ presented over 30 different seminars and workshops.
- Established training/performance improvement measurements to strengthen OD process.
- Developed annual training plans and budgets to meet organizational needs, and federal and state regulations governing sexual harassment, discrimination, substance abuse and safety.
- Negotiated with consultants and colleges to coordinate in-house courses in ESL, supervision and employee education.

Achievements:

- Introduced "Self-Directed Work Teams" and implemented "Performance Management" processes, delivering up to a 50% improvement in productivity, efficiency and organization performance.
  - Customer Service - Increased quality 40% and reduced attrition from 100% to 15%.
  - Distribution - Reduced customer complaints from 5/1000 to less than 1/1000 per month, developed cross-training matrix for 500 employees and improved morale 52%.
  - Advertising - Increased sales time 15%, exceeded sales goals 10%-15%.
  - Maintenance - Developed preventive program which reduced downtime 14.8%, implemented cross-training and improved morale 34%.
  - National Sales - Restructured organization while exceeding sales goals 8.6%.
  - Human Resources - Dramatically expanded level of HR service throughout organization with concurrent 30% reduction in HR staffing requirements.
- Transitioned corporate culture into a "learning and development" environment, fostering teamwork and high involvement employee processes resulting in substantive improvements in performance and communications..
- Increased number of internal training programs from four to more than 30 within a five-year period with enrollment increasing by more than 100%. Consistently received top-level course ratings throughout tenure.

Training & Organization Development Specialist 1983 to 1988
LOS ANGELES COUNTY TRANSIT AUTHORITY, Los Angeles, California

Led the organization's human resources development function and all training programs.

- Designed and implemented performance evaluation and development process, and all related training for executives, managers and supervisors.
- Audited actual performance evaluations and designed coaching techniques to improve quality of evaluations by up to 50%.
- Developed core management and supervisory development programs.
- Authored and edited internal management/supervisor newsletter to expand communication and documentation of pertinent training and OD initiatives.
- Consulted with executives and senior management teams on strategic development plans and implementation.

SARAH E. GREENE   **Page Three**

Corporate Manager - Human Resources Development   1981 to 1983
BRONSON & STURGIS, INC., Houston, Texas

Built a complete human resources training and development organization for this 45,000-employee international engineering and construction firm. Recruited, trained and supervised 14 training and organization development specialists providing craft and technical support, employee training and management development programs.

- Established management assessment and development program, including identification of high potential candidates, and the corporation's formal succession planning model.
- Authored management development and succession plan policies and procedures for the entire corporation. Travelled worldwide to facilitate plan implementation.
- Appointed to industry committee to reform Taft-Hartley and two other labor laws to promote "open shop" and "right to work" policies at the federal government level.

Human Resources Development Consultant   1979 to 1981
WINDSOR-WEST & ASSOCIATES, Orange, California

Marketed and presented custom-designed training and development programs to corporate, industrial and non-profit clients throughout the region.

Corporate Director of Training & Development   1977 to 1979
VSI CORPORATION, Pasadena, California

Led training, management development and performance appraisal programs for a 35,000-employee manufacturer. Developed "on-the-job" training techniques and provided technical training consultations.

Previous Professional Experience as **Director of Management Development & Training** for Fluor Corporation (established Human Resources Planning Center) and as **Vice President** of its for-profit training and organization development subsidiary (People Growth Inc.).

TEACHING EXPERIENCE:

- Instructor, Training & Development, University of California at Irvine
- Instructor, Human Relations & Industrial Supervision, Mt. San Antonio College

EDUCATION:

BA, University of Missouri
Dean's Honor Roll for Speech / Delta Sigma Rho (Speech Honor Society)

Certificate in Human Resources Management, University of California

PROFESSIONAL AFFILIATIONS:

American Society of Training and Development
The Association of Human Resources Professionals (PIRA)
Orange County Organization Development Network
Human Resources Independent Consultants (HRIC)

PAUL BOWLIN, CCP

P.O. Box 7613, 1330 Oak Knoll Trail   Home   (509) 587-7842
Yakima, Washington 99512-7613   Office   (509) 987-3214

SENIOR HUMAN RESOURCES EXECUTIVE

HR Generalist / Labor Relations Specialist / Organizational Development Strategist
Expert in Wage/Benefit Analysis & Cost Containment
Certified Compensation Professional (CCP)

Trusted management and employee confidante with expert qualifications in developing and leading comprehensive HR organizations. Strong record of performance in productivity and performance improvement, cost reduction, technology gains and leadership development. Enthusiastic with a positive management style.

PROFESSIONAL EXPERIENCE:

MOUNTAIN INDUSTRIAL COMPANY, Yakima, Washington   1994 to Present

Human Resources Director & Safety Director (1996 to Present)
Human Resources Director (1994 to 1996)

High-profile, senior-level management position leading the entire HR organization for this 325-employee corporation. Scope of responsibility is significant and includes all generalist HR affairs, compensation and incentives, employee relations, labor relations, loss control and HR information systems. Delivered strong performance results through expertise in HR leadership and organizational development.

Labor Relations Management:
- Negotiated comprehensive drug testing program with IBEW/USWA representatives in only 50 minutes.
- Appointed Spokesperson for USWA and IBEW contract negotiations. Successfully managed and resolved over 200 labor grievances and employee relations issues.

Organizational Development & Leadership:
- Pioneered the introduction of a series of innovative organizational development, performance management, quality improvement, change management and leadership development programs to strengthen workforce and enhance organizational competencies.
- Designed and led succession planning, litigation avoidance, workers' compensation, benefits, labor agreement, performance management, ADA and FLMA training for staff, management and union officials.

Staffing & Recruitment Management:
- Directed project team in the development of ADA compliant job descriptions, recruitment and screening programs, and hiring procedures for all levels throughout the organization (e.g., expatriate and national management, exempt professionals and technicians, non-exempt technicians, skilled craftworkers).
- Guided staffing and recruitment programs for field operations in Peru and Argentina.

Compensation & Benefits Management:
- Introduced workers' compensation cost containment techniques and reduced cash flow requirements by more than $745,000 (average of $1200 per employee per year savings). Captured medical benefit cost savings of more than $1 million (20%) over three years.
- Spearheaded implementation of first managed care program, integrated claims management and first report of injury procedures to provide enhanced quality of care throughout the organization.

Loss Control & Employee Relations Management:
- Created a proactive management, administration and training organization and facilitated joint effort between company and unions to develop a safety committee focused on reducing at-risk behavior. Educated union personnel and officials in loss control and compliance.
- Managed sensitive labor and crisis communications.

PAUL BOWLIN, CCP - *Page Two*

LONE STAR MINING COMPANY, Blackwater, Texas   1975 to 1994

Employee Services Director / Human Resources Director (1991 to 1994)
Industrial Relations Director / Employee Relations Director (1979 to 1991)
Environmental Director & Assistant Director - Public Affairs (1975 to 1979)

Advanced through a series of increasingly responsible management positions functioning as the #1/#2 HR Executive for 13 consecutive years. Managed a vast portfolio of HR, employee relations, technology, operations and infrastructure development projects. Led teams of up to 20.

Labor Relations Management:
- Favorably managed five major USWA contract negotiations and resolved 1100+ grievances, 60 arbitration cases and 1000 unemployment claims.
- Established cooperative working relationships with union representatives and officials, virtually eliminating all unnecessary grievances and creating common goals, objectives and performance standards.

Staffing & Recruitment Management:
- Spearheaded the entire recruitment, screening and hiring process for all personnel throughout the organization, from top-level national management teams through all exempt levels to hourly craftworkers and support personnel.
- Successfully thwarted two aggressive union organizing attempts while managing salaried workforce reduction programs.
- Led 64% reduction in HR staffing requirements while maintaining optimum service.

Organizational Development & Leadership:
- Developed and instructed management training sessions for over 500 management, staff, union and hourly personnel. Certified Management Development Trainer.
- Introduced change management, reorganization, process improvement and productivity/performance improvement programs.

Compensation & Benefits Management:
- Redesigned compensation system to replace antiquated hourly base pay system with 15 grades and a 1.5% wage grade spread to more equitably manage payroll and employee benefit programs.
- Implemented successful cost containment strategies to lower corporate expenses associated with workers' compensation, health insurance and other core benefit programs.

HR Information Systems (HRIS) Management:
- Facilitated regional implementation of $600,000 corporate-wide integrated payroll and HRIS to create a state-of-the-art HR management and reporting environment.

EDUCATION & PROFESSIONAL DEVELOPMENT:

BS (Commerce & Industry), University of Texas at Austin

CORNELL UNIVERSITY	Human Resources Executive Development Program
WASHINGTON EMPLOYERS COUNCIL	HR, Labor & Employee Relations Seminars
AMERICAN COMPENSATION ASSN.	Wage & Benefit Seminars; CCP Competency Exams
BEHAVIOR SCIENCE TECHNOLOGY	Safety Analysis & Injury Prevention Program
TEXAS LAW CONFERENCE	State Workplace Issues

PROFESSIONAL AFFILIATIONS:

President, Washington Employers' Group. Member, American Compensation Association.

LINDA S. SWAN   35 Last Desert Road   •   Phoenix, Arizona 78431   •   (602) 874-4512

PROFESSIONAL SKILLS & QUALIFICATIONS:

Human Services Professional with excellent qualifications in developing and managing specialized vocational, educational and training programs for challenging adult and youth populations. Excellent qualifications in facilitating cooperative relationships among private and public sector service agencies to enhance the quality and continuity of client care. Strong communications, interpersonal relations and crisis management skills.

- Vocational Rehabilitation
- Training Program Management
- Professional Staff Training
- Program Budgeting & Administration

- Social Services
- Placement
- Counseling & Guidance
- Testing & Evaluation

RELATED PROFESSIONAL EXPERIENCE:

Testing/Evaluation/Placement Consultant   V.I.P. SERVICES, Phoenix, AZ
- Screened, tested and evaluated trainable mentally handicapped adults for placement in vocational training programs. Completed two terms of employment with this organization throughout professional career.

Vocational Rehabilitation Consultant   WATSON REHABILITATION CENTER, San Antonio, TX
- Designed and administered a work activity program for trainable mentally handicapped adults. Focused program development on critical issues including daily living skills, physical exercise, social adaptation and communication.
- Developed and led physiological training programs to enhance fine and gross motor skills coordination.

Chief Vocational Evaluator   ARIZONA STATE MENTAL HOSPITAL, Phoenix, AZ
- Directed the start-up and subsequent management of a vocational evaluation unit to assess the training and development potential of patients prior to discharge.
- Established norms for standardized testing with a sample of 100 vocational/trade school students.

Teacher   SAN ANTONIO PUBLIC SCHOOL, San Antonio, TX
- Taught mathematics, vocational education and drivers education to educable mentally handicapped and learning disabled senior high school students.
- Evaluated the cognitive, social and emotional level of special education students to develop appropriate work study programs in the school and local community.
- Designed pilot program for testing and placement of trainable mentally handicapped students in a work adjustment environments.

OTHER EXPERIENCE:

Fifteen-year career (1980 to Present) in Supply, Materials, Equipment and Logistics Management for the U.S. Army. Advanced to **Deputy Director of Logistics** for a 60,000 person organization. Acquired extensive experience in mainframe and PC technologies. Completed assignments in the U.S., West Germany, Korea and Marshall Islands. Currently serve as a **Major** with the United States Army Reserve.

EDUCATION: **Master of Science in Vocational Rehabilitation**, UNIVERSITY OF TEXAS

Bachelor of Science in Industrial Arts, SAN ANTONIO STATE UNIVERSITY

Military Training & Education:
- Supply, Logistics Management Course
- Maintenance Officer Advanced Course
- Internal Review and Audit Course
- Maintenance Officer Basic Course
- Women's Army Corps Basic Course

JACQUES SAN MIGUEL
43 North End Avenue
Chicago, Illinois 60842
(847) 211-6471

INTERNATIONAL TRADE & IMPORT/EXPORT EXECUTIVE

Over 15 years experience in the structure and negotiation of **international trade, barter and import/ export** projects throughout the U.S., Europe, Russia, Far East and Middle East. Identified and capitalized upon market opportunities to profitably trade commodities, technologies, equipment and consumer products. Pioneer in barter trade management. Extensive qualifications in new venture start-up, joint venture and partnership negotiations, manufacturing and purchasing management. Multilingual with extensive worldwide travel.

PROFESSIONAL EXPERIENCE:

PIE R.F.P. ISRAEL / S.P.A., INC. USA   1987 to Present

Senior Operating Executive with this multinational corporation engaged in a diversity of independent and joint venture import/export, international trade, international business development, marketing and manufacturing opportunities worldwide. Key business units located in Israel, The Netherlands, Russia and the United States.

Promoted rapidly through a series of increasingly responsible international trade, operating and business management positions. Career highlights include:

General Manager - S.P.A., Inc. - New York/Russia/Europe (1990 to Present)
High-profile executive management position directing international trade and import/export programs worldwide. Collateral responsibility for strategic business planning, new business development, international business relations, plant operations, purchasing and revenue/profit contribution of several subsidiaries and joint ventures.

- Identified, structured and negotiated international trade and import/export projects with leading U.S. corporations in the automotive, food, textile, consumer products and children's products markets. Managed contracts, purchasing and all related logistics, transportation and distribution programs.

- Spearheaded development of international trade programs between U.S. and The Netherlands that generated multi-million dollars in transactions within first 18 months.

- Pioneered innovative trade bartering deals between Russian metals manufacturer and U.S. manufacturers, wholesalers and distributors (e.g., Chrysler, Magic Chef, Oleg Casini).

- Negotiated a unique partnership between Russian business partners and a U.S. pre-engineered steel building manufacturer for the research, development and manufacture of a large commercial facility for export and erection in St. Petersburg.

- Led start-up of wood products manufacturing plant in the Ural region of Russia. Introduced Western manufacturing practices, redesigned production cycle, installed U.S. manufactured technology, and built worldwide distribution function. Built business from start-up to over $2.3 million in annual revenues.

- Designed multi-faceted transportation and logistics program for new trade agreement between Russian manufacturer and U.S. finished goods assembler as business grew from start-up to over $7.5 million in first year sales.

General Manger - PIE S.P.A. - South Carolina (1989 to 1990)

Senior Operating Executive with full P&L responsibility for the planning, development, staffing, training, budgeting and bottom-line financial performance of a scrap aluminium production and distribution facility. Challenged to build and direct new ventures and deliver strong financial results.

- Negotiated lease with owners of dormant plant to re-start operations and rebuild market presence. Recruited and trained 100+ new workers, implemented labor relations and labor incentive programs, designed monthly and year-end management reporting systems, and coordinated a complex domestic and international logistics program to transport product from the U.S. and Japan.

- Built revenues from start-up to over $6 million in first year sales. Generated profits margins well above industry averages and 25% over projections.

General Manager - PIE S.P.A. - Israel (1987 to 1989)

Recruited to accelerate the corporation's import/export, international trade, manufacturing and construction projects throughout the international market. Spearheaded global research and feasibility studies to identify emerging market opportunities and coordinated operating unit start-up.

EQUIPMENT DEVELOPMENT LTD. - Israel   1983 to 1986

Executive President

Directed large-scale construction of metal and wood pre-engineered buildings for the Israeli Government. Planned, staffed, budgeted and managed several million dollars in annual construction and renovation projects. Worked with U.S. companies in design and construction of U.S. air base.

SUDANRIO LTD. - Israel   1979 to 1983

General Manager

Managed daily business operations of a diversified import/export company. Spearheaded several large-scale feasibility studies to investigate import/export and international trade opportunities in the former Yugoslavia and Brazil. Collateral responsibility for leasing, development, staffing, supply, logistics and distribution operations of large food manufacturing operation in Australia exporting products to Israel.

T. R. LAFIA LTD. - Israel   1977 to 1979

Operations Manager

Negotiated the import of corrugated carton boxes specially manufactured in Italy for the export of Israeli agricultural products to the U.S. and Europe. Managed a complex logistics, transportation and distribution management function.

DEVELOPMENT & CONSTRUCTION, INC. - Israel   1975 to 1977

Manager

Directed daily business operations for a diversified import/export and commercial construction company. Sourced and imported materials from Europe and the U.S. to support Israel during a period of rapid economic growth and expansion.

EDUCATION:

Bachelor of Science Degree, University of Indiana, Bloomfield, Indiana, 1974

KAREN M. LAWSON

500 Oakmont Court
St. Louis, Missouri 60000
Home (314) 300-2000   Office (314) 900-5000

INSURANCE INDUSTRY EXECUTIVE
Expertise in Marketing, Business Development & Business Management

Dynamic professional career building retail and wholesale businesses for leading insurance carriers. Extensive qualifications in new product/new plan development, strategic and tactical marketing, competitive market positioning, sales leadership and agent recruitment/training. Strong general management, P&L and teambuilding qualifications.

Captured millions of dollars in increased sales and premiums
within highly competitive markets.

PROFESSIONAL EXPERIENCE:

THE WHOLESALE AGENCY, St. Louis, Missouri   1989 to Present

PRESIDENT (1990 to Present)
VICE PRESIDENT (1989 to 1990)

Acquired 50% ownership of this wholesale insurance brokerage in 1989 and the additional 50% in 1990. Operate a unique insurance firm specializing in the recruitment, training and retention of independent agents to represent the products of major regional and national carriers.

As President and Senior Operating Executive, hold full P&L responsibility for the planning, development, staffing, financial affairs and production of the agency. Manage a corporate staff of 15. In addition to agency management, provide expert consultation to general agents nationwide relative to marketing, business development and strategic business management.

Achievements

- Delivered the strongest financial results in the history of the agency. Consistently qualified for incentive plans with all major carriers for the past six consecutive years.

- Launched a nationwide recruitment effort and built agency to over 400 general agents and 2500 agents nationwide.

- Negotiated representation agreements with major insurance carriers nationwide including Nationwide Insurance, Aetna Insurance Company, Provident Indemnity, Federal Home Life and Rockingham Mutual.

- Recently retained by Continental Life, recruited 100 agents within three months and launched the successful market introduction of a specialized health insurance product.

THE WHOLESALE AGENCY *(Continued)*:

- Created a portfolio of marketing, promotional and publicity materials to drive business development via agent recruitment and field sales/marketing. Designed tabletop, video and slide/video presentations, and marketing communications.

- Appointed to the National States Product Development Task Force challenged to identify market opportunities and drive the development of market-specific products, plans and coverages.

- Spearheaded selection and introduction of a Novell network to link agents nationwide.

MASS MUTUAL, St. Louis, Missouri   1983 to 1989

SALES REPRESENTATIVE

Top-producing sales associate with this diversified retail insurance brokerage. Marketed a complete line of life and health products to individuals and small groups throughout Iowa, Missouri and Illinois. Advanced rapidly and assumed additional responsibility as a Sales Trainer in 1988 to provide field training and support to newly hired agents.

Achievements

- Consistently exceeded annual sales goals and premium objectives. Closed 1988 and 1989 as the #1 producer and sales club qualifier.

- Independently managed the entire sales cycle, from initial client consultation, product presentation, pricing and contract negotiation through to final sales closing. Achieved top performance in account retention, add-on sales and growth.

- Represented the life and health products of four major carriers: National States Insurance Company, Guarantee Trust Life Insurance Company, Federal Home Life and American Integrity Insurance Company.

CIVIC & PROFESSIONAL AFFILIATIONS:

ST. LOUIS CHAMBER OF COMMERCE
Co-Founder, Partners with Industry Program (1995)
Participant, National Training & Development Program (1994 to 1995)
Employer of the Year (1994)
Participant, Transitional Employment Program (1993 to Present)

THE SMALL BUSINESS BOARD
Participant, Business Owner Forum (1994 to 1995)

MISSOURI NUMISMATIC SOCIETY
Committee Member (1990 to 1993)

EDUCATION: **B.A. Degree (History)**, Drake University, Des Moines, Iowa, 1983

THOMAS RICHARDSON
100 South Church Road
Baltimore, Maryland 21212

Phone (410) 800-5000   Office (410) 500-6000

INSURANCE INDUSTRY EXECUTIVE - CHAIRMAN / CEO / COO

Dynamic professional career as Chairman, CEO and COO of a high-growth division of a Fortune 500 company. Provided the strategic, tactical and operating leadership to meet challenging start-up, turnaround and high-growth ventures worldwide. Expert in wrap-up, retail and wholesale insurance, reinsurance and benefits consulting. Pioneer in international business expansion and globalization.

Strong qualifications and experience in structuring and negotiating profitable joint ventures and strategic alliances in both the insurance and entertainment industries. Effective in complex risk management programs and cross-cultural government affairs. Skilled crisis manager, negotiator and marketer. Extensive P&L experience.

PROFESSIONAL EXPERIENCE:

INTERNATIONAL IDEAS, INC.   1992 to Present

Chairman & CEO

Founded and currently direct a multi-discipline management consulting group with offices in the U.S. and Singapore. Capitalized upon lifelong experience and contacts in the insurance industry and 17 years of residing/operating in Asia/Middle East to build client relationships and win key consulting contracts. Completed engagements in the insurance and entertainment industries. Highlights include:

- Managed insurance bidding and award for several major wrap-ups including the $1.5 billion Caltex Refinery in Thailand, the $6 billion Boston Harbor Waste Water Treatment Facility and the $21 million China Beef & Lamb Company in Beijing.

- Retained by Bechtel Corporation to investigate and evaluate feasibility of a unique joint venture with Chinese-based insurance company. Evaluated financial, economic and political risks to corporation.

- Identified and capitalized upon emerging opportunities within the Far East for U.S. entertainment events. Acted as General Manager responsible for booking tours, coordinating international licensing and taxation, negotiating sites, managing logistics and directing advertising and promotions. Negotiated joint ventures, strategic alliances and other partnerships with John Denver, Michael Jackson, Tony Bennett, Phil Collins, Garth Brooks and the Everly Brothers.

- Appointed Chairman of American Golf Club USA, a Malaysian-based sports equipment and clothing manufacturer seeking to penetrate U.S. market. Provided strategic/tactical leadership for market development, negotiated licensing and trademark agreements, and coordinated U.S. registration.

- Provided strategic marketing and operational leadership to the National Back Injury Network, an on-line network designed to expedite injury claims processing nationwide. Delivered expertise in marketing, business development, partner development and service delivery.

MITCHELL & MITCHELL, INC.   1973 to 1992

Chairman, Director & CEO - Asian/Middle East Division (1987 to 1992)
Chairman & CEO - Middle East Ltd. (1979 to 1986)
Vice President & COO - Alexander & Alexander Massachusetts (1973 to 1979)

Promoted to Vice President within three months and led the organization through a period of rapid growth and expansion. Instrumental in the structure and successful negotiation of the largest wrap-up contract ever ($11 billion project in Saudi Arabia with 450 contractors, 5 insurance policies and 2 sites located 1000 miles apart). Following award, promoted and transferred to Saudi to provide on-site leadership for this project generating $20 million in fees to M&M.

MITCHELL & MITCHELL, INC. *(Continued):*

- Negotiated with Saudi Arabian government to fund 100% of start-up and mobilization costs with an "advance pay" contract. Provided M&M with the opportunity to enter the country with no cash outlay.

- Successfully negotiated contract against eight major worldwide competitors and won renewals for two five-year contracts.

Devoted the next seven years to establishing a full-service insurance brokerage throughout the Middle East. Held full P&L responsibility for building the entire organizational infrastructure, establishing strategic and tactical business plans, negotiating joint ventures and establishing wholly-owned subsidiaries. Established a significant and sustainable market presence throughout the region.

- Built Middle Eastern region from concept into a complex business organization generating $8.5 million in annual commission fees and over $2 million in annual profits.

Promoted in 1987 to Chairman, Director and CEO of the newly-formed Asian/Middle East Division. Challenged to continue to build Middle East while leading the turnaround of existing operations throughout Asia and the Indian Subcontinent. As the Senior Operating Executive, held full P&L responsibility for the strategic planning, development and leadership of the entire business organization.

Scope of responsibility was diverse and included annual business planning, financial affairs, government relations, international tax, legal affairs, risk management, human resources, MIS technology, business development, joint venture negotiations and executive administration. Operated autonomously with little HQ support. Held significant decision making responsibility.

- Brought Singapore regional operations from $1 million loss to breakeven within first 18 months and to subsequent $4+ million annual operating profit on $12 million in annual commission fees. Concurrent with turnaround, launched a massive market expansion effort throughout Asia and the Middle East, building Division to 21 countries with 850 employees.

- Established strategic alliances and joint ventures with financial institutions, commercial banks and merchant banks in all 13 major Asian countries to close the service gap in the globalization of the M&M.

- Structured, negotiated and won major contracts (including multi-million dollar wrap-ups) with large U.S. corporations including A. Brown Boveri, Westinghouse, Aramco, Parsons and Unilever.

- Member of an elite 8-person executive "globalization task force" challenged to transition the corporation from U.S. to international and capitalize upon emerging market opportunities worldwide.

- Appointed to numerous operating and management committees throughout tenure whose missions were to profitably build and expand specific products and markets worldwide (e.g., retail, wholesale, reinsurance, benefits consulting). Highlights included:

  — Board of Directors, Mitchell & Mitchell International
  — Board of Directors, Mitchell & Mitchell Global Retail Company
  — Operations Management Committee, Mitchell & Mitchell Australia/New Zealand
  — Board of Advisors, Mitchell & Mitchell London
  — Board of Directors of 13 operating subsidiaries of Mitchell & Mitchell in Asia/Middle East

AMERICAN INSURANCE   1968 to 1976

Director - Risk Management Services

Fast-track promotion through series of increasingly responsible assignments to final position as Director of Risk Management Services. Led cross-functional teams in the design, engineering, implementation and management of safety, fire prevention and security systems for corporate clients nationwide.

EDUCATION: **Towson State University**, Towson, Maryland

JAMES R. PETERSON
19 Cassatt Road
Boston, Massachusetts 03851
(617) 267-4541

TECHNOLOGY INDUSTRY EXECUTIVE
President / CEO / COO / Corporate Vice President

High-profile career spearheading the development, commercialization and market launch of emerging technologies worldwide. Combines expertise in strategic planning, P&L management, marketing and business development with sophisticated technology skills. Extensive experience in international joint ventures, technology transfer and commercialization, strategic alliances and other business partnerships. M.B.A. and Ph.D. degrees.

- Profiled in Business Week, Fortune, Science Digest, and more than 30 other international publications.
- Winner, Harvard Smithsonian Astrophysical Observatory Award (1979 to 1982)
- Outstanding Scientist of the Year, Maryland Academy of Sciences (1984)

PROFESSIONAL EXPERIENCE:

JRP INC., Lexington, Massachusetts / Columbia, Maryland   1996 to Present

President / CEO
Re-ignited management consulting firm founded in 1988 and specializing in technology development/ commercialization, business process reengineering and other corporate development projects. Current engagements include:

- **Chairman of the Board of PhotoTronics Corporation**, a privately-held technology venture developing on-line, interactive Internet photography for consumer/commercial markets. Currently negotiating partnerships with telecommunication, Internet content providers, photofinishers, cable stations and other "broadcast" media nationwide.
- **Technology Advisor** spearheading several high-profile technology transfer and commercialization projects from government into private sector.
- **Business & Financial Advisor** directing investment banking negotiations for proposed LBO transaction for emerging technology company.

POLAROID CORPORATION, Cambridge, Massachusetts   1991 to 1996

Vice President - Business Development (1995 to 1996)
Launched the start-up of Polaroid's newest venture, based upon technology invented as VP of Research & Technology. Given full P&L responsibility for building the business unit, acquiring/ developing the technology and identifying market opportunities worldwide. Collateral P&L responsibility for Far East and Middle East PhotoDocumentation and Identification (ID) Card Business Development initiatives.

- Created strategic business unit to penetrate the $1 billion electronic photography industry.
- Negotiated 12 worldwide alliances, partnerships and joint ventures in software, telecommunications, information processing, digital electronics and systems integration industries to build portfolio.
- Appointed to "Corporate Leadership Team," a multidisciplinary senior officer group including CEO, CFO and business unit Vice Presidents driving long-term strategic and tactical planning.

Vice President - Research & Technology (1991 to 1995)
Senior corporate officer recruited to plan/direct a comprehensive business process redesign of Polaroid's $160 million Research & Technology Division (2000 employees in seven locations responsible development/manufacture of silicon, GaAs and microelectronic devices; chemical engineering scale-up plants; and engineering design/development/manufacture of products). Streamlined processes, reduced costs and improved productivity while accelerating technology development and commercialization.

JAMES R. PETERSON - *Page Two*

- Led a massive corporate culture change, restructured product development teams into P&L-based business units, and transitioned from technology-driven to business process-driven organization. Captured a **30% reduction in cost and time to develop technology.**
- Identified opportunities, structured and negotiated 10 major domestic and international technology development joint ventures.
- Downsized Central Research from 500 to 100 scientists and doubled technology outsourcing.
- Influenced core business units to incorporate 70% of Polaroid's existing technology investment into their product development projects.

NOTE: Invented new, interactive Internet electronic photography system, won corporate funding and promoted to lead start-up of ImageNow strategic business unit.

JRP INC., Lexington, Massachusetts / Columbia, Maryland   1988 to 1991

President / CEO
Founded and directed successful management consulting firm working with public and private sector organizations worldwide. Completed more than 20 engagements in three years.

- Retained by the Republic of China (Taiwan) to facilitate development of their space, telecommunication and microelectronic technology acquisition and transfer program. Managed year-long project with top technology and government leaders.
- Assisted with $5 million initial funding for start-up software company, $10 million IPO and subsequent merger with larger, more established technology company.
- Guided product development and new business initiatives for five corporations, five universities and three national laboratories.

DEPARTMENT OF DEFENSE, Washington, D.C.   1984 to 1988

Director - Strategic Defense Initiative Organization
Challenged to create multi-million dollar technology development organization, recruit technical talent and establish business processes to acquire and incorporate advanced technology into highly sophisticated defense systems. Led a team of 100 professionals and managed a 4-year, $1 billion budget.

- Spearheaded joint venture programs with 200+ companies and 60 universities worldwide.
- Negotiated sophisticated technology transfer agreements with the private sector and influenced successful commercialization of over 50 new technologies.
- Won several prestigious awards including 1988 "Outstanding Performance Award," 1988 "Mission of the Year Award" and 1987 "Federal Government Top Manager Under Forty Award."

Project Scientist, NASA Goddard Space Flight Center   1978 to 1984
Adjunct Professor - Physics & Astronomy, University of Maryland   1978 to 1984

EDUCATION:

Ph.D., Applied Technology, University of Maryland, 1977
M.B.A., Engineering Technology, University of Michigan, 1975
M.S., Physics, University of Michigan, 1973
B.S., Math & Physics (High Honors), University of Michigan, 1972

PROFESSIONAL ACTIVITIES:

Affiliations
- Board of Governors, CalTech Center for Microelectronics
- Editorial Board, Photonics Spectra and R&D Magazine

Publications
- Authored 50+ articles in professional journals worldwide.

Athletics
- Member, U.S. World Championship Kayak Team (1970)

VICTORIA MATHESON
9832 West 45th Street
New York, New York 10021

Home (212) 930-6547

Office (201) 584-7364

INFORMATION TECHNOLOGY EXECUTIVE

Expert in the design, development and delivery of cost-effective, high-performance technology solutions to meet challenging business demands. Extensive qualifications in all facets of project lifecycle development, from initial feasibility analysis and conceptual design through documentation, implementation, user training and enhancement. Excellent organizational, leadership, team building and project management qualifications. Member of the Association of Information and Image Management.

PROFESSIONAL EXPERIENCE:

FIRST FIDELITY BANCORPORATION, Newark, New Jersey   1992 to Present

Senior Project Manager/Vice President - Information Systems & Technology

Recruited to accelerate First Fidelity's implementation of emerging technologies and manage enterprise-wide projects for the Distributed Computing Department. Scope of responsibility has included four major projects with total technological investment of more than $4 million:

— Document Imaging
— Mainframe COLD Application
— LAN-Based E-Mail System
— Corporate Purchasing Process (reengineering initiative)

Scope of responsibility is diverse and includes authoring and issuing RFI's and RFP's, directing the competitive vendor selection process and producing cost/benefit analyses to justify capital expenditures. Write business requirements and system specifications, and produce/manage deliverables through formal project plans. Lead cross-functional project teams and team meetings. Supervise project managers and technical staff.

• Led projects through multi-year R&D cycle to develop application-specific systems capable of meeting current and long-range information management requirements.

• Developed bank-wide imaging strategy and designed improved workflow processes for implementation via FileNet Document Imaging System with projected productivity gains of over 40% ($1.2 million over five years).

• Led development and pilot implementation of LAN-Based E-Mail with full roll-out designed for 3000+ users across six states.

CHASE MANHATTAN BANK, New York, New York   1979 to 1992

Fast-track promotion throughout 13-year career, advancing through a series of increasingly responsible operating and information systems technology positions. Career highlights included:

Project Manager/Assistant Vice President - Information Systems Development (1990 to 1992)

Planned, staffed, budgeted and directed software development efforts for various Automated Voice Response projects. Led cross-functional project teams through the entire development cycle, from initial needs assessment through specification, development, quality review and implementation.

CHASE MANHATTAN BANK *(Continued):*

- Introduced transfer functionality, electronic bill processing and an expanded information capability through a cooperative project effort with 12 mainframe systems development areas and representatives from Marketing, Business Operations, Data Center Operations and Business Support Units.

Senior Product Specialist/Assistant Vice President (1989 to 1990)

Spearheaded the development and implementation of new technologies, products, product enhancements and processes to expand product portfolio, increase competitive position within the market, and accelerate Chase's continued growth and expansion.

- Appointed Project Manager for the implementation and launch of the national Automated Voice Project. Authored an award-winning business specifications document integrating financial transfer functionality with this emerging technology.

- Developed operations standards and processes to support a new product offering targeted to high-end customer niche. Created comprehensive operations plan detailing recommendations for the establishment of several new business units throughout various divisions within the organization.

Project Manager/Assistant Vice President (1986 to 1989)

Planned and directed the simultaneous implementation of new ATM and teller systems projects throughout Chase's New York operations. Installed 387 ATMs at 153 sites and new teller systems at 93 branch locations for total technology investment of $23 million.

- Developed project plans, assigned project team responsibilities and matrix-managed activities of Facilities, Training, Marketing, Back Office and Area Offices to ensure timely implementation.

- Represented region at Division headquarters. Determined business requirements, established priorities and consulted with other regions, businesses and business support groups throughout the Chase national organization.

- Organized and led regional task force responsible for coordinating internal technology training programs for a 2500-person workforce.

Unit Manager - Branch Operations Department (1984 to 1986)

Managed 35+ employees in the Direct Mail, Mail Fulfillment and Sales Tracking Units. Controlled a $380,000 annual operating budget and the production/distribution of 500,000 direct mail pieces annually. Project Manager for all regional marketing and promotional campaigns.

Assistant Manager (1979 to 1984)

EDUCATION:

New York University - Information Systems Management (1995 to 1996)
Queens College - Biology Major (1977 to 1979)
Queensborough Community College - Biology Major (1976 to 1977)

Continuing Professional Studies in Document Imaging, Data Warehousing, COLD applications, E-Mail and other emerging technologies.

GEORGE D. ROBINSON
359 Main Street
Albany, New York 06548
(518) 847-6547

SENIOR TECHNOLOGY EXECUTIVE
Voice & Data Communications / Information Technologies / Data Center Operations
Executive & Project Management / Client/Server / Strategic & Operational Planning

Dynamic, creative and results-driven Technology Executive successful in building state-of-the-art, multi-technology organizations. Pioneer in sophisticated networking, client/server and telecommunications technologies. Energetic and decisive business leader able to merge disparate technologies and personnel into team-centered business units. Solid technical training, team building, management development and customer service skills.

PROFESSIONAL EXPERIENCE:

NATIONAL TESTING COMPANY, Albany, New York   1975 to Present
(Developer leading scholastic testing programs. Seven offices nationwide. Revenues of $360 million.)

Director - Communications & Information Processing (1989 to Present)
Director - Technical Support (1980 to 1989)
Assistant Director - Research & Development (1975 to 1980)

Technology Executive responsible for creating and directing a sophisticated voice, data and information technology organization. Beginning in 1975 with the introduction of mainframe systems technology, led the organization through a series of advanced system upgrades to capitalize upon emerging technologies and automate the entire corporation. Currently direct a staff of 123 and an annual operating/capital budget of $25 million.

Built a state-of-the-art data center, sophisticated client/server PC/LAN network and communications technologies to support both NTC and client organizations nationwide. Fully accountable for overall strategy for technology acquisition and integration, vendor selection and negotiation, technical and usage forecasting, workload planning, project budgeting and administration, software and hardware disaster/recovery, system software support, financial and administrative affairs, human resources, training and support, and daily system operations. Guide management in long-range planning.

Technology Achievements:

- Created a technologically-sophisticated and operationally-sound multi-site infrastructure with large-scale IBM and DEC mainframes, HP, UNIX, WINDOWS, MVS/ESA and SCO Unix operating system, voice and data communications, 50 servers supporting 3400 PC/MAC/SUN node BANYAN/VINES ethernet based LAN, 6 videoconferencing sites, T1 backbone, frame relay, ATM, ISDN, WEB site, Internet service provider and an operationally centralized client/server LAN.

- Integrated CMOS CPU and RAMAC storage to create a sophisticated mainframe infrastructure.

- Established and directed Help Desk operations and complete systems software support function for PCs, DB2, IDMS, TSO, ORACLE, AFP, TOTAL, ACF/VTAM/NCP, CICS and ACF2. Introduced sophisticated systems security standards and controls.

- Exploited multi-platform client/server technologies to lead the organization from mainframe centric computing topology to network centric topology.

- Managed an average of $6-$10 million in technology acquisition and investment each year.

- Quoted in <u>Communications Week</u> and <u>Computer World</u> for technological innovation. Featured as one of five technology "success stories" in a Northern Telecom video production.

NATIONAL TESTING COMPANY *(Continued)*:

Financial Achievements:

- Delivered a 40% reduction in Data center operating costs by renegotiating disaster recovery service contracts, reducing staffing requirements through process simplification, and evaluating alternative support and maintenance providers.

- Delivered an average of $4 million in annual labor and operating cost reductions.

- Spearheaded a number of service/product line expansions that increased revenues by more than $250,000 over the past five years.

- Designed financial and statistical models for technology cost/benefit analysis.

General Management Achievements:

- Negotiated contracts and managed long-term service/maintenance relationships with major technology vendors (e.g., IBM, Bell Atlantic, SUNGARD, MCI). Captured over $400,000 in vendor contract cost savings that contributed to overall 40% cost reduction initiative.

- Pioneered innovative team building and cross-functional project management techniques to expedite workflow, simplify processes and reduce operating costs.

- Initiated successful internal change management programs supporting technology advances, modifications to existing work processes, and realignment of supervisory and management teams.

- Appointed as one of three NTC technology representatives to the New Jersey State College Boards Association. Evaluated systems vision and strategy for centralized technology acquisition throughout state-operated colleges and universities.

> ***NOTE:***   *Currently directing the relocation of the corporate data center to a newly-constructed facility. Fully responsible for project P&L, budgeting, contractor management, facilities design, space configuration, installation planning and physical relocation.*

INTERNATIONAL DATA SYSTEMS, Bethpage, New York   1970 to 1975

Systems Programmer / Supervisor of Systems Implementation

Fast-track promotion to supervisory position responsible for a 14-person programming team.

EDUCATION:

M.S., Computer Science, Pratt Institute, 1970
B.S., Mathematics, State University of New York at Stony Brook, 1968

PROFESSIONAL ACTIVITIES:

Public Speaking	Extensive public speaking experience before the American Records Management Association, Data Processing Management Association, Communication Manager's Association and numerous private corporations.
Teaching	Adjunct Assistant Professor, Rider College Adjunct Instructor, Mercer and Bucks County Community Colleges
Affiliations	Association for Computing Machinery Mercer County Data Processing Advisory Committee Technology Representative, Lawrence Township Educational Foundation

ALLISON M. CARLSON

21 Boonsboro Road • Lynchburg, Virginia 24503 • (804) 300-4000

ATTORNEY / LEGAL COUNSEL

Environmental Law & Environmental Justice / Corporate & Business Law
Real Estate Law / Civil Law / Family Law / Criminal Law

Practicing Attorney with excellent qualifications in the independent planning, management and representation of client legal matters in District, State and Federal Courts. Expert in community outreach and legal advocacy, regulatory/legislative affairs, legal research and documentation, and court proceedings. Extensive experience providing legal representation to corporations, non-profit organizations and firm clients. Skilled public speaker and media liaison.

EDUCATION:

LL.M., Environmental Law, 1993
UNIVERSITY / CENTER FOR ENVIRONMENTAL LEGAL STUDIES, Lynchburg, Virginia

Activities: Research Assistant, The Energy Law Project
(Team member on demand side energy management research project and proposal for residential conservation techniques.)

Pro Bono Counsel, Community Coalition
(Led successful legal initiative to oppose development of natural gas power plant impacting the entire Lower River Valley.)

J.D., 1989
UNIVERSITY SCHOOL OF LAW, Lynchburg, Virginia

Honors: Public Policy Fellow, Foundation (1987)
City Mayor's Certificate (1987)
Activities: Founding Member, Latino-American Law Students Association

B.A., Political Science, 1985
STATE UNIVERSITY, Lynchburg, Virginia

Honors: Public Policy Fellow, Foundation (1985 to 1986)
Activities: L.I. Affirmative Action Council Certificate, Role Model for Minority/Women Entrepreneurs

BAR ADMISSION: State of Virginia

PROFESSIONAL EXPERIENCE:

Attorney   **PRIVATE LAW PRACTICE,** Lynchburg, Virginia
September 1993 to Present

Independent Legal Counsel specializing in criminal, civil, family, real estate and environmental protection law. Represent clients in Family, District and Supreme Court. Draft pleadings, motions, orders and legal contracts/agreements. Provide bilingual services to Spanish-speaking litigants.

Attorney   **U.S. ENVIRONMENTAL PROTECTION AGENCY,** Washington, D.C.
Summer 1993

Participated in a diversity of environmental law and environmental justice issues impacting the construction, operation and management of federal government and military facilities throughout the U.S. Negotiated hazardous waste remediation actions with military installations nationwide, and assessed relevant environmental justice issues impacting local and regional communities. Evaluated nationwide research to draft and present legislation for Congressional reauthorization of the Safe Drinking Water Act.

ALLISON M. CARLSON   *Page Two*

Legal Intern   **ENVIRONMENTAL CONSERVATION**, Lynchburg, Virginia
                          Spring 1993

Selected from a competitive group of LL.M. candidates for a four-month internship. Exposed to and provided legal guidance relative to environmental law and environmental justice issues. Participated in compliance conferences with potentially responsible parties under State Environmental Conservation Law and related statutes. Drafted proposed consent orders and memoranda of law. Conducted extensive legal research and prepared written documentation to support case proceedings and actions.

Staff Attorney   **THE LEGAL AID SOCIETY**, Lynchburg, Virginia
                          September 1990 to September 1992

Provided legal services, counseling and advocacy for plaintiffs and defendants in the Family and District Courts. Family Court responsibilities included bench trials on quasi-criminal cases and matters involving dependent and neglected children and children in need of supervision. Provided respondents with representation against the County (complaints, discovery, negotiation, settlement) in civil proceedings. District Court responsibilities included calendar (arraignment pretrial and trial), law and motion, preliminary examinations and bench trials.

Associate   **LARRY LAWYER, ESQ.**, Lynchburg, Virginia
                          June 1989 to September 1990

Associate in a general practice firm with principal caseload in education and real estate law. Drafted contracts of sale, purchase money notes and mortgages, research memoranda, pleadings and proposed legal orders. Managed a caseload averaging ten clients per month.

Attorney Assistant   **SAVINGS BANK, FSB**, Lynchburg, Virginia
                          December 1988 to June 1989

Working under the guidance of corporate counsel, managed legal affairs impacting the operations, customer base, administration, tax status and financial solvency of the institution. Evaluated civil and criminal motions and briefs concerning jurisdictional, discovery, pretrial and trial matters on behalf of this regional banking institution. Drafted Nominee Partnership Agreement to create tax exempt status for customers and reduce cost of taxes on every stock transfer.

Law Clerk   **PRESIDING JUDGE, SUPERIOR COURT**, Lynchburg, Virginia
                          May 1987 to September 1987

Reviewed transcripts of civil and criminal trials, analyzed points of appeal, and prepared pre-hearing memoranda for review by the judicial bench. Revised calendar system to reduce exponentially growing caseload for 15 County courts.

Executive Director   **LA UNION HISPANICA EN COUNTY, INC.**, Lynchburg, Virginia
                          September 1981 to December 1986

Directed a team of 25 employees and volunteers providing social services to County residents. Advocated and won funding from private and public sources to support program development, services delivery and agency administration. Personally managed budgeting, financial reporting, community outreach and advocacy, media relations and legislative affairs.

References Provided Upon Request

Confidential Resume

TODD McGUIRE

25 Tea Farm Road
Garden City, New York 11000
(516) 700-8000

SENIOR ASSOCIATE ATTORNEY / CORPORATE COUNSEL
Expert in Real Estate Law

Twelve-year career providing legal counsel and transactional expertise. Skilled negotiator, mediator and executive advisor. Consulting Counsel to more than 100 corporations, partnerships and investor groups.

PROFESSIONAL EXPERIENCE:

Senior Associate Attorney - Real Estate Practice   1989 to Present
DAVIDSON, CHARLES & SMITH, LLP, New York, New York

Senior Real Estate Associate of general practice law firm. Direct the real estate practice area and staff of paralegals and support personnel. Manage sale, purchase, mortgage and lease transactions valued from $25,000 to $10+ million on behalf of real estate purchasers, investors, shareholders, sellers, developers, landlords and tenants.

- Represent individual corporate, partnership, LLC and LP domestic and foreign sellers and purchasers, lessors, lessees, sublessors and sublessees of commercial and residential real property and cooperative apartments. Prepare, negotiate and review transactional and loan documents, and commercial, retail and residential leases and subleases. Address complicated title issues including commencement and prosecution of actions to extinguish mortgages and ancient mortgages of record. Represented ground lessees in purchase of underlying fees.

- Review, structure, negotiate and close on behalf of borrowers and lenders first and subordinate mortgage loans, and secured and unsecured libor and prime rate based lines of credit.

- Draft formation documents for corporations, partnerships, limited partnerships and limited liability companies.

- Participate in the firm's zoning practice including drafting and submission of applications to and appearances before the New York City Board of Standards and Appeals and the New York City Planning Commission.

- General Counsel to cooperative apartment corporations and condominiums. Prepare, amend and review corporate and condominium formation documents and meeting materials. Act as corporate representative at board of directors/board of managers and shareholder/unit owner meetings.

- Prepare legal documents, draft "No-Action Letters" for the New York State Department of Law, and serve as Transfer Agent. Represent in both litigated and non-litigated disputes with tenant-shareholders and/or unit owners. Act as counsel in refinancing underlying mortgages of cooperative apartment corporations.

- Act as General Counsel to sponsors of cooperative and condominium offering plans. Draft offering plans and amendments for submission to the New York State Department of Law.

Senior Associate Attorney - Real Estate Practice   1985 to 1989
HARRISON & WATSON, New York, New York

Senior Associate Attorney with a boutique real estate law firm.

- Conducted all phases of cooperative, condominium and condop conversions. Drafted and submitted to the New York State Department of Law more than 30 offering plans and 250 amendments, negotiated with tenants' associations, and supervised cooperative and condominium closings for building ranging in size from 50 to 300 units.

- Drafted leases, mortgages, easements, residential and commercial real property contracts, partnership agreements, certificates of incorporation, corporate by-laws and resolutions, Major Capital Improvements Rent Increase Applications, and J-51 Tax Abatement and Exemption Applications.

- Drafted and probated wills, administered estates, and provided general legal counsel to more than 100 clients.

Legal Research Assistant - Real Estate Law   1984 to 1985
RALPH JOHNSON, DEAN OF NEW YORK UNIVERSITY SCHOOL OF LAW, Jamaica, New York

Researched and assisted in the revision of treatises, practice commentaries and textbooks in the areas of trusts and estates, eminent domain, zoning, real property, real estate financing, real estate brokerage, cooperative and condominium housing, and homeowner associations, including *Nichols on Eminent Domain* and *Powell on Real Property*.

Conducted extensive legal research of local, county, state and national real estate laws, rules, regulations and legislative addenda. Assimilated, synthesized and edited data for final publication.

Law Clerk   Summer 1982
JOHNSON & JOHNSON, ESQ., Brooklyn, New York

Four-month legal clerkship with a general practice firm. Conducted primary and secondary legal research, filed court documents, coordinated serving process and handled general administrative affairs.

EDUCATION:

J.D.   **NEW YORK UNIVERSITY SCHOOL OF LAW**, Jamaica, New York, 1985
          Honors: Moot Court Senior Bar
          Activities: Phi Delta Phi Legal Fraternity

B.A.   **UNIVERSITY OF PENNSYLVANIA**, Philadelphia, Pennsylvania, 1982
          Major in History; Minor in Chemistry
          Activities: Featured Writer & Copy Editor, *The Daily Pennsylvania*
                           Elected Member, House Committee of Hill College House
                           Campus Tour Guide, Office of Undergraduate Admissions
                           Intramural Sports - Football, Softball & Tennis

PROFESSIONAL AFFILIATIONS:

- The Committee on Condominiums and Cooperatives of The New York State Bar Association
- Association of the Bar of The City of New York
- American Bar Association

MARK P. WRIGHT

194 Prairie Way
Houston, Texas 77381

Home   (713) 295-8434
Office   (713) 657-9447

CAREER PROFILE:

MARITIME INDUSTRY EXECUTIVE with over 15 years of progressively responsible experience building and directing integrated, vessel/terminal/intermodal operations. Combine strong planning, finance, sales, marketing and operating expertise with consistent achievement in improving customer service, reducing operating costs and increasing net profitability. Extensive travel throughout Europe, Pacific Rim, Middle East, Central & South America.

PROFESSIONAL EXPERIENCE:

MITSUI O.S.K. (AMERICA) LINES, INC.   **1995 to Present**

District Manager - Houston

Recruited to plan and direct a complete reengineering of all operations in Texas, Colorado, Oklahoma and Nebraska. Challenged to rebuild and strengthen Finance, Operations, Administration, Documentation, and Sales & Marketing affairs. Direct a staff of 24 and a $13 million annual operating budget.

Fully accountable for weekly vessel calls in Houston (Gulf to Northern Europe service with 20,000 TEUs annually) and weekly intermodal service to both the East and West Coasts. Concurrently, manage divisional sales office in Houston and satellite sales offices in Dallas and Denver.

- Exceeded 1996 Houston sales goal by 30% to close the year at 14,000 TEUs.

- Expanded and strengthened relationships with key accounts throughout the region including Exxon, DuPont, Kodak, Coors, Hoyer and Leschaco.

- Launched a complete reengineering of Customer Service and Documentation departments to more effectively meet customer needs and improve customer retention.

HAPAG LLOYD (AMERICA), INC.   **1991 to 1995**

Gulf Operations Manager

Senior Manager with full decision-making responsibility for Finance, Operational, Administrative and Documentation activities for intermodal container transportation throughout the U.S. Gulf Region. Directed a staff of 24 and administered a $17 million annual operating budget.

Operated principally in Houston with satellite hub facilities in San Antonio, Dallas, Memphis and New Orleans for vessels calling between the West Coast and Far East. Primary inbound customer base included Canon, Nissan, Sharp, Tandy, Kmart and other large manufacturers; primary outbound customer base included diverse commodities manufacturers and suppliers nationwide.

- Directed the start-up of this new organization to replace Hapag's previous reliance on local agents. Built the entire business unit, recruited management personnel, staffed and set up offices, introduced computer technology, and established operating policies and procedures.

- Reduced net operating costs by $1+ million by renegotiating vendor contracts, consolidating vendor services and coordinating a complete rerouting program.

- Integrated ship, rail and over-the-road transportation to build a regional intermodal network.

NEIDERMEIR LINES (USA) CORPORATION   1988 to 1991

Director of Operations - Gulf Division

Directed the start-up and profitable management of all operations within the Gulf region to transition from agency to company managed hubs in Houston and New Orleans. All water service included Houston to Europe and New Orleans/Houston to South America (containerized and break bulk freight). Controlled a $12 million annual operating budget.

- Upgraded the entire business organization and established internally-managed Equipment, Intermodal, Terminal, Maintenance and Repair operations through a seven-state region.

- Appointed as the U.S. representative to the Rotterdam Task Force established to enhance operations performance and improve worldwide market share.

BOARD OF COMMISSIONERS OF THE PORT OF NEW ORLEANS   1987 to 1988

Executive Assistant for Maritime Affairs

High-profile position as direct liaison between newly-appointed Port Director and maritime community. Drove forward new programs, services and operations to improve relationships with vessel operators, stevedores and other port users, and increase port trade within the highly-competitive Gulf market.

UNITED STATES LINES, INC.   1979 to 1987

Fast-track promotion through a series of increasingly responsible positions during eight-year tenure. Advanced from Material Specialist Trainee to Central American Terminal Manager (Panama) within first year; from Marine & Terminal Manager (Boston) to Operations Manager (Baltimore) within next two years. Final promotions included:

Port Manager, New Orleans, Louisiana (1985 to 1987)

Led the successful turnaround of a port operation with significant management problems and operational inefficiencies. Reengineered and restaffed the entire operation, introduced quality management strategies, realigned workflow, improved customer relationships and significantly improved the entire operation.

Directed Administration, Finance, Documentation and Operations for intermodal transportation between the East Coast and Far East, Europe, South Africa and South America. Managed a large company-owned railyard and contracted rail operations servicing both the East and West Coasts.

Divisional Container Operations Manager, Cranford, New Jersey (1984 to 1985)

Corporate headquarters position managing a land fleet of 44,000 containers and chassis. Directed 12 regional equipment managers throughout North America and a $93 million annual budget. Facilitated significant improvements in container operations through redesign of distribution, transportation, handling, maintenance and repair operations.

Terminal Operations Consultant, Rio Grande, Brazil (1985)

Completed a four-month special assignment with Container Transport Technology for the Port Authority of Brazil. Worked in cooperation with representatives from other major maritime organizations to facilitate container terminal design and handling systems for new operations.

EDUCATION: **B.A. Degree**, University of South Alabama, Mobile, Alabama, 1985

GILBERT T. WAINRIGHT

2942 Southern Drive
Savannah, Georgia 47652
(651) 496-8424

TRANSPORTATION INDUSTRY EXECUTIVE
Expertise in General Management and Sales/Marketing Leadership

Twenty years domestic and international experience in the shipping and freight consolidation industries. Combines expert qualifications in marketing, business development and key account management with equally strong operating unit and P&L management qualifications.

Delivered strong operating and financial gains within highly competitive markets worldwide.

PROFESSIONAL EXPERIENCE:

EAST LINE AMERICA, INC. 1991 to 1996

VICE PRESIDENT SALES - NORTH AMERICA
Recruited as the first new executive to join the existing management team following East Line's migration from agency to wholly-owned subsidiary. Challenged to rebuild and strengthen the corporation's sales, business development and account management organization to accelerate growth, solidify existing customer relationships and expand into new business markets. Directed a multinational staff of 140 sales and customer service personnel at 26 locations throughout North America. Devised innovative sales and business development programs to expand inbound and outbound lift from West Coast ports.

- Delivered strong financial gains despite capacity constraints and dissolution of all-water service. Increased total volume 46% and BCO Anera market share 220%.

- Built key account relationships with leading importers (e.g., Nike, Reebok, LA Gear, May Department Stores, Dollar General, Sears) and leading exporters (e.g., Sunkist, Haagen-Daaz, Union Carbide, IBP, Montfort).

- Led the start-up and managed five regional customer service departments to improve customer satisfaction, increase retention and relieve operating teams of direct customer contact. Established policies and procedures, defined service functions and recruited/trained a team of 42.

SEA-LAND SERVICE, INC. 1970 to 1990

General Manager - Sales (1987 to 1990)
Buyers & Shippers Enterprises, Inc. - Jacksonville, Florida
One of two senior operating executives with direct P&L for this worldwide freight consolidation company. Directed a 16-person sales and marketing organization, a 120,000 square foot West Coast freight consolidation facility, annual operating and capital expense budgeting, and long-range strategic planning. Executive-level responsibility for development and management of key account relationships throughout the U.S. and Canada.

- Instrumental in building volume from 25,000 to 45,000 containers (80%) from 175 customers within three years. Revitalized and strengthened relationships with key accounts (e.g., Reebok, Adidas, Meldisco, Avon, Kmart, The Limited, May Department Stores) to accelerate revenue growth and improve market position.

- Spearheaded start-up of ship direct programs for both U.S. and Asian operations, Asia-Europe freight consolidation service and West Coast deconsolidation and distribution operations.

- Successfully marketed ancillary product offerings including "Buy-Com," an innovative computer program designed for cargo tracking and reporting.

SEA-LAND SERVICE, INC. *(Continued)*:

Country Manager - Bangkok, Thailand (1984 to 1987)
Full P&L responsibility for Sea-Land's Thailand operations, including sales, marketing, advertising, marine/terminal, intra-Asia pricing and U.S./Asia interport trade. Directed a staff of 35, a trucking/stevedoring operating agent and a large foreign labor pool. Executive-level responsibility for new business development and all international account sales.

• Delivered revenue growth averaging 20% to 30% annually within a competitive market.

• Maintained a highly visible position within Thailand's maritime community. Appointed Chairman of the Thailand/Pacific Freight Conference, Chairman of the American Chamber of Commerce Transportation Committee and Secretary of the Bangkok Shippers & Agencies Association.

• Launched the successful start-up of a new Sea-Land agency operation in Djakarta, Indonesia.

General Manager - Caribbean (1981 to 1984)
Senior Executive with full P&L responsibility for the leadership of Sea-Land operations throughout the entire Caribbean region (Dominican Republic, Jamaica, Haiti, Curacao, Aruba, Trinidad and the Leeward Islands). Responsible for strategic and tactical management of sales, marketing, advertising, operations, marine/terminal, human resources, labor relations and administration. Directed six agencies and two offshore corporate offices with 200+ employees (including a five-person expatriate management team).

• Increased annual revenues to $35 million (20% gain). Achieved 400% growth in reefer revenue production.

• Launched the start-up of Dominican Republic operations as primary linehaul and feeder hub for Central and South Caribbean to Florida operations.

Sales Manager - Seoul, Korea (1978 to 1981)
Import Sales Manager - Hong Kong (1978)
International Account Manager - Taipei, Taiwan (1976 to 1977)
Rapid promotion through several increasingly responsible sales management positions within the Pacific Rim. Managed North American import and export trade, inter-Asia and Asian-Middle East sales, marketing and advertising. Led teams of up to 20 sales professionals and personally managed key account relationships.

• Increased regional sales revenues to $30 million annually.

Early Sea-Land Career (1970 to 1976)
Promoted from Sales Representative (Philadelphia) to Account Executive (Baltimore) to Sales Manager (Houston).

EDUCATION: **Princeton University - BA Degree, 1969**
                    Graduate, 100+ hours of professional sales, management and leadership training.

AFFILIATIONS: National Freight Transportation Association
                    Board of Directors, Friends of Princeton University Ice Hockey

KEITH GLASSTON
119 Old Stable Road
Lynchburg, Virginia 24503
(804) 384-4600

SENIOR OPERATIONS & MANUFACTURING EXECUTIVE
Start-Up, Turnaround & High-Growth Operations

"Hands-on" Operations Executive combining proven theoretical skills with expert qualifications in multi-site production management. Introduced leading edge technologies, systems and processes to create technically-advanced, cost-efficient and top-performing World Class Manufacturing operations. Strong contributions in driving organizational change and improvement.

APICS Certified in Integrated Resource Management (CIRM), 1993
APICS Certified in Production & Inventory Management (CPIM), 1982

PROFESSIONAL EXPERIENCE:

SURAMCO MANUFACTURING, INC., Bedford, VA   1994 to Present
($22 million, 300 employee, privately-owned and vertically integrated manufacturer of pneumatic devices for the transportation and industrial equipment industries.)

Manager of Materials
Senior Business Unit Executive with full responsibility for strategic planning, staffing, budgeting and operations of the corporation's complete materials management function. Direct 11 hourly and professional staff in production planning and scheduling, purchasing and stores. Turn $12.5 million annually in inventory, manage a $400,000 annual operating budget and direct $3+ million in annual purchasing expenditures.

- Pioneered corporation's transition to World Class Manufacturing techniques. Efforts impacted all key operating departments and business units throughout the corporation.
- Designed and implemented first-ever production planning and master scheduling processes. Results included 32% inventory reduction ($1.8 million), 13% improvement in on-time delivery and 21% personnel reduction.
- Appointed Project Team Leader facilitating the upgrade of MAPICS / IBM AS360 manufacturing and business technology.
- Captured $180,000+ in annual savings through series of internal design and business process improvements. Identified and currently facilitating implementation of new programs designed to further reduce costs while improving product quality and customer service.

INTERNATIONAL TECHNOLOGIES, INC., Orchard Park, NY & Tampa, FL   1981 to 1994
($30 million, 200 employee manufacturer of custom-designed electro-pneumatic controls and systems for the aerospace, defense and commercial airline industries.)

Manufacturing Support Reengineering Team (1991 to 1994)
Member of management team leading the company through a complete reorganization. Challenged to create "focused" factories segmented by business market in an effort to accelerate growth and diversification, reduce operating costs and improve quality/service.

- Pioneered innovative process improvements impacting all core business operations, manufacturing departments, and administrative/support functions. Trained process improvement teams in World Class Manufacturing, team building, team leadership and problem solving. Results included:
  — five-fold reduction in WIP inventories.
  — reduction of CNC machine set-up times from 4.5 hours to 20 minutes.
  — reduction of throughput times from 6 weeks to 8 days.
  — introduction of manufacturing cells and cross-functional project teams.

KEITH GLASSTON   *Page Two*

Materials Manager (1990 to 1991)
Production & Inventory Control Manager (1981 to 1989)
Directed a team of 7-18 hourly and staff personnel responsible for materials planning, production scheduling, stores, shipping, receiving and government property control.

- Led on-time and within-budget implementation of IBM / PICS MRP II system and 7-month conversion to Digital VAX / CINCOM integrated manufacturing and costing system.
- Achieved 99%+ inventory accuracy resulting in elimination of annual physical inventory.
- Promoted in 1990. Assumed responsibility for procurement function in addition to previous accountabilities. Appointed Acting Operations Manager in incumbent's extended absences.

WINSMITH (Division of UMC, Inc.), Springville, NY & Gainsville, GA   1973 to 1980
($25 million, 220 employee manufacturer of power drives for the capital equipment industry.)

Procurement & Planning Manager (1977 to 1980)
Planned, staffed, budgeted and directed all purchasing, materials management, inventory planning and master production scheduling for two manufacturing locations.

- Created and managed a centralized purchasing function for all operations to exploit volume purchasing and discount opportunities with vendors worldwide.
- Designed and implemented commodity contract establishing JIT deliveries for primary material supply. Eliminated 900 separate purchase orders annually and reduced floor stock inventory by $50,000.
- Saved $80,000 in pattern costs through strategic negotiations with foreign casting broker.

Production & Inventory Control Manager (1974 to 1976)
Led a team of nine salaried and hourly union personnel responsible for materials planning, production and assembly scheduling, stores, shipping and receiving.

- Designed specifications for company's first-ever MRP system.
- Established cycle count program which improved record accuracy to 96%.

Manufacturing & Facilities Engineer (1973 to 1974)
Project Engineer on various facility upgrades and manufacturing process improvements.

- Directed building expansion featuring high bay material storage and retrieval system.
- Established sub-assembly cell which increased final assembly output by 23% despite 6% personnel reduction.

Previous Professional Experience with Chevrolet-Buffalo (Division of General Motors Corporation). Progressed through increasingly responsible engineer and production management positions.

EDUCATION: **18 Credits Towards Masters of Manufacturing Management**, General Motors Institute
               B.S., Mechanical Engineering (Electrical Option), General Motors Institute

PROFESSIONAL AFFILIATIONS:

American Production & Inventory Control Society (APICS)
- Publications and APICS Conference Presentations (1982, 1984, 1987, 1991)
- Materials Management & Operations Management Course Instructor, State University of New York, Erie Community College, Virginia Western Community College (1986 to Present)
- Buffalo Chapter Education Committee (1984 to 1994)

ROBERT W. LEWIS

1093 St. Andrews Lane   Home   (513) 578-5735
Cleveland, Ohio 44052   Office   (513) 543-1169

CAREER PROFILE

Director of Operations / Director of Manufacturing / Plant & Production Manager
Start-Up, Turnaround, High-Growth & Multinational Operations

Top-Performing Business Manager with direct P&L responsibility for multi-site manufacturing, assembly and distribution operations. Delivered strong revenue and profit gains, multi-million dollar cost reductions and sustainable yield improvements. Expert in state-of-the-art manufacturing technologies and processes.

PROFESSIONAL EXPERIENCE:

THE DIAL CORPORATION, Cincinnati, Ohio   1995 to Present

Manufacturing Manager - Household Division
(Dial's fastest growing segment with $450 million in revenues)

Senior Manufacturing Director and Dial's only on-site management representative for five contract manufacturing facilities in Ohio, Illinois and Massachusetts. Hold full responsibility for the planning and management of all Dial business operations (e.g., inventory, materials, manufacturing, quality, logistics, packaging, distribution) for the Softsoap business line and for the administration of Dial/co-packer partnership contracts.

- Delivered 3.5% growth within a mature and highly competitive business market.
- Led integration of two new products into manufacturing operations, generating $7.5 million in new revenues within first year and poised for national launch into KMart and Wal-Mart. Facilitated product transition from Dial's product engineering teams into specific production, assembly and packaging operations in a tight, 16-week cycle.
- Spearheaded introduction of a series of continuous improvement initiatives that consistently strengthened productivity, product quality and customer satisfaction.

STORAGE SYSTEMS COMPANY, Cincinnati, Ohio   1994 to 1995

Business Unit Manager

Recruited by CEO to launch the start-up of a new business unit for this $5 million privately-owned distributor of material storage devices. Challenged to build new operation and establish market presence for introduction of ergonomically-designed material handling and logistics equipment.

- Successfully completed one-year contract. Brought business from initial planning through start-up and market launch. Negotiated preliminary relationships with manufacturers, assemblers and distributors throughout region and positioned company for strong market performance.

CAVU DISTRIBUTING, INC., Cincinnati, Ohio   1992 to 1994

Partner

Challenged to launch an entrepreneurial venture and capitalize upon core competencies in operations and distribution management. In cooperation with two other principals, directed start-up and initial management of new beverage distribution company.

- Transitioned company from concept through start-up to full-scale operations. Created all operating, business, financial, sales and service programs. Closed 100 accounts in first 60 days.
- Negotiated company sale to primary supplier and facilitated management transition.

REDKEN LABORATORIES, INC., Cincinnati, Ohio   1985 to 1992

Director of Manufacturing / General Manager of Eastern Operations

Senior Operating Executive (on-site) directing a sophisticated hair care products manufacturing and distribution facility. Held full P&L responsibility for the business unit. Directed a team of nine exempt and 100 non-exempt, non-union employees. Controlled assets valued in excess of $15 million. Administered $4 million in annual operating and capital budgets. Guided the annual strategic planning process.

Scope of responsibility was diverse and included materials planning, inventory, component manufacturing, process batch operations, industrial engineering, plant engineering, packaging, distribution, freight control, customer service, human resources, quality assurance and an aggressive continuous process improvement program.

- Produced 40 million units annually at 99.5% acceptance rate and 98% customer order accuracy.
- Led a $7 million construction program to expand facility from 35,000 to 150,000 sq. ft.
- Delivered over 35% ROI through implementation of vertical integration projects and bulk material purchasing programs.
- Appointed to numerous corporate task forces spearheading market integration programs, U.S./international manufacturing analysis, bar coding technology implementation and distribution network consolidation. Efforts improved ROI to 40%.
- Saved $75,000 annually in material costs through employee-driven scrap reduction program.

AVON PRODUCTS, INC., Cincinnati, Ohio & New York, New York   1977 to 1985

Operations Manager (1984 to 1985)
Group Manager (1981 to 1984)
Packaging Manager (1980 to 1981)
Section Manager (1977 to 1980)

Fast-track promotion through a series of increasingly responsible operating and production management positions with the world's largest cosmetics company. As **Operations Manager**, directed a staff of 50 exempt and 550 non-exempt, non-union employees in the operation of a state-of-the-art, 1.3 million sq. ft. manufacturing complex (60 different production lines).

- Delivered strong and sustainable operating gains:
  - 20% reduction in cost of "non-conformance" through Crosby quality programs.
  - 15% reduction in undistributed labor costs for a 300-employee direct labor workforce.
  - 5% reduction in indirect labor costs through internal industrial engineering techniques.
  - 18% improvement in equipment reliability.

As **Group Manager for Manufacturing Operations** (corporate HQ position), served as corporate liaison between manufacturing, marketing, new product development and product cost. Guided U.S. and international operating locations in industrial engineering, equipment design, methods improvement, TQM and financial control.

- Captured over $1 million in operating cost reductions.

JOSEPH E. SEAGRAMS & SONS, Lawrenceburg, Indiana   1974 to 1977

Maintenance Supervisor for multi-million dollar bottling operation.

EDUCATION: **PURDUE UNIVERSITY**, Lafayette, Indiana
B.S., Industrial Management, 1974

Continuing Education in Leadership, Communications and Management Decision Making.

CHARLES H. TAYLOR
946 Cedar Court
Cary, North Carolina 27253
(910) 278-6547

SENIOR OPERATING, MANUFACTURING & MANAGEMENT EXECUTIVE

Delivered strong operating and financial results in challenging start-up, turnaround and high-growth operations through expertise in:

- Strategic Business & Market Planning
- Quality & Performance Improvement
- Cost Reduction & Revenue Gain
- Customer Relationship Management
- Production Processes & Standards
- Multi-Site Manufacturing Operations
- Technology & Engineering
- Product Rationalization & Diversification
- Purchasing & Materials Management
- Contract Negotiations

PROFESSIONAL EXPERIENCE:

WIP SYSTEMS, Raleigh, North Carolina 1988 to Present
($3.5 billion electronics technology manufacturer with 20 plants worldwide)

Vice President / Plant Manager, Raleigh, North Carolina (1994 to Present)
Senior Operating Executive with full P&L responsibility for a 140,000 sq. ft. contract manufacturing facility with 400 employees and revenues of more than $120 million annually. Challenged to plan and direct the turnaround and return to profitability of the operation. Lead a six-person management team responsible for operations, manufacturing engineering, materials, quality, technical programs, human resources, finance and marketing.

- Achieved/surpassed all turnaround objectives and returned the operation to profitability within less than 12 months. Delivered strong and sustainable operating gains:
  — 70% improvement in operating efficiency.
  — 250% reduction in cycle times.
  — 75% increase in product quality.
  — 100% on-time customer delivery.
- Launched regional market expansion to penetrate emerging customer markets and achieve product diversification. Increased sales revenues from $80 million to $120 million (30% growth).
- Identified, negotiated and closed two major new contracts (Fortune 500 technology OEMs).
- Restored credibility with one customer generating over $30 million in revenues to WIP. Resolved long-standing quality and delivery issues, implemented key account management strategy and revitalized business relationship.
- Achieved ISO 9002 and QS9000 quality certifications.

Plant Manager, Rochester, New York (1988 to 1994)
Recruited to WIP to direct the operating turnaround of a start-up contract manufacturing facility established through a strategic business partnership with IBM. Scope of responsibility included all planning, operating, staffing, budgeting, technology and customer management programs for a 150,000 sq. ft. manufacturing facility with 550 employees. Challenged to rebuild the manufacturing function and restore credibility with IBM.

- Achieved successful turnaround within first year and positioned for long-term growth. Increased sales by 35% and profit contributions by 20%.
- Delivered significant improvements in quality, productivity, cycle time and cost control through implementation of advanced operating processes, on-time delivery and quality standards.

AMERICAN DEFENSE SYSTEMS, Pittsburgh, Pennsylvania   1986 to 1988

Director of Operations

Full P&L responsibility for a 100,000 sq. ft. manufacturing facility with 400 employees and revenues of $65+ million. Developed operational strategies to improve productivity, efficiency, quality and delivery of sophisticated electronics technology. Directed manufacturing, quality assurance, test, material/production control, purchasing, manufacturing/plant engineering and industrial relations.

- Captured an average 10% reduction in annual material and labor costs to accelerate profit growth while maintaining constant sales pricing.
- Directed a $5 million technology investment to automate production line, implemented MRP II system, and drove forward several other critical technology installations.
- Achieved 100% on-time customer delivery and restored customer confidence.

MEDICAL DIAGNOSTIC INSTRUMENTS, Nashua, New Hampshire   1982 to 1986

Vice President / Co-Founder

General Manager of start-up medical instrument company funded through private investor financing and structured as a limited partnership. Designed business development, marketing and operating systems to transition from R&D to full-scale manufacturing. Created budget and performance objectives, directed implementation of accounting and inventory control systems, and created the entire operating and technical support infrastructures.

- Directed clinical trials at 15 hospitals and health care facilities nationwide to position company for full-scale market launch with five year projections at $25+ million.
- Recruited and led a highly creative technical staff toward the timely design completion of complex medical equipment and technology.

SMITHKLINE INSTRUMENTS, Boston, Massachusetts   1980 to 1982

Director of Operations

Directed operations of a 225-employee ultrasonic scanning equipment manufacturer. Planned, staffed, budgeted and managed production, system test, product assurance, material/production control, purchasing, manufacturing engineering, plant engineering and field service/technical support.

- Delivered annual operating cost reductions averaging 20%+ to accelerate profit gains.
- Installed disciplined manufacturing processes and stringent quality controls to standardize production methods, increase manufacturing output and improve product reliability.

MICRO-CONDUCTOR CORPORATION, Morristown, New Jersey   1972 to 1980

Manufacturing Manager

P&L responsibility for high-volume, 175-employee microwave amplifier/component manufacturer. Launched successful start-up of off-shore microwave component manufacturing facility.

Previous Professional Experience: Fast-track promotion through a series of manufacturing, engineering and operations management positions with Lockheed Electronics, RCA and Kearfott/Singer.

EDUCATION: **M.S., Management Science**, Stevens Institute of Technology
                        B.S., Industrial Engineering, Fairleigh Dickinson University

PUBLICATIONS: - Co-Author, *"Computer Aided Design of Hybrid Microcircuits,"* National Electronic Packaging Conference.
                        - Author, *"Subtle Aspects of Micro-Packaging,"* Product Assurance Conference.

MILITARY SERVICE: Two-year tour of duty with the U.S. Navy.

WAYNE FARRELL
34952 North Wind Drive
Topeka, Kansas 65229
(913) 528-2494

MANUFACTURING MANAGER / OPERATIONS MANAGER / PLANT MANAGER
Start-Up, Turnaround, Fast-Track Growth & Multinational Corporations

Results-driven Operating Executive with 15+ years management experience. Strong general management qualifications in strategic planning, manufacturing, fabrication and assembly, production scheduling and control, inventory/materials management, project management, warehousing, distribution, budgeting/finance, human resource affairs and capital improvement. Pioneer in MRP, TQM, SPC and other productivity/performance improvement initiatives.

Reduced manufacturing costs by more than $4.5 million while increasing operating profits in excess of $4.6 million.

PROFESSIONAL EXPERIENCE:

1001 PRODUCTS, INC., Topeka, Kansas   1993 to 1997
($27 million multi-product manufacturer and distributor)

PLANT MANAGER

Senior Operating Executive with full P&L responsibility for the strategic planning, development, operating management and turnaround of this 300-employee manufacturing organization. Established procedures, developed business plans and managed all production operations/control, scheduling, quality, testing, shipping/receiving, materials, inventory, staffing and financial reporting.

Introduced a series of productivity improvement, process reengineering, cost reduction and performance management programs that consistently improved production output, product quality and customer satisfaction. Innovated unique solutions to complex operating problems.

- Returned the company to profitability within first four months of hire. **Increased operating profit to over $1.6 million**.
- Realigned staffing patterns, restructured production scheduling, introduced improved materials planning procedures, and **reduced indirect labor costs by $380,000**.
- Reduced scrap by 2.5% weekly for an **annual cost savings of $187,000**.
- **Improved on-time delivery from 67% to 95%** and restored customer confidence.

ARCHITECTURAL PRODUCTS CORPORATION, York, Pennsylvania   1988 to 1993
($40 million manufacturer of commercial products and components)

PROJECT MANAGER (1992 to 1993)

Promoted by President to a special assignment targeting the collection of past due receivables that had been outstanding for three to five years. Managed complex communications and negotiations with customers nationwide, and coordinated with attorneys for cases in litigation.

- Closed contracts on 35 "open" projects and **recovered $6 million in cash** to the corporation.

PLANT MANAGER (1990 to 1992)

Full P&L responsibility for a 350-employee production operation, multi-million dollar annual operating budget, all capital expenditures, and an aggressive productivity, quality and performance improvement initiative.

WAYNE FARRELL - *Page Two*

ARCHITECTURAL PRODUCTS CORPORATION *(Continued)*:

- Led successful turnaround from $200,000/month in losses to $200,000/month in profits. **Delivered full year profit contribution of $985,000**.
- **Decreased direct labor costs from 14.5% of total expenditures to 12.5%** through realignment of staffing, training and production scheduling programs.
- Orchestrated a dramatic consolidation and reduction in workforce in 1992.

SUPPORT PRODUCTION MANAGER (1988 to 1989)

Directed materials support for an 8-line, 400-employee operation. Responsible for receiving, raw materials processing, fabrication, paint operations, inventory control and warehousing. Managed 187 employees.

- Consolidated two shift operation into one which **reduced labor costs by $1.3 million annually** while sales revenues grew by $2.9 million over the previous year.
- **Increased productivity to 103% while reducing lost time accidents by 52%.**
- Reduced turnover to 1.19% annually, absenteeism to 3.1%, operating budgets by $331,000 and fabrication scrap by 40,000 pounds.
- Designed a completely new inventory control system, attained 98.2% accuracy and eliminated need for annual physical inventory.

KRESTMARK INDUSTRIES, Lewisville, Texas   1983 to 1987
($23 million finished products manufacturer and distributor)

PLANT MANAGER (1985 to 1987)
PRODUCTION MANAGER (1983 to 1985)

Full operating management responsibility for a 325-employee, high-volume production operation with 10-day lead time. Managed production planning and scheduling, materials management, inventory, manufacturing, assembly, test and packaging.

- Built production output to 2500 units/day to meet increased customer demand.

KAISER CORPORATION, Chalmette, Louisiana   1973 to 1985
(Largest U.S. aluminum manufacturer with $400 million in sales and 2600 employees)

PRODUCTION MANAGER - Louisiana
Promoted to Louisiana plant to facilitate a complete turnaround and return to profitability. Directed operations for 160 production cells with four supervisors and 60+ hourly personnel.

- Restructured the entire production operation and transitioned from $200,000/month loss to $200,000/month profit within two months. **Improved annual profitability by $2 million.**

PRODUCTION MANAGER - Washington

Fast-track promotion throughout a series of increasingly responsible plant operations, supervisory and management positions during 10-year career.

- Achieved record production and safety levels, won four corporate awards for performance improvement, and **cut lost time accident costs by $1.3 million annually**.

EDUCATION: **Business Administration**
LOUISIANA STATE UNIVERSITY / SOUTHEASTERN LOUISIANA UNIVERSITY

Continuing Professional Training in General Management, Management By Objectives, Communications, Computer Technology and Performance Management.

WILLIAM B. GRANGER

987 South Boston Street
Stamford, Connecticut 09134
(203) 647-1673

MARKETING / BUSINESS DEVELOPMENT / PRODUCT DEVELOPMENT EXECUTIVE
Expert in Competitively Positioning Products & Technologies Worldwide

Dynamic management career building and leading corporations through fast-track growth and global market expansion. Consistently successful in identifying and capitalizing upon market opportunities to drive revenue growth, expand market penetration and win dominant market share. Pioneer in strategic alliances, business partnerships and global distribution networks.

Equally strong qualifications in general management, organizational development, multi-site operations, R&D, corporate finance and human resource affairs. Dynamic leadership, team building and public speaking skills. MBA degree.

PROFESSIONAL EXPERIENCE:

PANTAK, INC., Stamford, Connecticut   1992 to Present
($15MM manufacturer of x-ray systems and technology for the health care & manufacturing industries)

Vice President / General Manager

Member of a 4-person executive team directing the financing and successful acquisition of a division of Pantak. Led the organization through the critical phases of reengineering and realignment to position as an independent corporation. Full strategic and management responsibility for operations, P&L, cash flow, technical and R&D activities, product development and global sales/marketing.

- Built business from less than $1MM to over $15MM in revenue on initial $1MM investment. Authored business plan to acquire start-up funding and subsequently arranged second $1MM round of financing with a major regional bank.
- Created an operating unit that delivered factory margins of 47% with 12% NPBT cash contribution. Pioneered introduction of leading edge MRP, quality, productivity and performance management systems.
- Accelerated the company's penetration throughout worldwide markets and built international revenues to 50% of total sales. Created market-specific, direct and indirect distribution networks and private label strategies to penetrate high-growth and emerging business worldwide.
- Negotiated complex licensing agreements with the FDA to market medical products in the U.S. Subsequently, expanded contracts to other export markets, including Eastern Europe and third world nations.
- Established Pantak as a leading worldwide supplier to the medical market. Currently ranked #1 in new product placements.

NYNEX COMPUTER SYSTEMS, White Plains, New York   1988 to 1992
($30MM provider of large scale systems integration, facilities management, and business and information management consulting services)

Vice President / General Manager

Recruited to this newly-formed, wholly-owned Nynex subsidiary to lead the company from start-up into a global systems consulting and integration firm. Given full autonomy for building the operating and business infrastructure, establishing strategic and tactical marketing plans, driving technology development and building a competitive presence.

WILLIAM B. GRANGER - *Page Two*

NYNEX COMPUTER SYSTEMS *(Continued):*

- Authored corporate business plan and won funding of $12MM to launch start-up. Over the next four years, built business at a rate of 30% with 8%+ profit margin.
- Recruited team of 120 business consultants, software/hardware engineers, computer programmers and telecommunications analysts to manage client engagements. Personally handled complex and high-profile customer relationships worldwide.
- Negotiated strategic alliances with major system manufacturers including IBM, Digital, Novell, Microsoft, Apple and others.
- Led the identification, justification, negotiation and acquisition of two high-tech companies and the rights to several key technologies to expand entry into new, high-growth business markets. Executed over $8MM in transactions.

Project Highlights & Achievements:

- Negotiated $12MM competitive contract for hardware, software and network systems design/implementation for several major metro airports.
- Completed $5MM contract for development of multi-kiosk interactive public access systems that delivered 18% profit margin to Nynex.
- Led several large-scale business reengineering and systems development/integration projects that captured an average 25% reduction in operating costs through process redesign and advanced automation.
- Directed design and implementation of a high-tech, interactive learning center for the Ellis Island Project. Honored with the Smithsonian Institute Humanitarian Award in 1992 for deployment of sophisticated technology to advance humanitarian needs.

CRYSTAL TECHNOLOGIES, INC., Syracuse, New York   1986 to 1988
($10MM supplier of leading edge, PC-driven executive workstations)

Vice President / General Manager

Recruited to provide the strategic and operational leadership to build this start-up company and position it as a viable competitor worldwide. Challenged to create a global sales and marketing organization, identify/capture business opportunities and build the entire operating infrastructure. Full P&L responsibility.

- Authored business plan, marketing plan and financial documentation critical in securing $12MM of venture capital equity investment to fund start-up and technology development.
- Transitioned business from concept into $10MM in revenues in two years. Built a worldwide distribution network to accelerate market penetration.
- Structured and negotiated $18MM in offshore manufacturing contracts and directed product development, manufacturing, packaging and distribution functions.
- Negotiated private label agreement with Olivetti that demonstrated significant revenue and market potential, and subsequently evolved into Olivetti's acquisition of Crystal Technologies.

PITNEY-BOWES, INC., Stamford, Connecticut   1969 to 1986
($2B mailing and business equipment manufacturer)

Fast-track promotion throughout 17-year management career. Delivered strong and sustainable revenue, market and profit gains through expertise in new business development, new product launch and market expansion. Earned distinguished awards including:

- *Pitney-Bowes Walter H. Wheeler Award (Employee of the Year)*
- *Pitney-Bowes Outstanding Performance Awards*

WILLIAM B. GRANGER - *Page Three*

PITNEY-BOWES, INC. *(Continued):*

Director, Marketing & Product Development (1984 to 1986)

Senior Operating Executive with full P&L responsibility for $325MM international business unit with a staff of 20 professionals and a $23MM annual operating budget. Complete strategic and tactical leadership of all product development, marketing and business development initiatives.

- Captured 18% increase in sales through realignment of global market distribution.
- Developed/launched 12 products delivering 15% sales increase and 30% profit gain.
- Increased aggregate profit from 4% to 9% and market share by 20%.
- Identified global market opportunities to expand product portfolio and market penetration, and negotiated multi-million dollar, multi-national OEM contracts to acquire new technology and products. Resulted in a 7% increase in new product ROI.

Business Unit Director (1982 to 1984)

Direct P&L responsibility for line management of a combined domestic shipping systems and international postal systems business unit with revenues of $200MM and an $18MM operating budget.

- Built worldwide Postal Systems business unit. Achieved 25% revenue increase and 30% profit growth in first year.
- Increased Shipping Systems market share from 2% to 55%.
- Negotiated and closed two major contracts for a total of $18MM in new business.
- Structured/negotiated successful OEM strategy which reduced annual operating costs by $3MM.

Director, New Business/Venture Development (1980 to 1982)

Spearheaded the company's successful entry into the worldwide business and mailing automation markets. Developed strategic business and marketing plans, negotiated world-wide product rights, executed technology acquisitions, and pioneered global distribution strategies.

Promoted rapidly through a series of increasingly responsible MIS management positions during early professional career with Pitney-Bowes (1969 to 1980). Advanced to **Director of Corporate MIS & Telecommunications.**

Prior to Pitney-Bowes, **Senior Programmer Analyst** with Sikorsky Aircraft (1967 to 1969).

EDUCATION:

MBA, University of New Haven, 1972
BS (Marketing & Computer Science), Quinnipiac College, 1966
Graduate, Pitney Bowes Executive & Advanced Management Programs

References Provided Upon Request

BRUCE GROSSMAN

3847 Outback Way
Dallas, Texas 83494-9713
(815) 834-9716

CORPORATE MARKETING & BUSINESS DEVELOPMENT EXECUTIVE
Expertise in Technology Development, Commercialization & Global Market Expansion

---

Dynamic management career leading start-up, turnaround and high-growth organizations through explosive market growth and unprecedented profitability. Combines extensive "hands-on" technical qualifications with consistent success in identifying opportunities for product launch, market penetration and accelerated growth. Strong general management, P&L management and HR leadership successes. MBA Degree.

PROFESSIONAL EXPERIENCE:

SOLVAY AMERICA, INC., Dallas, Texas   1983 to Present
(U.S. Division of Solvay S.A., Brussels, Belgium)

Solvay Enzymes, Inc., Indianapolis, Indiana
Vice President - International Business Development (1995 to Present)

Following an 11-year career with Solvay America, joined the Belgium parent corporation in April 1995 to spearhead development of a global marketing and business development initiative for the $100+ million Enzymes Division. Challenged to design strategy and implement systems/processes to create an integrated worldwide marketing function as part of the business group's aggressive turnaround program. Provide strategic and tactical marketing leadership to Group Presidents in North America, Germany, Australia, Argentina and the Far East.

- Positioned the Division to achieve its first profitable year since 1991. Currently projecting revenue growth of 20% in 1997.

- Launched a massive effort to globalize product development and commercialization throughout the R&D organization.

- Structured and negotiated cooperative ventures between Solvay operating divisions and product lines to leverage worldwide marketing capabilities.

- Investigated and managed preliminary negotiations for proposed joint venture in the PRC.

Solvay Interox, Dallas, Texas
Vice President - Marketing (1989 to 1995)
Vice President - Hydrogen Peroxide (1987 to 1989)
Marketing Director (1986 to 1987)
Technical Manager (1984 to 1986)
National Accounts Manager (1983 to 1984)

Recruited to Solvay America's Interox Division in 1983. During the next 11 years, built a global marketing organization that led the Division from revenues of less than $20 million to 1995 volume of $120+ million. Recruited and developed a talented team of marketing professionals that now serve as Solvay Interox's core marketing management team.

BRUCE GROSSMAN *Page Two*

SOLVAY AMERICA, INC. *(Continued):*

- Established the initial marketing function, all long-range strategic and short-term tactical marketing plans, a comprehensive market research function, and a complete marketing communications program.

   RESULT: Delivered 100% revenue growth within two years.

- Promoted to Vice President in 1987. Developed "value-based" strategy to transition Division from commodity basis to product functionality to accelerate applications development and market expansion. Full marketing, technology development and technical service responsibility for the largest business group (Hydrogen Peroxide).

   RESULT: Increased annual revenues by more than 50% through a combined program of product development, applications development and market development.

- Promoted to Vice President of Marketing in 1989 with full P&L responsibility for Solvay Interox's entire marketing, field sales, technology and applications development, technical service and product distribution functions. Led a professional team of 50+, a $9 million annual operating budget and the entire North American field sales organization.

   RESULT: Built Division revenues from $45 million to $120 million annually, achieved #1 market position in North America, and surpassed all profit goals for six consecutive years. Implemented customer focus strategy to drive applications/ technology development.

HOOKER CHEMICALS & PLASTICS CORP., Niagara Falls, New York   1972 to 1983
(Currently Occidental Chemical Corporation)

Fast-track promotion through a series of increasingly responsible research, commercial development, sales and marketing positions. Career highlights included:

Marketing Manager - Chlorine & Caustic Soda (1982 to 1983)

Senior Marketing Executive for commodity chemicals throughout the North American market. Direct P&L responsibility for annual sales of $100 million.

Sales Manager - Technology Licensing (1979 to 1982)

Chief Technology Licensing Manager with global responsibility for technology and equipment marketing, licensing and contractual agreements. Operated worldwide.

- Negotiated, closed and directed projects valued up to $30 million each.

Project Manager - Technology Licensing (1976 to 1979)

Directed large-scale chemical plant construction projects that embodied licensed technology. Completed over $200 million in projects in the U.S., Europe, Asia and Latin America.

EDUCATION: **MBA**, State University of New York at Buffalo, 1975
                         BS / Chemical Engineering, Syracuse University, 1972

PATENTS: U.S. Patent No. 4,985,267 - "Versatile Process for Generating Chloric Acid"
                       U.S. Patent No. 4,854,753 - "Removal of Chlorate Electrolytes From Cells"

GARY R. JORDAN
547 Southbend
Queens, New York 19734
(212) 967-6984

SENIOR MARKETING & BUSINESS DEVELOPMENT EXECUTIVE
NationsBank, M&M Mars, Hershey

Dynamic management career spearheading successful marketing and business development programs nationwide. Combines expertise in strategic market planning, organizational leadership and project management with strong qualifications in campaign design, new product/service development and market launch. Participative leadership style with excellent skills in cross-functional team building, quality performance and productivity improvement.

*Delivered the strategies and tactical development plans that drove
millions of dollars in revenue and profit growth.*

PROFESSIONAL EXPERIENCE:

Corporate Marketing Consultant   1992 to Present
THE CONSULTING GROUP, Queens, New York

Executive Marketing Advisor to corporate clients in the publishing, health care and dairy industries throughout New York and Connecticut.

- **New England Dairy**. Long-term consulting assignment developing objectives, strategies and tactics to expand market penetration of specialty product. Contributed to solid 15% annual growth to over $70 million annually. Concurrent responsibility for advising CEO on product and company acquisitions. Reviewed more than 25 potential opportunities and currently in final due diligence review with several.

- **Futura Medical Publishing**. Defined marketing objectives, evaluated existing programs, and developed a series of targeted promotions and direct mail marketing campaigns.

Vice President / Marketing Director   1977 to 1992
NATIONSBANK, New York, New York

Spearheaded Nationsbank's successful and profitable entry into the nationwide Bankcard Insurance market to capitalize upon emerging market opportunity and exploit core competencies. Created innovative marketing programs targeted to key consumer markets throughout the U.S. and established Nationsbank as a major player within the industry.

- **Transitioned business unit from concept into a full-scale marketing and business development organization that grew to $100 million in annual volume within eight years.**

Built the entire marketing infrastructure, defined short-term marketing goals and long-term market development plans, and created high-profile, market-specific business development initiatives. Provided a decisive course of action to accelerate revenue/market growth. Recognized by corporate executives for expertise in market plan development, management and goal attainment.

GARY R. JORDAN **Page Two**

NATIONSBANK *(Continued):*

- Conceived, developed, tested and introduced more than 20 new products and services to expedite market penetration, create strong revenue and profit streams, and gain a competitive market advantage.

  — Credit Insurance Product. $100 million in revenue in eight years.
  — Established Insurance Products. 20% annual growth.
  — Basic Life/Health Insurance Products. $1 million in two years.
  — "Buy By Mail" Savings Products. $500,000 in revenue in two years.
  — Airflight Insurance Product. Projected as second largest insurance revenue producer in Nationsbank's past 10 years.

- Revitalized Nationsbank's in-house insurance agency providing strategic and tactical marketing support for major consumer businesses (e.g., Bankcards, Choice Visa).

- Negotiated strategic partnerships and alliances across all business units to facilitate nationwide marketing and business development initiatives.

- Created innovative, distinctive and successful direct mail, telemarketing, advertising, promotion and business development campaigns.

- Led cross-functional project teams (e.g., strategic, financial, operating, creative design, production, marketing, sales).

- Built incremental revenue by 20% through expansion of third-party distribution network.

Product Manager - New Products 1975 to 1977
M&M/MARS, New York, New York

Spearheaded the development and market launch of a series of new products and line extensions for the Family Products Division.

- Led successful introduction of new brand which surpassed first year dollar and unit share objectives by 18%.

- Managed successful consumer research and testing to evaluate product potential.

Senior Brand Manager 1971 to 1975
HERSHEY COMPANY, INC., Hershey, Pennsylvani

Fast-track promotion through several brand management positions.

- Revised marketing campaign for "$100,000" bar and drove 250% increase in three years.

- Realigned marketing and brand management programs for Hershey's Syrup products, increasing revenues by up to 48% annually.

- Identified market opportunity and led the most profitable promotion in 12 years.

Assistant Account Executive 1969 to 1971
MATHEW BENDER & ASSOCIATES, New York, New York

Developed marketing strategy for "Payday" (#1 market position in 1971). Wrote marketing segments for Kelloggs' "Frosted Flakes" cereal (exceeded profit objectives by 12%). Directed successful test market launch of Kraft's "Macaroni & Cheese" line extension.

EDUCATION: **BA, Yale University**

Betsy Underwood

Route 12 Box 971
Radford, Virginia 29877
(540) 654-9841

Qualifications Summary:

Twelve years experience in **MEDICAL OFFICE MANAGEMENT**. Combines excellent planning, organizational and administrative skills with strong performance in staffing, productivity improvement and patient service/satisfaction. Qualifications include:

- Medical Office Technology
- Physician & Provider Relations
- Regulatory Affairs & Compliance
- Purchasing & Inventory Management
- Banking & Financial Negotiations

- Insurance Claims Management
- Accounts Payable & Receivable
- Budgeting & Cost Control
- Staff Training & Development
- Quality Control & Improvement

Strong oral and written communication skills. Effective in prioritizing workflow to meet patient needs and physician obligations. Precise and detail oriented with excellent leadership, motivational and public relations experience.

Professional Experience:

Office Manager   1984 to Present
RADFORD MEDICAL GROUP, Radford, Virginia

Joined Radford Medical in 1984 as the only administrative employee in a small primary care practice (25 patients daily). Built the entire administrative infrastructure as the practice has grown to four physicians, three nurses and 100+ patients daily. Currently manage a staff of six administrative, accounting, claims and support personnel.

Scope of responsibility includes the entire administrative organization, all human resource functions, office systems, finance and accounting affairs, marketing, public relations, patient relations, recordkeeping and regulatory affairs. Establish business policies and procedures, develop internal administrative and reporting systems, streamline documentation requirements, and work to create a professional office management capability.

Significant Responsibilities:

- Direct the entire human resource function including recruitment, hiring, training, scheduling and performance appraisal. Evaluate current and long-range staffing requirements to meet increasing patient demand.

- Manage accounts payable, accounts receivable, general ledger, payroll, financial recordkeeping and reporting, purchasing, vendor relations and internal financial controls. Coordinate communications with banks, accountants and investment firm to expedite financial transactions.

Betsy Underwood

RADFORD MEDICAL GROUP *(Continued)*:

- Represent the practice, and the rural health care community, on various advisory boards (e.g., Carelink, CAMC, PEIA, OMA) throughout the region to strengthen relationships between providers, regulatory agencies and insurance companies.

- Monitor changes in the health care systems through publications, seminars, networking and professional development activities.

- Identify areas of potential malpractice risk and institute policies and procedures to minimize impact.

- Serve as the direct liaison with physicians, insurance companies, attorneys, medical schools, advisory boards, hospitals and others throughout the regional health care community.

- Review patient charts and write correspondence to obtain authorization for procedures, referrals and insurance benefits.

Major Projects:

- Coordinated construction, interior design and space planning for a large addition to existing office facility. Brought project in on time and within budget despite several contractor delays.

- Managed the cost effective purchasing of more than $200,000 annually in general supplies, equipment and capital expenditures.

- Spearheaded initial computerization with Versyss Network (integrated health care management system) and several subsequent upgrades to fully automate all accounting, recordkeeping, reporting and patient database functions.

Pharmacy Assistant   1983 to 1984
REYNOLDS PHARMACY, Radford, Virginia

Worked with pharmacist to fill prescriptions. Processed insurance billings and collections, coordinated inventory planning and control, priced pharmaceuticals and medical supplies, and managed customer service.

Education:

Southwest Virginia Community College (Accounting)

Completed over 200 hours of continuing professional education on topics including health care regulations, PC software technology, supervisory skills, communications, organization, time management, project management and administration.

FELICIA JONES

34 NE 33rd Street
New York, New York 19836
(202) 987-3212

PROFESSIONAL QUALIFICATIONS:

Over 15 years experience in the planning and management of large-scale Office Services, Facilities Management Services, Purchasing and Administrative Support Functions for a Fortune 100 corporation. Consistently effective in streamlining and upgrading operations, improving productivity and reducing annual operating costs. Qualifications include:

- Mail & Messenger Services
- Contract Negotiations
- Inventory & Materials Management
- Equipment Leasing & Acquisition
- Staff Training & Supervision

- Property Management
- Fleet Administration
- Insurance Administration
- Purchasing Management
- Budget Administration

PROFESSIONAL EXPERIENCE:

TURNER BROADCASTING, INC., New York, New York   1984 to Present
($4 billion diversified entertainment conglomerate.)

Office Services Manager

Plan, staff, budget and direct the daily business operations of the Office Services Department, a support function servicing over 1200 employees located at corporate headquarters. Scope of responsibility includes all mail and shipping services, a large contracted messenger operation, and office support services throughout both facilities.

Hold concurrent responsibility for the management of Transportation Department operations for executive staff. Administer departmental policy, negotiate the purchase and sale of all vehicles, and manage related insurance programs. Currently control a 30-car corporate fleet.

Formulate and administer a $3.5 million annual operating budget. Train and supervise a staff of 26 Office Services and Facilities Management employees. Coordinate all related purchasing, materials management, vendor sourcing/selection, contract negotiations and inventory planning/management functions. In addition, manage production of monthly promotional mailings of 5000 to 50,000 pieces.

Achievements:

- Launched a complete reorganization of the Office Services department and cut annual operating expenses by 25%. Reduced staffing requirements, eliminated overtime and restructured messenger service programs.

- Integrated several independent operating departments into one Office Services organization for an annual savings of more than $75,000.

- Sourced vendors, prepared bid packages and negotiated cost-effective contracts for the outsourcing of mailroom and messenger services. Resulted in a substantial improvement in service delivery while reducing net operating costs by 25%.

FELICIA JONES

Page Two

TURNER BROADCASTING, INC. *(Continued)*:

- Introduced the use of presort mail, international mail and bulk mail services into the corporation for a substantial reduction in annual postage and handling costs.

- Negotiated favorable equipment leases and facilities contracts to expand in-house operating capabilities and support to 1200 employees.

- Coordinated transportation services for high-profile special events including Annual Stockholders Meetings, Board of Directors meetings and a series of national fundraising events.

Real Estate Assistant (1984 to 1987)

Fast-paced operations support position coordinating commercial, industrial and residential real estate projects for the corporation. Reported directly to the President.

- Orchestrated a national employee relocation program for the transfer of personnel throughout various Turner companies and locations. Negotiated the resale of homes in cooperation with local real estate brokers, coordinated home purchases and expedited physical relocations.

- Negotiated with management companies of Turner leased buildings throughout the U.S. to monitor daily operations, resolve tenant problems, evaluate rental costs and contracts, and coordinate service delivery.

- Assisted with the planning and implementation of plant closure programs. Reviewed consultant contracts and negotiated vendor, utility and contractor agreements. Monitored costs, maintained ledgers and identified/resolved cost overrides.

EDUCATION:

FORDHAM UNIVERSITY, New York, New York, 1985 to 1988
Coursework in Business Administration, Planning & Communications

Licensed Real Estate Sales Associate, State of New York, 1984

PROFESSIONAL AFFILIATIONS:

National Association of Fleet Administrators
Mail Systems Management Association
Postal Customers Council

JOHN P. MITCHELL
5378 Jefferson Avenue
Arlington, Virginia 22153
Email jmitchell@msn.com

Home (703) 351-5620   Work (202)267-5648

PUBLIC RELATIONS / MEDIA RELATIONS / COMMUNICATIONS / SPECIAL EVENTS

Talented Public Relations Strategist and Campaign Director with 10 years professional experience. Expertise in community/public outreach, multimedia communications, publications management and crisis management. Accomplished in managing relationships with major print and broadcast media nationwide. Skilled in large-scale event coordination/management. Consistently effective in meeting budget and schedule requirements.

PROFESSIONAL EXPERIENCE:

Public Relations Officer   1987 to 1995
UNITED STATES NAVY - Washington, D.C. / California / Virginia / Pennsylvania

Fast-track promotion through a series of increasingly responsible public relations / public affairs positions nationwide as one of only 200 designated spokespersons in the U.S. Navy. Won several distinguished commendations (2 Commendation Medals, Achievement Medal) for outstanding performance in the management of sensitive public relations programs and initiatives.

Public Relations / Public Affairs

- Rebuilt and revitalized non-active public relations function aboard the aircraft carrier USS Enterprise. Created innovative PR programs targeted to military and civilian personnel, re-established weekly newspaper and planned/hosted more than 10 special events.
- Developed course content and taught public relations training seminars to personnel throughout 12 Naval organizations.
- Publicized the Navy's assistance to victims of January 1994 earthquake in LA, winning positive media coverage and strengthening position of the Navy's response to domestic crises.
- Launched several high-profile public relations campaigns to recruit community board members and expand public information concerning two hazardous waste removal projects. Personally managed and responded to all public and local political inquiries.
- Wrote public relations guidelines for congressional visits emphasizing the management of high-profile events and strategies to leverage media exposure.
- Trained and supervised teams of up to 24, responsible for public relations, printing, graphic arts, photography, media relations, community outreach and administrative support.

Media / Press Relations

- Represented the Navy with major print and broadcast media nationwide including network affiliates, national and local correspondents, National Public Radio, Washington Post, New York Times, Los Angeles Times, Wall Street Journal, Time and Newsweek.
- Managed liaison affairs with local, national and international press, White House Press Office, Arlington National Cemetery and National Cathedral for national coverage of memorial services for the late Chief of Naval Operations and the late U.S. Commerce Secretary.
- Appointed spokesperson in regional and national media markets to handle high-visibility issues including base closures and related employee relocation issues, integration of women into combat assignments and emerging environmental concerns.
- Spearheaded communications with media nationwide to change negative reaction and media perception of large-scale environmental projects. Won positive coverage and support with major print and broadcast media.
- Responded to public and national media inquiries about the USS Iowa explosion at sea and operated the first "800" family information number (now standard in Navy crisis response).
- Coordinated media (including live segments on "Good Morning America") for the first U.S. port visit by Russian warships in 20 years. Managed affairs for 300+ media over a five-day period.

JOHN P. MITCHELL

Page Two

Public Relations Officer *(Continued)*:

Publications Management

- Editor of <u>Horizons</u>, a specialized publication with circulation of 9000+. Full responsibility for editorial content, story assignments, layout, design and outsourced printing contract.
- Editor and Sole Author of the only timely news service in the U.S. Navy. Wrote news and feature articles published weekly in Naval newspapers worldwide.

Multimedia Communications

- Designed and managed construction of renovated television and radio broadcast studio aboard the USS Enterprise. Directed programming, scheduling and transmission of broadcast services to 5000+ shipboard personnel.
- Led four-person editorial board responsible for content review and authorization of information posted on the USS Enterprise Internet Home Page.
- Authored press releases, news stories, articles, public outreach documents, correspondence, reports and other print communications.

Special Events

- Planned and directed educational tours aboard the USS Enterprise for thousands of U.S. and foreign visitors (e.g., general public, politicians, military personnel, visiting dignitaries, foreign attaches) during the vessel's travels throughout the U.S. and Latin America.
- Directed first-ever visits to Naval forces and a complete special events program for high-level government administrators and other noted dignitaries.
- Conceived, planned, staffed, publicized and directed 20+ special events throughout career.

Career Progression

Public Relations Officer - Naval District Washington Headquarters (1993 to 1995)
Public Relations Officer - USS Enterprise (1991 to 1993)
Asst Public Relations Officer - Naval District Washington Headquarters (1988 to 1991)
Asst Public Relations Officer - Pacific Fleet Headquarters (1985 to 1988)
Editor - Navy Internal Relations Activity (1983 to 1985)

EDUCATION:

B.S., Computer Science, Texas A&M University, 1983
(Distinguished Military Graduate - National Naval Officers Association)

Graduate, Public Affairs Officers Course, Defense Information School, 1983
(10-week, Graduate-Level Program Emphasizing Public Affairs/Communications)

References Provided Upon Request

MARSHA SMITH
943 Park Avenue
New York, New York 19436
(202) 971-6577

EXECUTIVE PROFILE

Corporate Communications / Marketing Communications / Advertising Communications

Top-flight management career building innovative marketing, communications and business development programs worldwide. Combines expert creative design, strategic and market positioning qualifications with strong general management, project management and financial accountabilities. Qualifications include:

- Print & Broadcast Media
- Market Positioning & Awareness
- Sales Promotions & Incentives
- Public Speaking & Public Relations
- Team Building & Team Leadership
- Crisis Communications

- Customer Marketing Communications
- Corporate Vision & Strategy
- Investor & Shareholder Communications
- Executive Presentations & Negotiations
- Business Process Reengineering
- Employee & Management Communications

- Awarded membership in YWCA Academy of Women Achievers, 1994.
- Woman of the Year Nominee, Business-Professional Womens Club, 1980
- Member, International Association of Business Communicators and New York Junior League

PROFESSIONAL EXPERIENCE

1994 to Present   **Managing Director - Corporate Communications, Advertising & Marketing**
CUSHMAN & WAKEFIELD, New York, New York

($300 million multi-service global real estate firm with operating units in financial services, leasing, asset services, outsourcing, valuation analysis and research services. Client base includes AT&T, Ford, Kraft, IBM, Hertz and J.P. Morgan.)

Recruited as the Senior Management Executive responsible for the strategic planning, development and leadership of the entire marketing, advertising and communications function. Manage a team-based organization with both in-house and contract marketing, communications, advertising, design, graphic arts and printing personnel. Manage a $2.5 million annual operating budget.

- Authored the firm's strategic communications plan and orchestrated successful effort to update corporate vision, mission and values statement. Transitioned marketing focus to core customer types and segments.

- Architected new corporate advertising and client testimonial trade campaigns which appeared in Forbes, Business Week, Fortune and other major national publications.

- Revitalized and expanded marketing communications program throughout Manhattan (company's largest market) utilizing industry-leading initiatives. Expanded editorial and advertising penetration from the "real estate" to "business" pages to increase market visibility with CEOs, CFOs and other top operating executives of target accounts.

- Launched development of global branding strategy to establish the firm as the preferred business-to-business real estate services provider. Leveraged existing client base as key partners in the firm's worldwide marketing and business development initiatives.

MARSHA SMITH - *Page Two*

1990 to 1993   **Corporate Communications, Marketing & Management Consultant**
                               ALLEN ASSOCIATES, San Francisco, California / New York, New York

Executive Consultant providing integrated marketing and communications advisory services to major corporate clients throughout the national market. Worked on a project-by-project basis with top operating management. Key engagements included:

ITT Corporation World Headquarters (New York)
- Consulted with ITT consumer, commercial finance and other business units on a broad range of internal/external communications, marketing and reengineering projects. Managed sensitive negotiations during union dispute, authored business plan for new operating unit, and designed process improvements for field and staff operations.

American Express (San Francisco & New York)
- Created and implemented marketing and promotional plans for Amex travel agencies throughout California, Arizona, Colorado, Illinois and Georgia. Recommended strategic and tactical action plans to increase market awareness and coordinated regional media affairs.

1984 to 1990   **Director - Corporate Communications**
                               ITT CORPORATION WORLD HEADQUARTERS, New York, New York

Senior Management Executive with responsibility for numerous ITT worldwide Corporate Communications Programs. Provided expertise counsel, strategic and tactical action programs for public relations, advertising, sales promotions, marketing and crisis communications for major ITT businesses, subsidiaries and operating units worldwide. Managed a $25+ million annual group operating budget.

- One of the highest ranked executive women within the ITT organization. Consistently earned highest performance ratings and several key promotions.

- Appointed Chairperson of the ITT Corporate Political Action Committee and the New York-Washington interface.

- Authored speeches for ITT Chairman, Board of Directors and executive management team. Managed various shareholder communications and annual reporting functions.

- Coordinated press, radio and television interviews during Chairman's 1989 media tour.

NOTE: Served as **Vice President of Operations** / **Board Member** for ITT's International Conference Center. Transitioned business from $10 million loss to $2+ million profit through a series of successful business process reengineering initiatives.

1976 to 1983   **Legislative Director / Legislative Assistant**
                               U.S. HOUSE OF REPRESENTATIVES, Washington, D.C.

Promoted from Legislative Assistant to Legislative Director for the Former Representative Beverly B. Byron. Served as the principal legislative policy advisor to the Member. Responsible for identifying and recommending legislative initiatives, training and supervising a team of legislative assistants and interns, and coordinating all legislative committee projects. Drafted major speeches, committee testimony and floor statements. Acquired substantial public speaking experience throughout the legislative, public interest communities and local districts.

EDUCATION

MBA in Marketing, NEW YORK UNIVERSITY / LEONARD N. STERN SCHOOL OF BUSINESS, 1993

MA in Legislative Affairs, GEORGE WASHINGTON UNIVERSITY, 1983

BA in Political Science, Honors Graduate, UNIVERSITY OF NORTH CAROLINA AT CHAPEL HILL, 1976

RALPH EVANSTON
3209 South Main Stree
Kalamazoo, Michigan 32878
(616) 641-6431

Public Affairs / Public Relations / Media Affairs / Community Relations
Corporate Communications / Customer Communications / VIP Relations / Special Events

Top-flight management career building high-profile public affairs organizations that have consistently enhanced competitive market positioning, won favorable media and customer recognition, and supported multi-million dollar revenue growth. Combine strong planning, organizational leadership and consensus building qualifications with creative design and writing skills.

Extensive general operating management qualifications in corporate restructuring, human resource affairs, budget administration, business planning and long-range strategic development.

PROFESSIONAL EXPERIENCE:

GTE CORPORATION, Michigan/Indiana   **1988 to Present**
(Nation's largest local exchange carrier and second largest cellular provider)

> *Fast-track promotion through a series of increasingly responsible management positions directing high-profile public affairs, public relations, corporate communications, special events and media relations programs. Achieved unprecedented cost reductions in each assignment and strengthened GTE's positioning within the highly competitive telecommunications industry. Career highlights include:*

Regional Public Affairs Director, Indiana-Michigan Region (1993 to Present)

Promoted to newly-created position in response to nationwide corporate consolidation and given full management responsibility for the entire public affairs program for a two-state region (1.7 million customers and over $450 million in annual revenues). Direct a staff of seven and $4 million in annual operating budgets.

- Maintained caliber, integrity and strength of public affairs and public relations initiatives despite downsizing and more limited financial resources. Successfully integrated multi-state operations into an integrated organization with common mission, strategy and vision.

- Orchestrated an integrated public affairs, media and VIP customer initiative to support the nationwide introduction of "World Class Networks" (leading edge infrastructure technology). Created a high-profile series of programs to win recognition, hosted major media events and an exclusive conference for GTE's top 250 accounts. Efforts resulted in hundreds of sales leads and significant revenue gains.

- Conceived and directed an innovative community relations tour featuring the "Airmen of Note" — premier jazz ensemble of the United States Air Force.

- Devised and implemented revenue-based measurement tools aligning public affairs resources with company goals and objectives to evaluate their direct impact upon the "bottom line."

*(NOTE: Promoted in Fall 1996 to **Regional Public Affairs Director** for Illinois, Indiana and Wisconsin. Scope of responsibility includes a $4.7 million budget and 14 staff supporting a region with 2.8 million customers and over $750 million in annual revenues.)*

RALPH EVANSTON - *Page Two*

State Public Affairs Director, Michigan (1991 to 1993)

Conceived, developed and directed top-flight public affairs programs throughout the State of Michigan (2500 employee organization with over $250 million in annual revenues). Led a professional staff of six and administered over $2.2 million in annual budgets.

- Managed sensitive state-wide media relations efforts during a significant employee reduction. Achieved neutral-to-positive coverage through intense media education campaigns, personal interviews and distinguished public relations/community events. Created companion internal communications programs to enhance management/employee relations during restructuring.

- Launched a massive media/employee communications plan to maximize the benefits of GTE's $450 million technology investment program. Won significant media coverage highlighting GTE's community and service commitment.

- Planned and hosted annual 4-day management conferences for over 1000 GTE personnel. Directed logistics, agenda, entertainment, sporting events, communications and awards programs.

- Conceived, developed and managed "Michigan Classics" public relations series featuring Ramsey Lewis and the Detroit Symphony Orchestra.

Community Relations Manager, Indiana (1988 to 1991)

Planned, designed and orchestrated community relations and special events to support GTE operations throughout a 10-state region. Identified and capitalized upon opportunities to enhance GTE's public image, improve customer relations and advance the company's competitive market positioning.

- Directed the award-winning GTE CHAMPIONSHIPS tennis tournament (voted "Tournament of the Year" 1988 through 1991 by the Association of Tennis Professionals). Designed stadium logo plan to maximize television exposure, resulting in over $2 million per year in equivalent advertising dollars. Hosted 1200 VIP guests, coordinated "Employee Night" with 1000 GTE personnel, and managed high-visibility participation of executive management team.

- Created and managed the "Target Districts" program designed specifically for regions with diminished company image. Spearheaded high-profile economic development, contributions, community relations, community services and local print advertising employee recognition programs to win customer support and improve customer perceived quality.

CALDWELL VANRIPER, Indianapolis, Indiana   **1986 to 1988**

Public Relations Account Manager for GTE, Mayflower, Paper Art Company, Charmglow Industries and Knauff Fiberglass. Managed Mayflower LPGA Classic Press Room.

EDUCATION: **BS / Majors in Journalism, Public Relations & Political Science, Magna Cum Laude,** 1985
BALL STATE UNIVERSITY, Muncie, Indiana

Graduate, "Leadership Michigan" Executive Training Program, 1992

PROFESSIONAL & COMMUNITY AFFILIATIONS:

Member, Michigan Rural Development Council Executive Steering Committee
Vice-Chair, Muskegon Economic Forum
Board Member, Wayne Sports Corporation
Industry Unit Captain, Greater Allen County United Way
Telecommunications Advisory Committee, Michigan Press Association

JASON A. WRIGHT
342 Twin Avenue • St. Paul, Minnesota 52348 • (612) 654-5547

PROJECT MANAGEMENT / PROCESS REENGINEERING / INTERNAL CONSULTING
Domestic & International Business Operations

Talented young professional with three years' experience in the conceptualization, design and leadership of pioneering efforts in process, productivity, efficiency and quality improvement. Provided the strategic and tactical actions that delivered millions of dollars in revenue gains and cost savings through organizational development and workforce optimization. Strong qualifications in team building and team leadership.

PROFESSIONAL EXPERIENCE:

PROCESS ENGINEER - 3M COMPANY, OPTIMIZED OPERATIONS   1993 to Present

Fast-track promotion through a series of increasingly responsible positions in 3M's internal consulting group, a specialty business unit providing process redesign, reengineering, change management and project management services to 3M operations in 60 countries worldwide. Major projects have included:

Corporate Marketing & Public Affairs - St. Paul, Minnesota
Project Leader for Customer Connect, a new initiative launched to create a seamless customer response network integrating the Internet, phone, fax and paper communications. Currently leading an 8-person cross-functional team (e.g., logistics, product management, marketing, IT, technical service) challenged to create the strategic and tactical processes to drive program development and implementation. Potential savings are forecasted at $70+ million through improved revenue, productivity and customer retention.

Corporate Communication Services - St. Paul, Minnesota
Facilitated cross-functional team that optimized 3M's deployment of this internal communication services business unit. Focused on organizational structure, financial systems, outsourcing and strategic planning. Spearheaded effort to standardize terms and conditions for 4500+ vendors of multi-media communication services/technologies. Long-term savings projected at $8 million.

3M South Africa - Johannesburg, South Africa
Directed two cross-functional teams developing of focused factory layouts. Pilot implementation resulted in 20% space reduction, 40% decrease in in-process inventory and 35% increase in production output.

3M Brazil - Sumare, Brazil
Short-term exploratory project to identify methods to improve processes, expand production and integrate cellular manufacturing methodologies. Project served as a model for worldwide implementation.

Knoxville Manufacturing Plant - Knoxville, Iowa
Implemented inventory reduction strategies to accommodate 200% production growth without increasing warehousing or personnel requirements. Designed computer simulation to optimize materials flow.

St. Paul Tape Manufacturing Plant - St. Paul, Minnesota
Environmental engineering assignment responsible for proposal development to reduce air emissions for the EPA Early Reductions Program (favorable corporate initiative providing significant cost savings). Negotiated directly with EPA officials.

ENGINEERING INTERN - 3M COMPANY   Summers 1990 to 1992

Participated in SPC, process improvement and quality assurance projects throughout the corporation.

EDUCATION:

B.S., Industrial Engineering, Northwestern University, June 1993
Presented to President Bush's Council of Advisors on Science and Technology; Senior Academic & Leadership Honor Society; President, Alpha Delta Phi Fraternity; Executive Vice President, Interfraternity Council; National Merit Finalist (Eastman Kodak Scholarship); College of Arts and Sciences Dean's Award for Art.

LAWRENCE FAIRFIELD
934 East End Avenue
Newark, New Jersey 09843
(609) 654-6431

SENIOR PURCHASING DIRECTOR
MRO & Capital Equipment Purchasing / Materials Management / Inventory Planning & Control
Multi-Site Warehousing / Regional & National Distribution / Barter & Trade Operations

Delivered over $100 million in total cost savings throughout career through expertise in planning, staffing, budgeting and directing large-scale domestic and offshore purchasing operations. Spearheaded development of regional and national purchasing programs, fixed price contracts, and vendor sourcing plans to expand supplier base and reduce acquisition costs. Keen negotiation and vendor/subcontractor management skills.

PROFESSIONAL EXPERIENCE:

FARBERWARE, INC., New York, New York   1990 to Present
($120 million consumer products manufacturer)

Director of Purchasing

Promoted from Purchasing Manager to Director with full responsibility for the planning, staffing, budgeting and operations of a diversified purchasing and inventory management function (e.g., stainless steel, aluminum, parts, packaging, MRO, POP). Managed a large off-shore purchasing and vendor management program. Directed a staff of six purchasing agents, buyers and support personnel. Negotiated $55+ million in annual purchasing contracts.

- Introduced MRP technology (BCPS system) to the corporation to upgrade the quality, control and availability of parts, equipment and support services. Resulted in a 14% reduction in annual inventory volume/costs.

- Structured/negotiated multi-year, fixed price contacts for major raw material expenditures, resale goods and components. Resulted in 18% reduction ($1.7 million) in purchasing costs.

- Spearheaded the transfer of parts manufacturing from U.S. to offshore facilities, significantly enhanced design performance, and saved 12% in annual purchasing and subcontractor costs.

- Directed a $10 million addition to physical plant. Brought project in on time and within budget despite problems with contractor performance and materials availability.

ALL-BILT UNIFORM CORPORATION, New York, New York   1987 to 1990
($18 million, privately-held custom uniform & career apparel manufacturer)

Director of Operations & Sales

Recruited to this family-owned business to introduce sound operation, purchasing and general management strategies as part of the management team's commitment to accelerated growth. Challenged to introduce the systems, processes and operations to support expansion and improve financial performance. Demonstrated success within a fast-paced, entrepreneurial and customer-driven organization.

Held full planning, budgeting and operating management responsibility for purchasing, inventory control, warehousing, subcontract production, scheduling, customer service, mail order processing and fulfillment, shipping and receiving, and divisional sales.

- Negotiated over $10 million annually in subcontractor manufacturing agreements and an additional $3 million in general purchasing contracts.

- Launched an aggressive expansion of computer technology to automate general business, customer service, purchasing, inventory and distribution management functions.

HERTZ CORPORATION, New York, New York   1980 to 1987
($2 billion automotive rental & fleet management company)

Director of Purchasing & Distribution

Directed the purchase of over $250 million in parts, components, equipment and support services utilizing a centralized national contracts system. Supported three major corporate facilities and three major operating divisions generating $2+ billion in annual sales revenues. Concurrently, directed all purchasing, vendor relations and subcontractor negotiations for the purchase of direct mail, promotional, printing and fulfillment programs.

- Delivered a 3% annual reduction in purchasing costs ($6-$7 million) through the introduction of the corporation's first regional and national purchasing contracts with complete internal purchasing audit function. Negotiated firm fixed price contracts to control accelerating costs and expanded vendor sourcing worldwide.

- Assumed additional responsibility for the planning, staffing, budgeting and management of telecommunications, support services, invoice audit and travel departments.

RYDER SYSTEM, INC.   1973 to 1980

Director - Field Purchasing & Administrative Services (1974 to 1980)
Ryder Truck Rental, Inc., Miami, Florida *($3 billion corporation)*

Led the start-up of a complete purchasing function as Ryder transitioned from third party to in-house materials management. Recruited/trained 12 buyers and support personnel responsible for the cost-effective acquisition of parts, replacement equipment, tires, shop equipment, chemicals and fuel storage/dispensing equipment.

Assumed concurrent responsibility for management of the Administrative Services function (e.g., accounting, graphic arts, records management, word processing, micro-graphics, mail & supply space planning, facilities management, inventory control). Directed Services team of 25-30.

- Structured, negotiated and executed $150 million annually in national and regional purchasing contracts. Supported company growth from $900 million to $3+ billion in revenues.

Director of Purchasing (1973 to 1974)
Supplyline, Inc., Miami, Florida

Joined newly-created subsidiary established to provide a national buying source for the entire Ryder system. Directed $25+ million in annual purchasing volume and operated four distribution centers nationwide supplying over 600 locations. NOTE: Company was liquidated in 1974 and all purchasing functions were transitioned in-house to Ryder System.

Previous Professional Experience:

Purchasing Manager, Southern Railroad, Inc., Atlanta, Georgia
Purchasing Agent to Superintendent, Monsanto Company, St. Louis, Missouri

EDUCATION:

POLYTECHNIC INSTITUTE OF BROOKLYN - B.S., Chemical Engineering
HARVARD UNIVERSITY - NAPM Executive Purchasing Program
AMERICAN INTERNATIONAL COLLEGE - MBA Program
REGISTERED PROFESSIONAL ENGINEER - Missouri & Georgia
CERTIFIED PURCHASING MANAGER (CPM)

AUGUSTA BINER

9329 Model T Drive
Flint, Michigan 46973
(313) 649-7498

CAREER PROFILE:

CORPORATE PURCHASING MANAGER with over 15 years experience in leading a multi-million dollar purchasing network for a Fortune 500 corporation. Consistently successful in controlling purchasing costs and improving net profitability while continuing to support critical operations. Established innovative vendor partnership programs that have dramatically improved product quality and positioned corporation as a forerunner within the industry.

Certified Purchasing Manager, National Association of Purchasing Managers, 1988 & 1994

PROFESSIONAL EXPERIENCE:

QUAKER CHEMICAL CORPORATION, Detroit, Michigan   1976 to Present

PURCHASING MANAGER

Promoted through several increasingly responsible purchasing assignments to current position as Purchasing Manager directing purchasing activities for Quaker's North American Division. Accountable for over $80 million in annual purchases from more than 350 vendors (national manufacturers, international manufacturers, local distributors).

Scope of responsibility is expansive and includes procurement of thousands of products (e.g., raw materials for chemical production, plant equipment, lab equipment, instrumentation, computer hardware/ software, facilities maintenance supplies, office supplies/materials, service contracts). Act as a direct liaison to all department heads throughout the corporation to identify and obtain their specific product requirements at best price/best quality. Personally handle large dollar purchasing negotiations and major vendor relationships. Train/supervise division's purchasing and administrative support staff.

Plant-wide management responsibilities include appointment as on-site Administrative Manager supervising the entire administrative operation during management's absence for union contract negotiations (50+ sessions), strategic and contingency planning for potential strikes/work stoppages, training/development of staff and college interns, and active participation in corporate litigation. Appointed as one of only four Internal Quality Lead Auditors in the North American Division.

Significant Achievements:

- Driving force behind the development of the North American Division's purchasing organization. Built department from virtual start-up to its current $80 million annual volume. Established policies/procedures, coordinated development of supporting data processing systems, implemented quality controls criteria, and created an autonomous business function supporting the entire corporation.

- Achieved profit improvements through aggressive control of annual purchasing costs. Negotiated vendor rebates, rescinded price increases and extended terms for an average annual net savings of $600,000. Reduced surplus raw materials by 57% and reduced long-term inventory through implementation of economic ordering quantity methodologies and JIT purchasing systems.

- Orchestrated the introduction of vendor quality, rating and management programs designed to foster a unique relationship between Quaker and its primary vendors. Objective was to instill a sense of personal commitment by vendors to the quality of Quaker's finished products. Included design/ development of a vendor rating program (based upon Quaker's quality expectations), implementation of quality audit programs, creation of an innovative shelf life information exchange program (first of its kind in the chemical industry), and establishment of vendor partnership agreements.

PROFESSIONAL EXPERIENCE *(Continued):*

- Appointed Lead Team Member representing Quaker's Purchasing Department for several on-site customer audits (e.g., ISO, Ford Q1, Caterpillar, Double Eagle, S.I.S.A.P.) Chosen by Ford Motor Company as a benchmark for supplier management and on-site demonstration facility for both Ford customers and its internal purchasing/materials management organization.

- Designed and led a series of corporate training programs (e.g., cross training in purchasing, vendor performance rating, price/quality negotiations, policy/procedure changes). Established cooperative working relationships with Quaker purchasing and personnel throughout the U.S. to provide ongoing management consulting/support.

- Facilitated the development/implementation of computerized employee inventory purchasing system to ensure accountability of all employee-based expenditures (primarily plant safety equipment). In addition, directed the design of a user-friendly committed/spent dollars budget variance analysis program to provide actual purchasing expenditure information on a department-by-department basis.

- Appointed to the Visionary Planning Group, a top management team formed to establish short and long term goals for each critical department to ensure that their operations are supportive of the corporation's overall vision for quality, achievement and profitability. Personally directed the visionary planning process for the administrative staff.

- Appointed to the Joint Application Development Team, working in cooperation with information systems consulting group to ensure that all data processing systems development efforts are implemented in support of the corporation's visionary planning process while effectively meeting current operational needs and objectives.

- Team Leader responsible for orchestrating the corporation's 75th anniversary celebration for the Detroit facility. Independently handled all special events and celebration planning functions. Member of Quaker's Global Anniversary Team in cooperation with facilities worldwide.

- Appointed to joint task force comprised of product managers, chemists and R&D personnel challenged to identify $300,000 in cost savings through redesign of product development cycle.

EDUCATION:

Candidate for Bachelor of Science in Business Administration & Labor Relations, 1986 to Present
WAYNE STATE UNIVERSITY, Detroit, Michigan

Associate Degree in Business Administration, Magna Cum Laude Graduate, 1987
HENRY FORD COMMUNITY COLLEGE, Dearborn, Michigan

Highlights of Continuing Professional Education:

- Lead Assessor of Quality Systems *(preparation for ISO Auditor)*, Perry Johnson
- Win-Win Negotiations, National Association of Purchasing Managers
- Cost Value Analysis, National Association of Purchasing Managers
- International Purchasing & Countertrade, National Association of Purchasing Managers
- International Purchasing Conferences (4), National Association of Purchasing Managers
- Statistical Process Control (SPC), Lawrence Institute of Technology
- Managerial Modeling, Organization Dimensions
- Public Speaking and Human Relations, Dale Carnegie (2 Achievement Awards)
- Leadership Training for Managers, Dale Carnegie

PROFESSIONAL AFFILIATIONS:

National Association of Purchasing Management
Purchasing Management Association of Detroit

MELISSA SPRINGFORD

6498 Bay Street
San Francisco, California
(615) 697-7982

PROPERTY DEVELOPMENT & MANAGEMENT PROFESSIONAL

*Multi-Family Housing / Senior Housing / Commercial Office / Medical Office / Industrial
Strip & Mall Retail / Sports & Recreational / Hotels & Resorts*

Distinguished management career in Property Management and Construction Management. Consistently successful in maximizing asset value through measurable gains in occupancy, tenant satisfaction, retention and operating cost reduction. Managed 100+ properties (5.3 million sq. ft. valued at $340+ million) and directed over $4.8 million in construction, renovation and retrofit projects. Strong general/P&L management, budgeting, financial reporting, training and leadership qualifications. Expert negotiator and "deal maker." PC proficient.

Professional Credentials

Executive Certified Property Manager (CPM) for Accredited Management Organization (AMO)
California Real Estate Broker

PROFESSIONAL EXPERIENCE:

Director of Property Management / Partner   March 1993 to December 1996
KTB REALTY PARTNERS, INC., San Francisco, California

> *Portfolio:* 14 residential properties (553 units) and 69 retail stores
> 600,000 sq. ft. industrial property
> 900,000 sq. ft. public facilities; 285,000 sq. ft. office space
> 96-room hotel with 500-seat live theater and ground floor retail
> 123,000 sq. ft. medical and health club facilities

Recruited to this diversified real estate investment, development and asset management company to build their property management portfolio. Established relationships with property owners, builders and developers throughout the region, and negotiated favorable, multi-year management contracts.

- Built portfolio by adding 2.6 million sq. ft. over two years. Structured, negotiated and closed major contracts with Bank of America (32 properties) and Resolution Trust Corporation (distressed multi-family property and 12 distressed commercial properties). Revitalized relationship and restored credibility with the San Francisco Redevelopment Agency.
- Created a complete property management function, recruited experienced personnel, designed accounting and financial reporting processes, and implemented PC technologies for expanded portfolio analysis and management reporting capabilities.
- Launched start-up of new contract maintenance services division that generated $75,000+ in first year revenue.
- Directed start-up of satellite property management office to expand market reach.
- Achieved the prestigious Accredited Management Organization (AMO) status for KTB.

President / Owner   June 1987 to February 1993
SAN FRANCISCO PROPERTY COMPANY, San Francisco, California

> *Portfolio:* 5 residential properties (783 units) and 200,000 sq. ft. retail space
> 296,000 sq. ft. commercial office and medical office space
> 2 hotels (246 rooms) and 107,000 sq. ft. mixed-use facility

Founded property management firm and built from start-up into a 1.3 million sq. ft. portfolio of mixed-use, multi-family, industrial, retail, commercial office, medical office and hotel properties. Recruited and directed a staff of 30. Developed all administrative, accounting, financial and reporting systems. Achieved AMO status for company.

MELISSA SPRINGFORD   *Page Two*

SAN FRANCISCO PROPERTY COMPANY *(Continued)*:

- Managed more than 17 properties and over $4 million in construction and renovation projects, including a large environmental treatment project (saved $5000+ annually), start-up of new security and maintenance operations, correction of major construction and structural defects, renovation of electrical and mechanical systems, renovation of historic properties, ADA compliance projects and countless tenant improvement upgrades.
- Identified opportunities, built relationships and negotiated/closed over 17 property management contracts over six years.
- Won the first-ever property management contract awarded by the City of Sausalito.
- Achieved 100% lease up for several new construction and renovation projects.
- Designed tenant service programs that increased residential and commercial retention by 20%.
- Directed installation of PC network to link all properties with company headquarters.

Regional Property Manager   January 1982 to June 1987
TAYLOR WOODROW, San Francisco, California

Recruited to join this international real estate developer and general contractor to manage a $18 million, 500,000 sq. ft. portfolio of commercial office and retail space. Collateral responsibility as Construction Manager for major tenant improvement projects.

- Significantly improved tenant mix of several commercial office and retail properties, enhancing asset value and subsequent sale price.
- Coordinated joint venture with San Francisco Redevelopment Agency for construction/lease up of 900 residential units, 20,000 sq. ft. of office space and 40,000 sq. ft. of retail.

Property Manager   March 1977 to December 1981
NORRIS, BEGGS AND SIMPSON, Los Angeles, California

Managed a $48 million, 1.2 million sq. ft. portfolio of commercial office and retail space. Directed tenant improvement projects and the mechanical system retrofit for 40,000 sq. ft. office building.

Club Manager   January 1972 to February 1977
LOS ANGELES ATHLETIC CLUB, Los Angeles, California

Directed all administrative, property management, front desk, accounting and food service functions for four affluent private clubs. Trained and supervised a staff of 92. Managed three major construction and facilities renovation projects.

PROFESSIONAL DEVELOPMENT:

- Completed all educational requirements for Broker's License and CPM (with AMO designation).
- Graduate of 200+ hours of professional training and development seminars, courses and workshops.
- Annual attendance at ULI national conventions, IREM local chapter meetings and seminars, and NNCREW national convention seminars for 10+ years.

PROFESSIONAL AFFILIATIONS:

Institute of Real Estate Management (IREM)
Building Owners and Managers Association (BOMA)
Urban Land Institute (ULI) — Full Member
National Network of Commercial Real Estate Women (NNCREW)
International Council of Shopping Centers (ICSC)

PAUL BERNSTEIN

3845 Shoreview Lane
Malibu, California 97381
(415) 967-8513

REAL ESTATE INDUSTRY EXECUTIVE

Property Acquisition / Finance / Leasing / Brokerage / Management / Divestiture

Well-qualified industry professional with extensive career building and managing profitable, mixed-use real estate portfolios, partnerships and syndications. Delivered consistent increases in portfolio valuation through innovative debt management, marketing and property operations. Expert negotiations experience.

PROFESSIONAL EXPERIENCE:

REALTY CENTER MANAGEMENT, INC., Los Angeles, California   1989 to Present

President & Chief Executive Officer
Managing General Partner (12 Real Estate Partnerships)

Recruited by Board of Directors to assume full P&L and operational management responsibility for a small property management company. Built firm from four employees to 100+ personnel managing a $250 million property portfolio throughout the U.S. (2500 apartment units and one million square feet of office and retail space).

Created corporate infrastructure, recruited qualified management personnel, introduced quality and productivity improvement initiatives, and established a united service goal at each property. Designed and implemented sound fiscal policies, budgetary systems and financial reporting structures. Established all policies, procedures and performance objectives.

- **Transitioned company from loss to breakeven within second year.** Achieved average annual profit growth of 100% throughout the past three years.

- **Increased average occupancy from 75% to 96%** through a series of strategic marketing initiatives.

- **Led the successful start-up of three new business divisions** (leasing, brokerage and construction) to expand the scope of RCMI's operations and provide comprehensive property management services to major account base.

- **Identified profitable opportunity to acquire, rehab and lease-up earthquake damaged apartments.** Acquired $1.6 million in funds from private investors for the acquisition of $4+ million in property, and orchestrated development, construction and marketing for the entire project. Current ROI averages 50% annually.

Serve as **Managing General Partner** for the firm's 12 real estate partnerships. Direct the acquisition (including due diligence), financial structuring, leasing, property management and divestiture activities for a $250 million mixed-use portfolio (four commercial office buildings, ten apartment complexes and two retail shopping centers).

- **Spearheaded an aggressive initiative to refinance troubled loans.** Negotiated new debt terms with lenders and creditors nationwide which reduced loan obligations by $40 million.

- **Structured debt relief transactions to minimize tax liabilities** and negotiated numerous Section 1031 tax free exchanges.

- **Provided expert witness testimony in bankruptcy court** regarding property valuations and feasibility of restructure/debt reduction plans.

PAUL BERNSTEIN

Page Two

PROFESSIONAL EXPERIENCE *(Continued)*:

PARKS, PALMER, TURNER & YEMENIDJIAN, Los Angeles, California   1980 to 1988

Partner

Fast-track promotion from Senior Accountant to Supervising Accountant to Manager to Partner (youngest ever in the history of this 12th largest public accounting firm in LA). Directed a $1 million tax practice servicing major real estate syndicators throughout the region. Concurrently, managed all tax planning, administration and management functions for the firm's 12 in-house real estate partnerships. Recruited, trained and supervised a 20-person professional and support staff.

Provided expert tax consultation for IPOs, foreign business ventures, high net worth individuals, publishers and high-technology development/manufacturing companies.

PEAT MARWICK MITCHELL & CO., Los Angeles, California   1978 to 1980

Staff Auditor/Senior Auditor

Planned and supervised audit engagements for clients in the manufacturing and entertainment industries.

EDUCATION & CERTIFICATIONS:

Masters in Business Taxation, University of Southern California, 1985

Bachelors in Economics (Magna Cum Laude), University of California, 1978

Certified Public Accountant, 1980

California Real Estate Broker License, 1981

References Provided Upon Request

JILL CLARKE

2514 Tree Line Drive
Cherry Hill, New Jersey 07896
(609) 654-8572

REAL ESTATE INDUSTRY PROFESSIONAL
Property Management / Leasing / Marketing / Tenant Relations

Twenty years experience in commercial and residential real estate. Consistently successful in increasing revenues, occupancy and income through expertise in building tenant relations and responding to tenant needs. Extensive qualifications in property/site renovation and construction, multi-year competitive leasing, multi-site property management and cost control/reduction. Outstanding communication and interpersonal relations skills.

PROFESSIONAL EXPERIENCE:

Broker of Record / Property Manager 1992 to Present
USI PROPERTY MANAGEMENT, INC., Clifton, New Jersey

Portfolio: *163,000 square feet of prime office space in a 3-building complex on 9 acres with large parking lots and extensive landscaping. Asset value of $13.5 million.*

Recruited as the Senior Broker and Property Manager with full P&L responsibility for the entire portfolio. Scope of responsibility includes daily operations management, marketing, leasing, construction, renovation, tenant relations, tenant retention, collections, outsourcing, contract negotiations, purchasing, ADA compliance, monthly financial reporting and general office/administrative affairs.

- Increased occupancy from 29% to 73% in less than three years.
- Negotiated a 10-year contract with Linens & Things for corporate headquarters operation. Instrumental in negotiation of long-term (minimum of 5-year), high-yield leases with McGraw Hill/ Dodge, New York Life/Sanus, and numerous other corporations.
- Managed $1.5 million renovation with responsibility for the entire project cycle, from initial consultations with architects/designers through bid and contract award to project planning, scheduling, costing and on-site supervision. Delivered project on-time and within budget.
- Planned and directed implementation of fiber optic cables in partnership with New Jersey Bell to ensure the latest in telecommunications technology for tenant companies.
- Negotiated outsourcing contracts for facilities maintenance/repair, janitorial services and property security. Consistently reduced expenditures while increasing quality and tenant satisfaction.

Vice President / Broker of Record / Property Manager 1991 to 1992
THE KAMSON CORPORATION, Englewood Cliffs, New Jersey

Portfolio: *230,000 square feet comprised of 3 office buildings and 11 luxury garden apartment complexes. Asset value of $200 million.*

Led the successful turnaround of the portfolio to meet investor and owner financial objectives. Held full responsibility for leasing, marketing, construction and renovation, tenant relations, cash flow management, financial reporting, ROI analysis and general administrative affairs. Spearheaded a high-profile marketing and public relations initiative to upgrade tenant quality. Directed staff of 30.

- Increased occupancy by 25% despite overall downward trend of real estate industry. Personally negotiated and closed over $750,000 in commercial leasing commitments within last six months.
- Managed a large-scale renovation to upgrade the facilities, properties and common areas of the portfolio as part of the initiative to increase tenant retention and improve market competitiveness.
- Negotiated and directed all maintenance and improvement work including electrical systems, HVAC conversions, elevators and grounds.

JILL CLARKE

Page Two

Association Manager   1988 to 1991
HILLS VILLAGE MASTER ASSOCIATION, Bedminster, New Jersey

   Portfolio: *153-acre, 1492-unit Association with 4000+ residents. Asset value of $4.5 million.*

Managed a master community association for one of the largest planned urban developments (PUD) in the U.S. Established policies and procedures, developed organizational infrastructure and created cooperative working relationships between home owners, builders and investors.

   • Launched a massive and successful public relations initiative (including Association TV channel) to expand communication between Association leadership and owners.
   • Personally negotiated and resolved a number of issues negatively impacting the Association, the owners and the PUD. Created definitive documents to educate owners regarding Association rules and responsibilities to enhance quality of life.

President / Broker / Managing Partner / Property Manager   1979 to 1988
BERGER MANAGEMENT COMPANY, Montclair, New Jersey

As President of The Berger Group, represented sellers, buyers and investors in commercial real estate sales transactions totalling several million dollars. As President of Berger Management Company, held full P&L responsibility for the leasing, marketing and management of 2500 residential and commercial units at 12 properties throughout the region.

Broker / Residential Manager / Sales Representative   1971 to 1979
LEO, DIAZ AND PICA, Bloomfield, New Jersey

   Brokered, marketed and leased residential and light commercial properties.

EDUCATION & PROFESSIONAL CERTIFICATIONS:

Certified Property Manager (CPM) Candidate, Institute of Real Estate Management, Current
Real Property Administrator (RPA), Building Owners and Managers Association, 1993
Registered Property Manager (RPM), International Real Estate Institute, 1993
Certified Real Estate Brokerage Manager (CRB), National Association of Realtors, 1985
Graduate Realtor Institute Designation (GRI), Bergen Community College, 1973
Licensed Real Estate Broker, State of New Jersey, Since 1975

PROFESSIONAL AFFILIATIONS:

National Association of Corporate Real Estate Executives (NACORE)
Building Owners and Managers Association International (BOMA)
Institute of Real Estate Management (IREM)
Industrial and Commercial Real Estate Women (ICREW)
International Real Estate Institute (IREI)
Community Association Institute (CAI)
Property Owners Association of New Jersey (POA)

ANN MARIE WASHINGTON
243 Front Road Apt. #45
Knoxville, Tennessee 64476
(423) 976-8748

CAREER OBJECTIVE:

Challenging **Laboratory Research / Research Management** position with a high-growth pharmaceutical or biotechnology company committed to pioneering research and product development.

SUMMARY OF QUALIFICATIONS:

Well-qualified and technically-proficient Research Scientist with more than five years laboratory experience and strong academic qualifications. Expertise in molecular diagnostics and microbiology, lab and field research, data collection/analysis and project management. Substantial experience in sophisticated research techniques and technologies.

Strong planning, organizational and communications skills. Extensive experience working with cross-functional engineering, scientific and research teams.

Clinical Laboratory Skills:	DNA purification, cloning, restriction enzyme analysis, PCR, transformation, gel electrophoresis, Western/Southern and slot blotting, plant/animal tissue culture, ELISA, colorimetric assays and radioactive materials management/control.
Computer Technology:	Excel, PowerPoint, Designer, SigmaPlot, Word, database applications and Internet tools.

EDUCATION:

Master of Science Degree / Major in Environmental Toxicology, July 1995
UNIVERSITY OF TENNESSEE, Knoxville, TN

> **Master's Thesis:** *"Bioavailability of Dissolved Organic Carbon in Surface Water by Surface and Subsurface Environmental Bacteria"*

Bachelor of Science Degree / Major in Biotechnology, May 1991
ROCHESTER INSTITUTE OF TECHNOLOGY, Rochester, NY

Associate of Applied Science Degree / Major in Chemistry, May 1988
DUTCHESS COMMUNITY COLLEGE, Poughkeepsie, NY

PROFESSIONAL EXPERIENCE:

Laboratory Research Assistant   1994 to Present
UNIVERSITY OF TENNESSEE (Center for Environmental Biotechnology), Knoxville, TN

Work in cooperation with a multi-disciplinary scientific and research team involved in the investigation/development of long-term strategies for the development of biotechnology systems for hazardous waste remediation. Utilize leading edge microbiological and molecular diagnostic techniques, procedures and technologies.

ANN MARIE WASHINGTON　　　　　　　　　　　　　　　　　　　　**Page Two**

UNIVERSITY OF TENNESSEE *(Continued)*

Analyze lab strain bacterial DNA and develop efficient/cost-effective methods for their rapid detection and impact upon the bacterial ecosystem. Currently working on the construction of a chromosomally integrated tod-lux gene fusion to develop an improved bioluminescent reporter strain for process monitoring and optimization of cometabolic TCE degradation.

Graduate Researcher　　　　　　　　　　　　　　　　　　　　1993 to 1994
OAK RIDGE NATIONAL LABORATORY / UNIVERSITY OF TENNESSEE, Oak Ridge, TN

Planned and conducted a series of microbiology and bioremediation research projects to gather data for Master's thesis. Directed experimentation, data analysis and results reporting over a 20-month period.

Focused research on the analysis of subsurface heterotrophic bacteria, its ability to metabolize dissolved organic carbon in surface water, and its effects on the cometabolization of organic pollutants.

Pharmaceutical Research Intern　　　　　　　　　　　　　　　1989 to 1990
BRISTOL-MYERS SQUIBB COMPANY, Syracuse, NY

Worked in cooperation with multi-functional product teams developing pharmaceuticals. Utilized sophisticated chromatographic and transfer system technologies to purify and quantify proteins used in various product development programs. (Summer 1990)

Participated in high-level research and toxicity analysis of antiviral drugs on murine hematopoietic progenitor stem cells. (Fall 1989/Winter 1990)

Research Intern　　　　　　　　　　　　　　　　　　　　　　1987 to 1988
IBM CORPORATION, East Fishkill, NY

Collected and analyzed water and air samples from solid state chip and electronic manufacturing facilities to determine composition of organic compounds, heavy metals and other characteristics. Operated within a stringent regulatory environment.

PROFESSIONAL ACTIVITIES:

Affiliation	Member, American Society for Microbiology
Public Speaking	Invited Presenter, "Comparison of the Availability of Dissolved Organic Carbon," slide presentation at the 94th General Meeting of the American Society for Microbiology, Las Vegas, May 1994
Military Service	U.S. Army National Guard (1985 to Present). Graduate, Officer Candidate School. Graduate, 15+ hours of management training. Earned six promotions within 10 years and numerous commendations.

PERSONAL PROFILE:

Born June 1, 1967. U.S. Citizen/Resident since 1974. Multilingual.

WILLIAM MICHAEL BROWN
349 Riverbend Road
Hackensack, New Jersey 09874
(609) 654-6887

OBJECTIVE

Seeking a management opportunity with a high-tech corporation in need of expert scientific knowledge to advance product development, accelerate business diversification, direct regulatory affairs and reduce potential risk/liability.

PROFESSIONAL PROFILE

Scientist / Researcher / Consultant with extensive qualifications in advanced technology, biotechnology and pharmacology for Johnson & Johnson, Bristol-Myers Squibb, NIH and world-renowned health care institutions. Transitioned career from advanced scientific and medical research to current focus on ethical and legal affairs associated with sophisticated technologies and medical devices.

Strong technological, research, project management and product liability litigation experience. Published Author and Public Speaker. B.Sc. and Ph.D. Degrees. Pending award of M.B.A. and J.D. Degrees.

PROFESSIONAL EXPERIENCE

Scientific Consultant - Pharmaceutical and Medical Devices
SILLS CUMMIS RADIN TISCHMAN EPSTEIN & GROSS, P.A., Newark, NJ
1994 to Present

Retained by Senior Partner to provide scientific expertise and research skills in the areas of pharmaceutical and medical devices product liability, regulatory affairs and medical malpractice.

• **Bristol-Myers Squibb**. Member of an exclusive national scientific research team providing guidance and backup for the legal teams representing client in hundreds of breast implant litigation cases. Review transcripts of depositions, trial testimony and interrogatories of expert witnesses and attending physicians in similar litigation cases to extrapolate relevant data and favorably position BMS. Prepare expert witnesses for depositions and trials. Prepare cross-examination outlines and briefing books. Research, analyze and report on scientific papers, statements and documentation. Utilize Westlaw, Dialog, Medline, Lexis/Nexis and WWW on-line research systems.

NOTE: *Manage full-time law firm responsibilities concurrent with pursuit of M.B.A. and J.D. degrees.*

Postdoctoral Fellow - Immunogenetics Laboratory
MEMORIAL SLOAN-KETTERING CANCER CENTER, New York, NY
1993 to 1994

Led an advanced research project on the immunogenetic characteristics and factors influencing the success of bone marrow transplantation.

Postdoctoral Fellow - Biological Research Laboratory
JOHNSON & JOHNSON, Raritan, NJ
1992 to 1993

Completed two advanced biological research studies through a funded research fellowship at J&J's Skin Biology Research Center.

WILLIAM MICHAEL BROWN - *Page Two*

Research Fellow in Neurology / NIH Visiting Fellow
HARVARD / BRIGHAM & WOMEN'S HOSPITAL / NIH
1991 to 1992

Joint appointment between Harvard Medical School, Brigham & Women's Center for Neurologic Diseases and the National Institutes of Health to investigate neurological factors impacting Alzheimer's Disease.

EDUCATION

J.D., New York Law School. Expected graduation in 1998.
M.B.A., Farleigh Dickinson University. Expected graduation in 1997.
Ph.D., University of Southampton, England, 1991. Clinical Neurological Sciences.
B.Sc., University of Southampton, England, 1988. Biochemistry & Chemistry.

Advanced Scientific Training at leading universities, biological laboratories and technology institutes in the U.K., Sweden, Germany, Spain and Italy.

HONORS, AWARDS & NOTABLE DISTINCTIONS

New York Law School Law Review (1995 to 1996)
Irving Mariash Scholarship (1994 to 1996)
NIH Visiting Research Fellowship (1991)
G.A. Kerkut Prize for Biochemistry (1988)
Wellcome Trust Research Scholarship (1987)

PROFESSIONAL AFFILIATIONS

American Management Association
American Assn. for the Advancement of Science
American Society for Quality Control
American Chemical Society
Regulatory Affairs Professional Society
Drug Information Association
International Society of Pharmaceutical Eng.

Royal Society of Chemistry
New York Academy of Sciences
Biochemical Society
Society for Clinical Trials
American Assn. of Pharmaceutical Scientists
Institute of Biology
Royal Microscopical Society

PUBLICATIONS

Author/Co-Author of 20+ journal articles and invited reviews, published in journals including the *Journal of Biological Chemistry, Cell, European Journal of Biochemistry, Biochemistry, Journal of Immunology* and *BioEssays*. Co-Author of a major monograph regarding the blood protein "Fetuin," published in 1995. Full listing provided upon request.

PHILLIP NEWTON
643 The Marshlands
Hilton Head Island, South Carolina 64731
(805) 647-1316

Resort Operator with successful career in Real Estate Sales & Marketing. Operated Private Equity and Semi-Private Country Clubs Nationwide.

Dynamic management career leading successful start-up, turnaround and high-growth resort and real estate operations nationwide. Combines expertise in strategic planning, sales, marketing and property development with an excellent track record in operations and P&L management, staffing and project coordination. Delivered strong and sustained revenue, asset, portfolio and profit gains within highly competitive markets. Bilingual English and Spanish.

- "General Manager of the Year" for Club Resorts (1993).
- Gubernatorial Appointment as Chairman of the Arizona State Tourism & Recreation Commission (1992-93).
- Certified Hotel Administrator (1992).

PROFESSIONAL EXPERIENCE:

President   1995 to Present
LONDON DOWNS, Hilton Head, South Carolina

> Promoted from Shangri-La by joint venture investment group (CCA/Melrose). Challenged to lead this 350-acre residential community with 18-hole Weiskopf/Morrish golf course through recapitalization, sales and marketing to final sell-out with projected revenues of $24 million. Responsible for operations and P&L including the development and marketing of riverfront and oceanfront lots targeted to an upscale clientele nationwide. Direct a staff of 40.

- Currently marketing equity memberships in affluent golf club projected to generate an additional $7 million in revenues at close-out. Finalized membership documents, authorized by-laws and regulations, and spearheaded initial market launch.
- Negotiated lines of credit with regional banking institutions to fund development of speculative housing product line.
- Reengineered core marketing and management processes resulting in 15% cost reduction.
- Created a successful property owner referral and incentive program.

> Currently finalizing planning stages of a limited partnership offering for a 7600 sq. ft. private clubhouse scheduled for construction in the Summer of 1997. In addition, completed planning development of tennis courts, pool, housing products and a high-end condominium project.

Vice President / General Manager   1990 to 1995
SHANGRI-LA RESORT, Phoenix, Arizona

> Recruited as General Manager to rebuild, revitalize and transition this property (800 acres with 400 lodge rooms, condominiums and private residences, conference facilities for 2000, and two 18-hole championship golf courses) out of bankruptcy and return to profitability. Finalized multi-million dollar refurbishment and complete reengineering of the entire organization, all sales and marketing programs, development, construction and operations. Led a team of 400 employees.

- Achieved turnaround objectives, reversing $1 million loss. Delivered $1+ million profit in two years.
- Identified opportunity, structured and negotiated joint venture with major development company with initial phase projected at $16 million in revenue; phase two at $55 million.
- Developed fractional fee project for golf course property to accelerate property sales.
- Renegotiated permanent property loan and saved 2% in annual interest expense. Successfully converted balance sheet loans to equity during loan restructuring.
- Promoted to Vice President. Authored real estate development and marketing plan.

PHILLIP NEWTON - *Page Two*

Executive Vice President & General Manager - Fairfield Glade   1988 to 1990
FAIRFIELD COMMUNITIES, Knoxville, Tennessee

Senior Operating Executive with full P&L responsibility for a diversified real estate and resort property, including lodge, country club, four golf courses, two full-service restaurants and 300+ residential units. Created strategic marketing, business and operations plans for the entire property, rental program and real estate operations (e.g., lots, construction, timeshare and residential home construction). Serviced a membership of 20,000+ owners, timeshare tenants and guests. Led a team of 750 employees.

- Increased operating profits by 6% despite downward economic trends within the real estate industry.
- Created high-profile sales and marketing campaigns to gain competitive advantage.
- Authored and instructed training programs in real estate, sales and resort management.
- Promoted to Corporate VP of Operations in six months to facilitate introduction of similar programs, services and operations throughout Fairfield's nationwide real estate and resort communities ($60 million division).

Senior Vice President - Acquisitions   1985 to 1988
FIRST RESORTS, INC., Telluride, Colorado

Dual responsibility for the sale/marketing of property management contracts to owners, developers and investors, and for the operating management of a $75 million portfolio of resort properties.

- Structured, negotiated and closed $6.5 million in contract acquisitions.
- Authored operating and marketing plans for complex turnaround resorts and associations. Co-developed real estate properties in the U.S. and Mexico, guided developers in preparing/closing financing documentation, and redesigned core business processes to reverse losses and accelerate revenue gains.

Vice President - Operations   1984 to 1985
MILES & COFFEE, Bangor, Maine

Senior Operating Manager of 220-room Sheraton Hotel with 20,000 sq. ft. of conference space. Developed new, 265-room Ramada Hotel ($19 million project) with full responsibility for staffing, start-up operations and grand opening marketing/promotions. Key participant in several other large development and acquisition projects.

Senior Vice President - Operations   1981 to 1984
C.E. PROPERTIES, New Orleans, Louisiana

Planned, budgeted and directed more than 12 renovation projects of hotels, resorts and condominiums owned and operated by this $100 million real estate syndicator. Managed acquisition projects, structured limited partnerships, and prepared/executed operating and marketing plans.

EDUCATION:

Business Administration - University of Akron
Graduate - Disney Approach to Quality Service
American Management Association

PROFESSIONAL AFFILIATIONS:

American Hotel/Motel Association (National Committee for Environmental Affairs)
Board of Directors, Arizona Hotel/Motel Association
Board of Directors, State Chamber of Commerce

ROBERT JACKSON
432 Jefferson Pike
Alexandria, Virginia 23455
(703) 647-6137

RETAIL SALES & OPERATIONS MANAGER
Building & Managing Multi-Site, High-Growth, High-Profit Operations

PROFESSIONAL EXPERIENCE:

BOAT / U.S. - RETAIL DIVISION, Alexandria, Virginia   1991 to Present

Fast-track promotion through a series of increasingly responsible sales and sales management positions with one of the nation's largest marine products retail corporations. Advanced rapidly based upon consistent increases in sales growth, profit improvement, merchandising, advertising and customer service/satisfaction.

Introduced a number of sales and operating strategies, procedures and programs that have subsequently been adopted throughout the corporation (e.g., SKU numbering system for ease in stock location, add-on sales promotions, project sales concepts), each of which has contributed to significant revenue improvement. Played a key management role in the planning, staffing and start-up of seven new retail stores nationwide. Position highlights include:

Manager - Atlanta Marine Center (1993 to Present)

Senior Sales and Operations Manager with full P&L accountability for a 10-employee, 10,000 square foot retail center. Scope of responsibility includes personnel recruitment and training, employee scheduling, sales, merchandising, product management, pricing, advertising, customer/member services, general accounting, budgeting, financial reporting and facilities management.

- Led the store through a critical and long-term computer conversion that adversely effected operations. Successfully directed sales and customer service functions despite administrative turmoil, introduced improved management practices to offset negative impact, and consistently outperformed previous year financial results.

- Brought store from #19 in overall performance (sales and gross margin) to #5 within one year. Delivered sales of $1.9 million and profits of 3.7% over previous year.

- Ranked #1 in the district (7 stores) for new member development, dollars per transaction, increase in gross margin and largest increase in sales for special incentive programs. Consistently ranked in the top five in the nationwide chain (34 stores).

- Reduced inventory shrinkage from $40,000 in first half of 1993 to less than $19,000 in second half through introduction of stringent product control, internal security and documentation procedures.

Manager - Los Angeles Marine Center (1992 to 1993)

Promoted to direct the start-up and subsequent management of the company's first-ever retail sales operation on the West Coast. Responsible for initial market penetration, gross margin performance, sales growth, expense control and inventory/product management.

- Brought store from start-up to $800,000 in sales within first year. Second year projections forecasted at $1.6 million.

- Consulted regarding the opening, staffing and advertising for two new West Coast start-ups.

- Received a commendation from the U.S. Coast Guard Auxiliary for contributions to boating safety.

ROBERT JACKSON - *Page Two*

BOAT / U.S. - RETAIL DIVISION *(Continued)*:

Assistant Manager - Chicago Marine Center (1991 to 1992)

Co-managed the chain's newest and largest retail operation (12,000 square feet with 18 employees). Instrumental in positioning the store for the most successful grand opening in the company's history with first day sales of $123,000 (projections of only $60,000).

- Achieved annual sales goal of $1 million within first 53 days of operation.

- Appointed to Special Projects Team that opened two new store locations within 10 days (from shell to full-scale operation).

Sales Associate / Assistant Manager in Training / Assistant Manager (1991)

Recruited as a Sales Associate in Atlanta. Promoted within 30 days to Assistant Manager in Training and within next 30 days to Assistant Manager responsible for personnel, scheduling, shipping, receiving, merchandising and in-store retail sales operations.

Previous Professional Experience (1988 to 1991) included positions in outside sales for a professional services company, trust administration for a large commercial bank, and customer/member relations with an exclusive private club.

EDUCATION:

BBA / Major in Marketing / Minor in Advertising, 1988
GEORGIA SOUTHERN COLLEGE, Statesboro, Georgia

References Provided Upon Request

RICHARD K. DILLARD

959 Fifth Avenue
New York, New York 13642
(212) 874-6416

EXECUTIVE PROFILE

Technically astute **Risk Management Professional** with expert qualifications in strategic risk financing strategies and management plans. Delivered strong and sustainable cost reductions while expanding coverages, maximizing premiums, reducing exposures and limiting liabilities. Talented negotiator and team leader with substantial contributions in problem solving, decision making and crisis management. Top-level advisor to executive operating, management, financial and legal teams worldwide.

PROFESSIONAL EXPERIENCE:

METLIFE INSURANCE COMPANY, New York, New York   1991 to Present
(Diversified insurance, financial services and real estate corporation with $180 billion total assets)

Manager of Risk Management

Led MetLife's Risk Management Organization through a period of significant internal change and reorganization to modernize, upgrade and enhance capabilities. Introduced leading edge information technologies to automate processes and expedite workflow. Designed training programs to enhance employee competencies and strengthen professional culture.

Scope of responsibility is diverse and includes strategic planning functions, technical operations, contract negotiations and renewals, automation, budgeting and staffing. Manage insurance for 300 company owned properties valued at $13 billion and for an additional $14 billion in mortgaged properties. Control $8 million in annual claims and litigation costs.

- Transformed Risk Management from a "white tower" function into a participative management culture and proactive business partner to Human Resources, Safety and Operations.
- Created template insurance requirements subsequently implemented throughout the entire corporation by MetLife's legal and operating units.
- Introduced a construction wrap-up program and innovative safety program that captured $4 million in cost savings on a $200 million renovation project.
- Pioneered innovative and expense reducing insurance programs and coverages including owner-controlled program for asbestos abatement liabilities, pilot program to integrate foreclosed properties, and several post-injury/return to work programs.
- Structured and formalized $35 million annual allocation system.
- Performed complex due diligence for large corporate merger and planned/directed subsequent risk management and financing programs.

SARASOTA COUNTY, Sarasota, Florida & **LEE COUNTY**, Fort Myers, Florida   1988 to 1991

Risk Manager

Directed property, casualty and employee benefit insurance programs for two large municipalities. Scope of responsibility covered law enforcement, fire, parks, public transportation, utility, 911, environmental services, Minnesota Twins Baseball Stadium and affiliated operations. Significantly improved coverages, expanded limits and reduced premiums each consecutive year. Managed all related litigation to successful conclusion.

- Restructured each organization's $13 million annual budget on an actuarially sound basis.
- Pioneered a proactive stance to safety management with design/instruction of safety training programs that consistently achieved regulatory compliance and reduced/removed exposures.
- Directed all risk management functions and related contractual agreements for construction of baseball stadium and $63 million bridge.
- Modernized benefit plans with implementation of Section 125 pre-tax premium plan, cafeteria plan and self-funded health plan.

RICHARD K. DILLARD   **Page Two**

SINGER CORPORATION, Stamford, Connecticut   1980 to 1988
(Diversified aerospace, automotive, furniture, gas meter, sewing products, simulator and tool manufacturer with sales of $2.4 billion)

Director of Risk Management (1988)
Manager of Risk Management (1980 to 1987)

Senior Risk Management Professional directing risk financing and claims administration with $19.5 million annual budget for 23 domestic and 10 international manufacturing locations. Coordinated contracts, leases and construction projects as direct intermediary with management and corporate legal counsel. Directed high-profile environmental litigation, acquisition and divestiture programs.

Supervised renewals for aircraft hull and liability, aircraft products, bonds, casualty, directors and officers, key man life, marine, nuclear liability, political risk, products liability, property and travel accident insurance. Travelled throughout the U.S. and Europe to manage carrier negotiations.

• Instituted sophisticated off-shore risk financing vehicles (e.g., ACE, Tortuga I & II) and managed the corporation's captive insurance subsidiary.
• Researched, documented and recovered a $15 million property and business interruption claim.
• Created global insurance program with a solid 30% reduction in annual premium costs.
• Reengineered core business processes within the risk management function and reduced staffing requirements while maintaining productivity.
• Rewrote corporate insurance manual, implemented premium reducing loss prevention engineering recommendations, and drove development of company-wide safety policies and regulations.

TECHNICON CORPORATION *(Revlon Subsidiary)*, Tarrytown, New York   1976 to 1980
(Multinational manufacturer of computerized blood analysis equipment with sales of $300 million)

Risk Manager

Recruited to launch the start-up of the corporation's first Risk Management Department. Given full autonomy for creating worldwide risk management program, administering corporate-wide employee benefit/retirement plans, directing loss prevention and managing OSHA compliance.

• Spearheaded an aggressive change management program. Redesigned employee loan accounting, replaced pension plan trustee, negotiated profit sharing investment fund rates, redesigned medical claims processing procedures and developed SPDs.
• Guided executive management in the development of optimal risk financing techniques.
• Appointed Chairman of the Products Liability and Corporate Safety Committees.

CHEMICAL CONSTRUCTION CORPORATION, New York, New York   1974 to 1976
(Wholly-owned subsidiary of General Tire Corporation)

Risk Manager

Designed and directed risk management programs with a $9 million insurance budget for 18 major projects worldwide. Concurrent responsibility for additional $7 million insurance program for the world's largest foreign liquid natural gas construction project.

• Created retro plan and reserve analysis audits yielding significant savings. Restructured insurance broker network from 7 to 2 to reduce costs and improve coverage. Launched development and leadership of Corporate Safety Committee.

EDUCATION:

B.S., Finance *(Magna Cum Laude Graduate)*
MARYMOUNT COLLEGE, Tarrytown, New York

WENDELL BROWN

94034 Ranchers Way
Richardson, Texas 65448
(654) 465-5441

EXECUTIVE SUMMARY:

SENIOR SALES & MARKETING EXECUTIVE
Advanced Information & Communications Technologies

Top-Producing Management Executive with more than 15 years experience directing national sales, marketing and technical service/support organizations. Combined expertise in leading edge technologies, strategic marketing, tactical sales and key account management. Outstanding record of achievement in complex account and contract negotiations. Multi-channel experience leading both direct sales teams and reseller networks nationwide.

PROFESSIONAL EXPERIENCE:

1989 to Present   **Director of Sales**, Connectware, Richardson, Texas

Technologies: Switches, Bridges, Routers, Hubs, Network Interface Cards & Network Management Software

Retained by AMP Incorporated following their 1993 acquisition of Netronix and start-up of Connectware. Challenged to build and lead a national sales organization of VARs and system integrators marketing Connectware technologies throughout the commercial and government markets.

Hold concurrent management accountability for nine sales managers directing key account relationships. Provide strategic planning and tactical support for major account negotiations and closings.

- Built Connectware's nationwide sales and marketing network to three national resellers producing $5+ million in annual sales.
- Delivered annual growth averaging 23% in a highly-competitive national market.
- Championed the development and spearheaded the market launch of several new technologies with cumulative revenues of $2 million annually.
- Guided sales managers/key account managers through several complex contract negotiations and closings.

Vice President of Sales, Netronix, Petaluma, California

Technologies: Bridges, Routers & Network Interface Cards

Recruited to build/lead a national sales and service/support organization with three regional managers, two support engineers, and a nationwide VAR and OEM network.

- Built revenues to $3.5 million annually with average annual sales growth of 53%. Captured an additional 7% in market share.
- Developed national reseller and OEM networks from ground floor to 50+ accounts.

1983 to 1989   **General Manager - National Accounts**, Businessland Inc., San Jose, California

Technologies: MIS Outsourcing

Promoted within the Businessland sales organization to launch the start-up of the corporation's first-ever technology outsourcing program. Created a turnkey business unit supplying packaged workstations, LAN products, service and training to world-wide locations of major corporate accounts.

WENDELL BROWN   *Page Two*

General Manager - National Accounts, Businessland Inc. *(Continued)*:

Developed the business infrastructure, wrote marketing plan, researched market opportunities and developed account relationships. Led cross-functional project teams from Businessland's technology, sales, service and support organizations in the development and delivery of client programs.

- Built new business venture from start-up to $15 million in revenue in two years.
- Structured, negotiated and closed customized outsourcing contracts with Chevron, Bank of America, Transamerica and Safeway.
- Established strong competitive position within this rapidly emerging market.

General Manager, Businessland Inc., San Francisco, California

Technologies: PC Workstations, Service & Training

Managed a combined corporate and retail sales center marketing technologies throughout the Bay Area. Directed a staff of three line managers (Sales, Service, Administration) and 31 sales, technical, training and administrative personnel.

- Built sales from $8 million to $14+ million with profitable key accounts throughout the corporate and municipal markets.
- Recruited and trained several of the top ranked sales associates in the corporation.

1981 to 1983   **District Manager**, Nixdorf Computer Corporation, San Mateo, California

Technologies: AS/400 Compatible Mainframes, Data Entry Mini Systems, Banking Terminals & POS Terminals

Full P&L responsibility for sales and branch offices in San Francisco, Denver, Seattle and Sacramento. Directed a staff of three line managers (Sales, Support, Administration) and 15 employees.

- Delivered 70%+ annual revenue growth in increasingly competitive markets.
- Personally negotiated and closed a $7 million sale (largest in Nixdorf's history).

1980 to 1981   **Branch Manager**, Pertec Computer Corporation, San Francisco, California

Technologies: Large Data Entry Minicomputer Systems

Managed branch and sales offices, key account relationships, new business development, technical support and sales recruitment/training programs in San Francisco, Sacramento and Denver. Directed a team of 15.

- Ranked as the #1 branch in the U.S. (35 total) with first year revenue growth of 30%+.
- Honored as the 1980 "Marketing Manager of the Year."

1969 to 1974   **Previous Professional Experience** in a series of increasingly responsible sales, marketing, branch management and national account management positions. Marketed mainframes, terminals and printers throughout California, Colorado, Utah, Montana and New Mexico.

- Top Revenue Producer with IBM, Decision Data Computer Corporation and Northern Telecom Systems Corporation.

EDUCATION:

UNIVERSITY OF CALIFORNIA AT LOS ANGELES (UCLA)
MBA Candidate (completed first year), 1969 to 1971
MS Degree / Engineering, 1968
BS Degree / Engineering, 1967

NORMAN SHWARTZ
839 Mountain View Terrace
Denver, Colorado 34165
(303) 885-6548

SENIOR SALES, MARKETING & BUSINESS DEVELOPMENT EXECUTIVE
Strong General Management and P&L Management Qualifications

Dynamic 17-year sales and marketing management career across broad industries, markets and accounts. Expert qualifications in identifying and capturing market opportunities to accelerate expansion, increase revenues and improve profit contributions. Extensive background in new product launch and product management.

Equally strong qualifications in financial planning/analysis, manufacturing and distribution operations management, human resources, training and development, administration, quality and change management. Excellent team building, team leadership and interpersonal relations skills.

PROFESSIONAL EXPERIENCE:

MOUNTAIN FRANCHISE, INC., Denver, Colorado   1995 to Present
(Developer of "Mountain Mike" Restaurants)

President

Challenged to launch an entrepreneurial venture, combining expertise in sales, marketing and general business management. Successfully negotiated rights with franchisor for five business locations throughout the Denver metro region. Researched specific areas throughout the region to identify prime markets for acquisition and/or start-up.

- Acquired first site in September 1995. Restructured service operations, implemented quality standards, designed unique marketing and advertising campaigns, and achieved 20% revenue growth over five months.
- Designed and instructed sales and customer service training programs for all personnel.
- Produced print, radio and television advertisements to expand market penetration.

BETTER LIVING COMPANY, Denver, Colorado   1994 to 1995
(Manufacturer of biomagnetic devices and electronics technology)

President / Director of Sales & Marketing

Senior Executive leading the start-up of a new manufacturing and distribution company marketing leading edge technology devices throughout emerging health care markets. Led company through complex R&D cycle, established manufacturing operations, recruited sales and marketing teams, designed administrative infrastructure, and accelerated business start-up.

- Transitioned business from concept to $750,000 in sales revenues within one year.
- Created an innovative distributor sales and incentive program that drove revenue growth 120% within six months.
- Demonstrated viability of the technology, created the appropriate marketing and promotional communications, and captured key accounts nationwide.
- Designed all internal financial, budgeting, sales management, customer management, technical support and operating policies and procedures.
- Set-up a complete and fully-functional manufacturing facility.
- Negotiated sale of corporation to major competitor for significant return to investor group.

NORMAN SHWARTZ

Page Two

DYNO NOBEL, INC., Denver, Colorado   1993 to 1994
($1 billion Norwegian manufacturer)

Regional Sales & Marketing Manager / Product Manager

Recruited by executive management to revitalize Western U.S. sales distribution network and facilitate new product launch throughout North America. Planned strategies and directed a team of eight sales distributors generating $200+ million in annual revenue throughout the Western U.S. Personally managed all key account sales presentations, negotiations and contract closings. Concurrently, led the market introduction of new products and technologies to 35 distributors throughout the U.S. and Canada.

- Achieved 12% revenue growth in one year to close 1994 at $225 million.
- Increased market share by 20% against strong international competition.
- Created marketing strategy for new product introduction and launched campaign that drove $600,000 in new revenue within first year.
- Ranked as a top business leader for success in virtually outplacing major competitor and positioning Dyno Nobel for strong, sustainable and long-term revenue/market growth.

PEABODY HOLDING COMPANY, Various Locations   1979 to 1992
($1 billion dollar diversified products manufacturer)

Fast-track promotion from Industrial Engineer to Buyer to Senior Buyer to Purchasing Manager to:

Vice President/General Manager - Sales & Marketing

Planned, implemented and directed all sales, marketing, new business development and customer service/retention programs for a wholly-owned, $20 million manufacturing subsidiary. Directed a field sales organization of seven.

- Delivered 55% revenue growth within two years.
- Realigned sales focus on emerging growth markets nationwide, increasing profitability 26% and IBIT to 10%.
- Introduced sales training and leadership development programs for field sales team.
- Restructured all sales administration and reporting processes to increase sales team's "time to sell" and further accelerate revenue growth.

EDUCATION:

B.S., Industrial Technology, Southern Illinois University, 1981
A.S., Mining Technology, Rendlake College, Illinois, 1978

Graduate of more than 100 hours of professional sales and marketing training.

References Provided Upon Request

NINA EL DORADO
8547 Central Park West
New York, New York 18549
(212) 984-5351

SENIOR OPERATING & MANAGEMENT EXECUTIVE
President / Vice President / Regional Director / General Manager

---

Dynamic management career building market presence, establishing profitable businesses and driving revenue growth throughout domestic and international markets. Combines general management, P&L and operating management experience with core competencies in marketing, business development and cross-cultural business management. Expertise in start-up, turnaround and high-growth organizations.

PROFESSIONAL EXPERIENCE:

ESTÉE LAUDER INTERNATIONAL, INC., New York, New York   1990 to 1995

Vice President / Regional Director - Asia/Pacific

Recruited by previous employer to return to the corporation and assume full P&L, operating and marketing management responsibility for their fastest growing and most profitable business region. Lived and worked in Hong Kong, Singapore, Sydney, Brussels and New York.

- **Accelerated market growth and built sales from $124 million to $300 million (130% gain).**

Scope of responsibility includes 11 Country Managers/General Managers, 3000+ employees and operations worldwide. Portfolio included two large manufacturing facilities and complete sales, marketing, MIS, human resources, distribution and administrative operations in all countries.

- Delivered strong and sustainable revenue gains in all markets: Australia (55%), China (100%), Hong Kong (31%), Indonesia (150%), Korea (740%), Malaysia (39%), New Zealand (59%), Philippines (50%), Singapore (29%), South Africa (67%), Taiwan (428%) and Thailand (201%).

- Launched the start-up of operations in Korea and Thailand (transition from independent distributor to affiliate), building total revenues to more than $24 million in four years. Steered Korean affiliate through crisis involving government officials not favorably disposed to foreign companies.

- As Managing Director of Australian company (1991), rebuilt management team, and introduced a series of productivity improvement and cost reduction programs. Managed worldwide press relations and crisis communications resulting from critical product issues.

- As Managing Director of Belgium affiliate (1990), restructured sales terms for significant profit gain to local company, recruited replacement management team, and facilitated merger of three markets into new affiliate.

- Restructured trading terms for Hong Kong affiliate and saved $100,000 annually.

- Restructured discount programs to brand-driven rebates with the largest South African trading partner. Resulted in a $300,000+ annual cost savings to Estée Lauder.

NINA EL DORADO - *Page Two*

CALVIN KLEIN COSMETICS CORPORATION, New York, New York   1987 to 1989

Vice President - International
Senior Operating Executive with full P&L responsibility for Calvin Klein Cosmetics' International Division. Led a team of 500 throughout the U.S., Canada and Europe.

- Increased sales from $3 million to $13 million within first year.

- Launched the start-up of Canadian subsidiary and achieved profit within first year.

- Transitioned U.K. operation from subsidiary to affiliate to rejuvenate market penetration and brought to profitability within first year.

- Structured/negotiated with French company to manage distribution in Western Europe.

CHOCOLATERIE CORNE TOISON DOR USA, INC., New York, New York   1982 to 1987

President
Challenged to launch an entrepreneurial venture and build new markets throughout the U.S. and Canada. Acquired exclusive distribution rights with famous Belgian confectionery and negotiated leasing agreement in the Trump Tower. Established the entire operating infrastructure, created order processing and distribution management policies, and launched high-profile marketing and business development programs targeted to upscale, affluent consumers.

- Built company from start-up to over $1.5 million in annual revenues (35% average growth rate).

- Won placement in retail accounts including Neiman Marcus, Bloomingdale's and I. Magnin.

ESTÉE LAUDER INTERNATIONAL, INC.   1974 to 1982

Area Director - Europe (1980 to 1982)
Promoted to revitalize and expand presence throughout nine major European markets for the complete portfolio of Estée Lauder, Aramis and Clinique products. Challenged to identify and capitalize upon opportunities to build revenues, increase earnings and outperform competition.

- Directed a multinational business group with marketing and management expertise throughout multiple foreign markets/cultures. Drove sustained revenue growth.

General Manager - South Africa (1974 to 1980)
Recruited to build an organization for the manufacture, packaging and marketing of Estée Lauder, Aramis and Clinique products throughout the South African market. Led project from concept through site selection, operations start-up, market launch and accelerated growth.

- Grew company by 830% with revenues increasing from less than $1 million to $10+ million. Achieved #2 industry ranking.

- Increased prime store distribution by 500% through expertise in key account development, relationship management and retention.

- Planned and executed one of the most successful new product introductions in the history of South Africa (Clinique).

Early Professional Experience:

Marketing Manager/Production Manager, Coty, Inc., South Africa   1969 to 1974
Assistant Plant Manager, Pfizer Laboratories, Inc., South Africa   1967 to 1969

EDUCATION: **B.S., Pharmacy**, Rhodes University
HONORS: Who's Who of South Africa
CITIZENSHIP: U.S.A.

PAUL REDPATH

854 Spring Garden   Home   (310) 654-9897
Placentia, California 98354   Office (310) 381-9957

SENIOR SALES / MARKETING / BUSINESS DEVELOPMENT EXECUTIVE
Health Care Industry

Dynamic domestic and international marketing career spanning 63 countries worldwide. Expertise in identifying and capitalizing upon market opportunity to introduce new products, reposition existing product lines and drive sustained revenue, market and earnings growth. Launched global introduction of 30+ products throughout career and negotiated high-profile partnerships with leading health care providers worldwide.

PROFESSIONAL EXPERIENCE:

DENTSPLY INTERNATIONAL IMPLANT DIVISION, Encino, California   1995 to Present
(Manufacturer of dental equipment and devices)

International Business Director

Full P&L responsibility for all sales, marketing and business development programs for Dentsply implant international operations. Direct international market development manager, international sales/marketing coordinators, support staff and 40 distributors in 40 countries worldwide. Challenged to reengineer existing marketing operations, refocus strategic plans and expand inter-company sales programs to accelerate revenue growth and improve competitive market position.

- Transitioned international division from 15% below previous year to 15% over within first six months to close 1995 at $12 million in sales. Opened four new markets during first nine months.

- Created a distribution partner evaluation process and model to identify top performers and reengineer distribution network. Concurrently, introduced recognition and incentive programs to further drive revenue growth.

- Designed internal, performance-based incentive programs for Dentsply sales teams.

IOLAB CORPORATION (Johnson & Johnson Company), Claremont, California   1985 to 1995
(Manufacturer of ophthalmic devices, equipment and pharmaceuticals)

Director of International Business Development (1994 to 1995)

Directed worldwide marketing programs for the affiliate and its independent distributor networks in 63 countries. Led market research, market planning, product launch, campaign management and advertising/promotions. Travelled worldwide.

- Designed and implemented an international product support matrix process to standardize and expedite product launches. Expanded communications structure between headquarters and worldwide sales organizations to respond to specific marketing, advertising, regulatory and promotional needs.

- Established framework to develop a network of international product development champions in Europe, Australia and Canada. Personally negotiated relationships with leading surgeons to advance IOLAB's product marketing and global launch initiatives.

Marketing Manager, Small Incision Devices (1992 to 1994)

Senior Management Executive responsible for the strategic planning and leadership of a global marketing initiative for $50 million product line. Held collateral executive-level responsibility for providing marketing direction for conventional cataract surgery implant product line (additional $10 million annually in worldwide sales). Led cross-functional project teams responsible for product development and market launch. Impacted markets in 63 countries on 5 continents.

PAUL REDPATH   *Page Two*

IOLAB CORPORATION *(Continued):*

Directed the complete marketing programs for both product lines. Developed marketing plans, prepared financial and product forecasts, analyzed competitor activity and market trends, and created integrated campaigns (e.g., advertising, direct sales, direct mail, trade shows, promotions). Negotiated patent licensure agreements and developed high-impact affiliate training/support opportunities.

- Grew small incision device market share from less than 5% to 22.9% (5 points higher than overall national share of all IOLAB products).

- Launched the introduction of 15 new products which grew to 35%+ of total surgery revenues.

- Transitioned cross-functional strategic planning process from corporate to business segment level for a substantial improvement in product development and marketing capabilities.

- Formalized product line identification process to create a standardized model for use throughout the corporation and all major operating divisions.

- Developed and implemented a forecast by product segment process, reducing complexity, expediting budgeting and saving substantial labor costs.

- Spearheaded development of a product champion concept, negotiated alliances with leading surgeons nationwide, and provided platform for product promotion and market expansion.

Product Director, 3 Piece Intraocular Lenses (1988 to 1991)

High-profile position leading the development, diversification, marketing and management of a high-growth product line. Consulted with surgeons nationwide to identify their specific product requirements and facilitated product development with manufacturing and engineering teams. Authored marketing plans, business plans, sales forecasts and other management tools.

- Led development and launch of 3 piece PMMA product line (now $15+ million in annual sales).

- Introduced seven new product models for the Prolene line (additional $4 million in sales).

- Streamlined product initiation process and forecasting model to reduce development cycle by more than six weeks.

- Created new hire orientation and sales training process.

Sales Representative (1985 to 1988). Increased territory from $10,000 to $90,000 per month. Appointed as one of only 10 field sales associates to Sales Rep Advisory Board (internal focus group providing critical direction for new product development, pricing and marketing).

3M CORPORATION, Nashville, Tennessee   1981 to 1985

Sales Representative - Dental Products. Built territory from $400,000 to $1.2 million in sales. Exceeded quota by 20%+ per year. Sales Trainer for new hires.

EDUCATION: **B.S., Mass Communications**, Middle Tennessee State University, 1980

Medical Marketing Course, UCLA
Total Quality Management Training, IOLAB Corporation
Xerox PSS II & III Sales Training, 3M Corporation & IOLAB Corporation

MARGARET WELLINGTON

2343 Kennedy Street
Arlington, Virginia 29771
(703) 644-9854

SENIOR SALES & MARKETING MANAGEMENT EXECUTIVE
Expert in New Business Development, Key Account Management & Account Retention

Top-performing Sales & Marketing Executive with 15 years experience building market presence and driving revenue growth within highly competitive markets nationwide. Delivered strong and sustainable revenue gains through combined expertise in organizational leadership, sales training and development, application selling and customer relationship management. Natural communicator and team leader with strong motivational skills and the ability to build, produce and succeed.

PROFESSIONAL EXPERIENCE:

AT&T BUSINESS MULTIMEDIA GROUPWARE SERVICES
(Acquired Western Union Business Communication Services)

1990 to 1996

Regional Vice President - Washington, D.C.

Senior Sales & Marketing Executive with full P&L responsibility for the leadership of all business development, account management and relationship management programs for AT&T business throughout the Eastern U.S., Central U.S. and Puerto Rico.

Scope of responsibility included six branch managers and a 100-person field sales and technical support organization. Defined annual marketing and revenue goals, developed sales plans and MBO's, created new profit centers and designed internal training and incentive programs.

Sales & Marketing Achievements

- Led the region through a period of sustained growth and expansion with revenues increasing from $35 million in 1990 to $60+ million in 1995. Delivered 50% revenue growth within vertically aligned sales branches.
- Developed and deployed business-wide methodology for revenue forecasting and goal attainment. Resulted in a 15%+ improvement in close ratio, 25%-30% annual revenue growth and 10% gain in market share.
- Created alternative distribution channel (via resellers and agents) with 100% annual revenue growth for three consecutive years.
- Directed successful negotiations for 10 multi-million dollar customer accounts (e.g., Pepperidge Farm, The American Red Cross, Morgan Stanley, State Street Bank, Tupperware, New York Times, Carnival Cruise Lines, Intercorp/Cigna).

Organizational Leadership & Management Achievements

- Devised innovative sales contests and incentives that drove $8 million in incremental revenue.
- Spearheaded creation of career ladder concept focusing on certification for all account executives and technical support personnel.
- Qualified over 60% of branch managers and account executives for AT&T President's Club.
- Created a portfolio of first-time marketing strategies and sales programs to gain competitive wins.

MARGARET WELLINGTON   *Page Two*

WESTERN UNION BUSINESS COMMUNICATION SERVICES   1981 to 1990

Fast-track promotion through a series of increasingly responsible sales management positions delivering sophisticated telecommunications solutions to commercial and industrial accounts. Career highlights included:

Branch Manager - Washington, D.C. (1988 to 1990)

Full P&L responsibility for the strategic planning, development, marketing, staffing, budgeting and operating leadership of a 20-person sales, marketing and service organization. Marketed a complete portfolio of teleprocessing services including E-Mail, EDI, voice and data communications.

- Consistently exceeded revenue plan and qualified for three consecutive "Pro Club" awards.
- Awarded the 1989 "Top Branch Manager of the Year" for highest sales performance nationwide.
- Negotiated GSA contract and schedule for telecommunications services to expand Western Union's penetration within the federal government market.

Branch Sales Manager - Boston, Massachusetts (1987 to 1988)

Led a team of eight sales professionals marketing complete telecommunications services, products and technologies to high-end key accounts throughout New England. Full P&L responsibility for revenue growth and performance.

- Built sales by 15% within first year through introduction of application sales techniques and associated training programs.
- Pioneered innovative account management program integrating pre-call planning, objective setting and relationship management strategies.

National Account Manager - Phoenix, Arizona (1985 to 1986)

Independently managed sales, service and expansion of Western Union's largest commercial account (American Express). Led cross-functional project, technical and sales team.

- Built account revenue by $4 million and retained customer despite aggressive competition. Qualified for "Pro Club" each year.

District Sales Manager - San Diego, California (1983 to 1984)

Led a 10-person sales, marketing and service team managing customer relationships throughout Southern California and Arizona.

- Ranked #1 in the Western Region for revenue growth. Qualified for "Pro Club."

Account Executive - Los Angeles, California & Phoenix, Arizona (1981 to 1983)

- Ranked #1 in new business development. Qualified for "Pro Club" in 1981 and 1982.

EDUCATION: **BBA Degree**, University of Iowa, 1980
                   MBA Program, AT&T Headquarters, 1992

JOHN POWELL

4012 South 12th Street
Federal Way, Washington 55124
(205) 314-4731

SECURITY PROFESSIONAL

Fifteen years of increasingly responsible management experience as Criminal Investigator and Administrator. Combines strong field experience with excellent qualifications in departmental management, budgeting, resource allocation and reporting. Expert in law enforcement training and inter-agency relations. Extensive experience in the U.S. and abroad. Hold direct responsibility for:

- Asset & Personnel Protection
- Emergency Planning & Preparedness
- Crisis Response & Crowd Control
- VIP Protection Services
- Community Outreach & Education

- Electronic Surveillance
- Interviewing & Investigations
- Fraud Investigation & Documentation
- Discreet Surveillance
- Tactical Field Operations

PROFESSIONAL EXPERIENCE:

THE GENESIS CORPORATION, INTERNATIONAL, Marysville, Washington   1994 to Present

Founded and currently operate an exclusive training firm specializing in security, leadership, supervisory development and safety education for law enforcement agencies nationwide.

- Completed numerous training engagements including presentations to 47 law enforcement agencies throughout the State of Washington.

- Currently pending certification with Police Officers Standards & Training Commission (POST).

EVERETT POLICE DEPARTMENT, Everett, Washington   1986 to 1994

Supervisor of Detectives (1992 to 1994)
Operations Supervisor (1989 to 1992)
Patrol Officer / Special Operations Unit (1986 to 1989)
Promoted rapidly through a series of increasingly responsible law enforcement and management positions in this 75,000-resident community. Earned several commendations for outstanding service to the department and local residents.

- As Supervisor of Detectives, challenged to reorganize and streamline the operations of a detective section downsized in response to budgetary constraints. Restructured and expanded operations despite shortage of fiscal and personnel resources. Managed all property crime investigations for the department (e.g., fraud, robbery, theft, burglary). Worked cooperatively with other state and federal law enforcement agencies.

- Conducted a large-scale investigation of welfare fraud throughout the State of Washington. Reported findings to the State Capital and detailed specific actions to resolve abuse. Resulted in $14 million savings to the State.

- Designed, developed and instructed a series of community outreach programs designed to increase resident knowledge of safety and security. Led hundreds of presentations to fraternal groups, business groups, schools and non-profit organizations. Won the "City Employee of the Month" award for training efforts.

JOHN POWELL - Page Two

CITY OF GREEN RIVER POLICE DEPARTMENT, Green River, Wyoming   1982 to 1985

Narcotics Detective / Patrol Officer
Provided patrol/undercover surveillance in this 10,000-resident community and regional drug trafficking center. Served as Relief Watch Commander responsible for the operations bureau.

- Designed and led training for narcotics and the tactical unit (SWAT).
- Presented and lobbied before the Senate Subcommittee for successful passage of law enforcement bill to protect the rights and lives of police officers.

MILITARY SERVICE:

U.S. NAVY RESERVES (1992 to Present)

Leadership position with an elite group of Naval Reservists supporting full-time, active duty Naval forces worldwide. Secret Security Clearance (pending).

U.S. ARMY - ACTIVE DUTY (1975 to 1980)

Completed three-year tour of duty in Germany and tour at Fort Leavenworth, Kansas. Prepared and administered multi-million dollar operating budget for 1600 enlisted personnel and officers. Designed and directed implementation of a Professionalism Program, Equal Opportunity/Race Relations Seminars and numerous job training workshops. Honorably discharged.

- Won the 1979 "European Soldier of the Year Award."

U.S. MARINE CORPS - ACTIVE DUTY (1967 to 1971)

Long Range Patrol Leader/Reconnaissance Team Leader. Completed two-year tour of duty in Vietnam. Honorably discharged.

MILITARY HONORS & AWARDS

Earned numerous military honors and awards for outstanding leadership skills and field performance. A brief listing includes:

- Naval Commendation Medal
- Combat Action Ribbon
- Vietnamese Service Medal (one silver star and two bronze stars)
- Vietnamese Cross of Gallantry
- Vietnamese Civil Action w/palm
- Vietnamese Campaign Medal
- Army Commendation Medal w/oak leaf cluster
- Air Assault Wings

EDUCATION:

CENTRAL WASHINGTON UNIVERSITY, Edmonds, Washington
Major in Public Administration (B.S. Candidate), 1992 to 1993

WESTERN WYOMING COLLEGE, Rock Springs, Wyoming
A.A. Degree in Law & Justice, 1984
Student of the Year Award, 1983

DOUGLAS McDANIELS

938 Manassas Trail
Fairfax, Virginia 23754
(703) 232-6413

SENIOR OPERATING & MANAGEMENT EXECUTIVE

Dynamic management career building and leading successful corporations through complex start-up, turnaround and high-growth cycles. Sixteen years of progressively responsible management and P&L experience. MBA Degree. Fluent Spanish. Expertise includes:

- Strategic Business Planning
- Marketing & Business Development
- Staffing & Management Development
- Advertising, Promotions & Incentives
- Quality & Productivity Improvement

- Corporate Finance & Budgeting
- Acquisition & Divestiture Negotiations
- Multi-Site Operating Management
- Cost Containment & Profit Growth
- Customer Service & Retention

Delivered strong and sustainable revenue and profit gains within
highly competitive markets nationwide.

PROFESSIONAL EXPERIENCE:

STEUART PETROLEUM COMPANY, Washington, D.C.   1988 to 1996

Vice President (1990 to 1996)
General Manager (1988 to 1990)

Senior Operating Executive leading this corporation's largest division through tremendous growth, from 10 operating locations generating $20 million in annual revenue to 78 locations with revenues surpassing $150 million. Held full P&L responsibility, all strategic and business planning functions, finance and budgeting, operating management, marketing, human resources, MIS and administrative affairs.

Financial Achievements:

- Delivered annual revenue growth up to 30% annually within a highly competitive market.
- Launched an aggressive reengineering of existing operations to reduce costs, improve service and accelerate profit gains. Reduced operating costs by more than 8%.
- Orchestrated an aggressive acquisition program totalling over $10 million annually to fund expansion and capital improvement. Personally led and/or participated in 57 acquisitions during a two-year period.
- Accelerated cash flow by more than $700,000 within just one year.

Operating Achievements:

- Developed dynamic organizational infrastructure responsive to the constantly changing market, financial and customer demands.
- Created high-profile marketing, advertising, service and employee incentive programs critical to the company's sustained growth cycle.
- Spearheaded successful corporate culture change to partner operations with field sales and improve customer service delivery. Created new positions and pioneered employee process ownership, team building and participative management strategies.
- Appointed to Executive Committee in 1991, providing strategic and operating support for $500 million corporation.

NOTE: Negotiated sale of operating units to six buyers in 1996. Designed strategies to position units, identified buyers, managed negotiations and closed transactions.

DOUGLAS McDANIELS

Page Two

EXXON COMPANY USA, Houston, Texas   1980 to 1988

Fast-track advancement through a series of increasingly responsible management positions. Promoted rapidly based upon consistent contributions to revenue and profit improvement.

Marketing Advisor - HQ Staff (1987 to 1988)

Spearheaded nationwide marketing program to launch the development and introduction of customer-driven service programs to improve Exxon's competitive positioning nationwide. Led project from concept through extensive market research to development of all marketing, promotional and business development campaigns. Designed associated training programs, incentives and fee structures to introduce throughout more than 5000 operating units nationwide.

District Manager (1984 to 1987)

Senior Operating Manager with full P&L responsibility for 45 company-owned operating locations throughout the Houston metro region. Challenged to improve customer retention and gain market share within this well-established $100 million business. Led a team of 300 through five direct reports.

- Delivered a 50% improvement in annual profit margins through a series of well-orchestrated staff reductions, renegotiation of key vendor contracts and introduction of a number of operating efficiency/productivity programs.
- Created a portfolio of top-producing customer promotions and employee incentives.
- Guided corporate HQ in the evaluation of investment decisions and the selection of specific sites for business expansion.

Store Supervisor (1983 to 1984)

Directed a five-site, 70-employee chain generating $10 million annually. Scope of responsibility included multi-unit operations, human resources, budgeting, financial reporting, marketing, advertising and customer service.

Marketing Analyst (1981 to 1983)

Transitioned expertise from field to corporate HQ to facilitate the automation and improvement of field and staff functions. Introduced fully-integrated MIS system and advanced order entry technology.

Construction Maintenance Engineer (1980 to 1981)

Coordinated construction programs within a six-state region during a period of rapid growth and corporate expansion.

EDUCATION:

MBA (Management), Loyola College, Baltimore, Maryland, 1983
BS (Civil Engineering), Drexel University, Philadelphia, Pennsylvania, 1980

PETER CAVANAUGH
934 Old Mexico Trail
Albuquerque, New Mexico 55971
(915) 644-3221

SENIOR OPERATING & MANAGEMENT EXECUTIVE
Building Corporate Value & Increasing Corporate Earnings

*Strategic Business Planning / Multi-Site Operations Management / Corporate Finance & Investment
Sales & Marketing Leadership / Human Resources / Negotiations / Worldwide Business Affairs*

Results-driven Management Executive with 20 years experience leading successful start-up and high-growth companies, acquisitions, divestitures and partnerships. Consistently successful in identifying and capitalizing upon market opportunities to drive revenue and profit growth. Strong general management, P&L management, negotiations and deal making experience.

PROFESSIONAL EXPERIENCE:

President   1994 to 1996
D3 IMAGE, INC., Santa Fe, New Mexico

Led start-up company through R&D and initial product launch of new digital technology for non-traditional business markets. Positioned technology for commercialization and global market sale throughout the printmaking and photography industries (global $5 billion industry).

Built initial operating infrastructure of the corporation, recruited technology team, spearheaded initial marketing efforts, and identified/closed key sales agreements.

NOTE: Negotiated the profitable sale to the Vaughan Morgan Company of Dallas in October 1996.

President   1981 to 1994
DRI EQUITY CORPORATION, Kansas City, Missouri

Founded and managed a new commercial venture specializing in real estate development, construction and property management. Built company from concept into a multi-million dollar enterprise. Scope of responsibility was diverse and included:

Strategic Planning & Business Development

- Authored strategic business, financial and marketing plans to facilitate company start-up, accelerate market growth and strengthen financial returns. Designed operating policies and procedures for all core operations.

Marketing & Business Development

- Led the corporation through explosive growth and award of 20+ major development contracts throughout the Midwest and California. Completed over $100 million in projects on time and within budget. Spearheaded innovative marketing, business development, sales and promotional campaigns to gain competitive market advantage.

Lending & Investment Management

- Structured and negotiated complex financing, investment and lending agreements/partnerships with financial institutions throughout the U.S., Canada, Germany and Japan. Built and managed long-term investment and partnership agreements with Shearson Lehman, E.F. Hutton and other leaders within the financial services industry.

PETER CAVANAUGH - *Page Two*

DRI EQUITY CORPORATION *(Continued):*

Corporate Accounting & Finance

- Designed and implemented budgeting, general accounting, project accounting, financial analysis and financial reporting systems to meet the changing requirements of the corporation and individual partnership agreements.

Human Resources Management

- Created all HR policies and management systems for 20+ permanent employees and several hundred subcontractors. Designed benefit and compensation plans, administered insurance coverages and developed recordkeeping procedures. Implemented incentive programs which consistently increased productivity, cost-efficiency and quality of operations.

Operating Management

- Developed and directed all general management functions, including purchasing, vendor sourcing, legal affairs, external accounting and auditing, information technology, and administration.

Board Member / General Partner   1981 to 1985
FIRST CITIBANK, Olathe, Kansas

Member of a six-person investment partnership that applied for and received a new bank charter from the State of Kansas Banking Commission in a highly-competitive award process. Facilitated complex strategic, business, financial and market planning to launch start-up and build the organization. Recruited senior operating team, established lending and credit policies, managed investment and asset growth, and spearheaded marketing initiatives.

- Instrumental in building the institution from assets of $1.5 million to over $18 million within first two years of operation.

President   1974 to 1980
FRONTIER REALTORS, Olathe, Kansas

Following college graduation, founded a real estate brokerage which grew to become one of the most successful in the region. Personally recruited and trained 30+ agents. Managed all marketing and business development functions, sales, leasing, contract negotiations, financing and banking transactions. Designed operating policies and procedures, budgets, financial reporting and sales tracking systems, and all general administrative/management functions.

- Built sales volume to more than $50 million annually and positioned Frontier as the #1 real estate sales organization in the market.

NOTE: Negotiated the profitable sale to a well-established Kansas City brokerage in 1980.

PROFESSIONAL ACTIVITIES:

Member of the Board of Directors, Chairperson and/or Management Consultant with numerous for-profit and non-profit organizations throughout career. A brief listing includes:

- Chairman, Johnson County Safe Home Shelter
- Member, President Reagan's Republican Inner Circle
- President, Johnson County Planning Commission
- Board of Directors, Missouri Bank & Trust
- Board Member/Volunteer, Kansas City Art Institute (Trustee for Fine Arts College), Kansas City Lyric Theater, Children's Mercy Hospital, Crippled Children's Nursery School, Nelson Art Gallery.

EDUCATION: **Bachelor of General Studies Degree**, University of Kansas, 1973

JEFFREY COLLINS
9403 Overland Pass
Portland, Oregon 96884
(651) 648-6515

SENIOR-LEVEL OPERATING & MANAGEMENT EXECUTIVE
Sales & Marketing / Global Expansion / Operations / Administration / P&L Management

Dynamic 20+ year management career leading successful start-up, turnaround, transition and high-growth corporations. Expert in identifying and capitalizing upon market opportunity to build revenue, capture key accounts and outperform competition. Strong presentation, negotiation and transactional skills.

- Strategic & Marketing Planning
- Corporate Finance & Investment
- Corporate Administration
- Human Resource Affairs
- Information Systems Technology

- Acquisition & Divestiture Transactions
- Multi-Million Dollar Buy/Sell Transactions
- Engineering & Project Management
- Regulatory & Legislative Affairs
- Quality & Productivity Improvement

PROFESSIONAL EXPERIENCE:

President & CEO   1983 to Present
PACIFIC UTILITIES MGMT., INC.

Led start-up company from incorporation to market success with over $57 million in annual sales revenues. Established presence in the U.S. and Pacific Rim as a pioneer in turnkey micro-utility™ services and trademarked new business market.

Hold full strategic planning, operating and P&L responsibility for the corporation. Accountable for business planning and development, sales/marketing, engineering, technical services, administration, finance, accounting, MIS and human resources. Direct large, multi-million dollar engineered-to-order construction projects.

- Built relationships with major corporate customers, including Marriott Corporation, Hilton Hotels, Westin Hotels, Kyocera Industries and Goodyear.

- Personally structured, negotiated and closed a $48 million contract with additional $27 million in long-term service and operating maintenance revenues.

- Developed 26 operating locations throughout the U.S. and Pacific Rim (total investment of more than $95 million).

- Transacted successful acquisition of a marginally profitable multiple services company. Structured and negotiated 100% stock buy-out using termed earned out strategy (allows seller to pay based on long-term performance). Acquired company with no cash outlay, launched aggressive reorganization, increased profitability from 5% to 27% and profitably resold in less than one year.

- Spearheaded the design and development of leading edge, real-time proprietary software to optimize and automate operations, and directed installation throughout all company facilities. Subsequently established systems consulting group and closed $4 million in customer contracts.

- Negotiated the successful divestiture of $27 million in corporate assets.

- Appointed Chairman of the 5-member Board of Directors in 1984.

Vice President - Operations 1981 to 1983
CALIFORNIA EDISON UTILITIES, INC.

Recruited by CEO and given full P&L responsibility for the operations and market expansion of this "in transition" diversified services company. Three-year old company had saturated its primary market and revenues had stagnated. Launched a series of customer-driven products and services that rapidly expanded market penetration and generated significant revenue growth.

Managed entire business and finance organization, all strategic planning, service design and delivery, sales/marketing, construction, engineering and senior project management functions. Concurrently, directed all financial, administration, regulatory and human resource affairs (90 employees).

- Increased annual sales revenues from $600,000 to $6 million within first year. Personally negotiated and closed the company's first multi-million dollar sale.

- Pioneered innovative product offerings that effectively positioned company against competition.

- Structured transaction and guided negotiations for the company's successful $7.5 million acquisition by a Fortune 500 corporation.

- Earned equity position, full partnership and Boards of Directors membership.

Vice President & General Manager 1979 to 1981
THE SOLEDYNE CORPORATION, INC.

Recruited to plan and direct the turnaround and return to profitability of this state-of-the-art energy technology and services company. Given full autonomy for reengineering the entire business infrastructure, refocusing market penetration, implementing financial standards and controls, and strengthening management team.

- Surpassed all turnaround objectives and transitioned corporation from $25,000 loss to $350,000 profit within first year.

- Launched a series of high-impact sales, marketing and business development programs that drove revenues from $200,000 to approximately $1 million annually.

- Positioned company for successful acquisition by Natkin Industries in 1981.

- Earned equity position and full partnership.

Previous Professional Experience with The Pacific Telephone Company. Promoted rapidly through increasingly responsible operating and senior management positions to final tenure as **General Manager**. Directed business units with up to 1223 employees and multi-million dollar annual operating budgets.

Scope of responsibility included plant construction, engineering, purchasing, inventory control, safety, security, quality control, union relations/negotiations, finance, training, customer service and all budgeting, financial planning and financial reporting functions.

- Travelled nationwide on public speaking tours to represent the company at shareholder meetings, industry conferences, association conventions and other events.

- Managed large-scale operations at nine Pacific Telephone subsidiaries nationwide.

EDUCATION:

SAN DIEGO STATE UNIVERSITY
Doctoral Candidate, 1972 to 1973
Bachelor of Science Degree, 1971

FRED C. GIEGERTY

2579 Center Square Court
Baltimore, MD 20817
Email FGiegerty@prodigy.com

Home (410) 768-4734
Fax (410) 768-9853
Office (301) 202-7354

PRESIDENT / CEO / BOARD OF DIRECTORS
Cross-Functional Expertise / Cross-Industry Experience
Start-Up Ventures & High-Growth Organizations
Harvard University MBA Degree

- Strategic Business/Profit Planning
- New Business/Market Development
- Organization Design/Development
- Advertising/Public Relations

- Acquisition Management
- Capital Raising & Financing
- Investor & Shareholder Relations
- Human Resource Affairs

PROFESSIONAL EXPERIENCE:

INTERPLASTY, INC., Baltimore, Maryland   1993 to Present

Chief Executive Officer

Member of 5-person new venture team developing business plan for the start-up of a nationwide network facilities providing revolutionary laser surgery. Selected by group as CEO to lead transition from strategic plan through funding, staffing and operations start-up. Built organizational infrastructure, developed strategic and tactical business plans, spearheaded nationwide marketing and business development initiatives, and guided corporation into a full-scale operation.

- **Raised $11 million in seed capital from 330 private investors to fund business start-up while awaiting FDA approval.**
- **Brought business from concept to $8.5 million in first year revenues with the start-up of 10 centers in 6 states and 70 employees. Currently projecting second year revenues of $18 million from 13 centers.**
- **Negotiated sale of privately-held company to Canadian venture seeking expansion throughout North America. Under contract with new company to facilitate ownership transition.**

BROWN JOHNSON, Alexandria, Virginia   1988 to 1993

President / Chief Operating Officer (1988 to 1993)
Board of Directors (1986 to 1994)

Accepted full-time executive position (after three-year tenure on the Board of Directors) to lead this advertising, public relations and direct marketing organization through a period of rapid growth and expansion. Built a complete corporate infrastructure integrating accounting, finance, legal, information systems, human resource and administrative operations.

- **Transitioned corporation from $1 million loss in 1988 to $3+ million profit in 1993.**
- **Negotiated and managed six major acquisitions, enabling company to grow from billings of $250 million to $425 million within four years. Led diversification and/or complete reorganization of non-performing business units.**
- **Introduced database technology as a viable tool for market research/segmentation. Built business from start-up to $1 million in first year.**

FRED C. GIEGERTY

Page Two

THE RESEARCH GROUP, Chevy Chase, Maryland   1969 to 1988
(Management Consulting & Training Corporation)

Chairman / Chief Executive Officer / Board of Directors (1975 to 1988)
Project Director / Division Director / Chief Operating Officer (1969 to 1975)

CEO at age 29 with full P&L, operational and decision-making responsibility for the organization. Directed the entire project management cycle, from initial planning and contract negotiations through funding, development and field implementation. Managed corporate affairs including strategic business planning, finance/accounting, budgeting, human resources, MIS, legal affairs and administration.

- **Built corporation from 50 employees and $3 million in annual revenues to 250+ personnel and over $15 million in annual revenues (600% growth in both sales and profits).**

EDUCATION:

MBA Degree, Harvard University Graduate School of Business Administration, 1968
BS Degree in Operations Research, Columbia University, 1966

PROFESSIONAL RECOGNITION:

Certified Management Consultant (CMC), Institute of Management Consultants.

Who's Who in America, the World, Health Care, Advertising, Finance & Industry, and the East.

Outstanding Young Men of America Award.

Published Author, "The New York Times," "The Washington Post," "The New Republic" and numerous books, magazines and trade journals.

PROFESSIONAL AFFILIATIONS *(past & present)*:

World Presidents' Organization
Young Presidents' Organization (Founding Chairman, Washington Metro Chapter)
American Association of Advertising Agencies
The Washington Board of Trade
Harvard Business School Club of Washington

BOARD OF DIRECTORS APPOINTMENTS:

Active leadership role in the start-up and/or executive leadership of diverse business ventures in the high-technology, consumer products, banking/finance, transportation, advertising, market research, economic development, human services and non-profit industries.

COLLIN T. PRICE
3643 Vineyard Alley
Sacramento, California 98314
(415) 654-7547

SENIOR OPERATING & MANAGEMENT EXECUTIVE
Technologically-Sophisticated Start-Up, Turnaround & High-Growth Corporations

Talented Management Executive with 15+ years experience building profitable manufacturing, sales and service organizations worldwide. Expert in identifying and capturing market opportunities, building international alliances, and driving long-term revenue growth. Equally effective in reorganizing, streamlining and strengthening existing operations. Team-based leadership style with excellent interpersonal skills.

PROFESSIONAL EXPERIENCE:

ROMED RESEARCH & DEVELOPMENT, INC., Sacramento, CA   June 1995 to Present

President
Recruited to transition this company from medical technology R&D into a full-scale operating unit with sales, marketing, administration, contracts, licensing, human resources and accounting/finance functions. Currently working to facilitate transformation from a scientific laboratory into a for-profit business venture. Within first six months:

- Led company's successful launch into the U.S. and European commercial markets. Closed over $500,000 in revenues with 1997 projections at $2+ million.
- Negotiated several key marketing and manufacturing alliances with companies in the U.S., U.K. and Italy to deliver products into $2 billion global market.

B&G CHEMICAL, INC., Colorado Springs, CO   1985 to 1995

President/CEO
Senior Operating Executive with full P&L responsibility for the strategic planning, development and leadership of a $125 million, 2-division, privately-held, bio-medical manufacturer. Directed sales/marketing, finance, human resources, R&D, manufacturing, MIS, purchasing, contracts, quality and regulatory affairs. Managed a team of 700 employees through four vice presidents.

- Led corporation through a period of rapid growth, from $5 million in 1985 to $125 million in 1995. Accelerated R&D efforts and launched over 10 new products (accounted for 90% of revenue growth). Returned annual net profits averaging 11%+.
- Achieved ISO and FDA certifications, implemented a successful TQM program, and led teams through development of manufacturing process improvements to simplify methods, increase productivity and improve net earnings.
- Restructured the corporation into three distinct operating units and negotiated their profitable sale to Bristol Myers Squibb, Dow Chemical and Warner Lambert.

ACUITY SYSTEMS, INC., London, England   1978 to 1985

Managing Director - Europe & Middle East

Recruited to this $200 million manufacturer of medical equipment and technology to launch the start-up of sales and service operations throughout Europe and the Middle East. Created organization from start-up into an 800-employee manufacturing and sales division. Established business infrastructure, sales and service network, recruited management teams, built multi-channel distribution networks and aggressively penetrated the international market. Held P&L responsibility.

ACUITY SYSTEMS, INC. *(Continued):*

- Built division from start-up over $100 million in annual revenue. Positioned as the most profitable division in the company with annual margin contributions averaging 14%.
- Established a sophisticated manufacturing operation in the U.K., and assumed complete general management and P&L responsibilities for the facility. Achieved ISO certification and approval through complex European FDA regulatory procedures.
- Captured over $1 million in cost reductions through a series of process redesign and simplification procedures. Served as model for introduction at corporate manufacturing facility and contributed an additional $1.5 million to the bottom line.
- Personally negotiated $50 million contract with the Saudi Arabian Ministry of Health for the sale of advanced medical equipment and technology. Delivered $25 million to net profit.

UNITED KINGDOM MEDICAL, LTD., London, England   1975 to 1978
(Merged with CCI Life Systems, Inc. in 1976)

<u>**President - CCI U.K.**</u> (1976 to 1978)
<u>**President / CEO - United Kingdom Medical**</u> (1975 to 1976)
Joined this $10 million medical technology and device company in 1975. Given full P&L responsibility for the entire manufacturing and sales/marketing organizations. Subsequently led merger with U.S. based company and reorganization into a 1500-employee operating subsidiary, with $200 million in revenue.

- Led the organization from $10 million to $200 million in annual revenues as a result of merger and through an aggressive expansion within Europe. Delivered 10% net profit.
- Achieved worldwide regulatory approval and launched the introduction of more than 10 new products ($190 million in combined new revenues).
- Negotiated the profitable sale of the corporation to Dutch medical technology company.

ALPHA MEDIX, INC., Palo Alto, California   1970 to 1975

<u>**Vice President / General Manager**</u> (1973 to 1975)
<u>**Vice President - Marketing & Sales**</u> (1970 to 1973)
Recruited to start-up medical equipment and device manufacturer. Launched four new products through FDA regulatory approval, negotiated licensing agreements in Japan and Germany, and established a global distribution network. Built company from start-up to $50 million in annual sales with a global market presence.

HARLECO, INC., Philadelphia, Pennsylvania   1967 to 1970

<u>**Pacific Rim Director**</u> (1967 to 1970)
<u>**Regional Manager**</u> (1967)
<u>**Sales Representative**</u> (1967)
Promoted from Sales Representative to Regional Manager to Pacific Rim Director within first year of hire. Challenged to build and direct a multi-channel distribution system throughout Asia and Australia. Won the 1967 Excalibur Award for most productive global business region. Honored as top sales producer, top regional manager and top international manager.

EDUCATION:

B.A., Business, Economics & Chemistry, Wichita State University

Wharton School/University of Pennsylvania - Finance for Non-Financial Managers
Stanford University - Operations Management & Financial Analysis
Amos Tuck School of Business/Dartmouth University - Managing in Hyper-Competitive Industries

THOMAS ANDERSON

329 Prairie Wind
Omaha, Nebraska 43469
(642) 643-2113

SENIOR OPERATING & MANAGEMENT EXECUTIVE
Leading Edge Cable, Broadcast & Telecommunications Technologies

Distinguished management career in the delivery of sophisticated technologies to build market share, drive revenue growth and outperform competition. Pioneered innovative operating strategies, broadcast productions, advertising programs and public relations initiatives to build new revenue streams. Strong general management and P&L management qualifications.

PROFESSIONAL EXPERIENCE:

GHOSTOWN MEDIA GROUP, Omaha, Nebraska   1995 to Present

Principal

Founded and currently building an exclusive consulting group specializing in multi-media broadcast operations, sales and marketing, business development, process reengineering, administration and revenue/profit growth.

- Completed several engagements with a multiple system operator and regional broadcaster.

- Currently spearheading the development, funding, technology and operations of pioneering broadcast and cable systems for nationwide implementation into emerging consumer market.

SKY CABLE TV, Omaha, Nebraska   1994 to 1995

General Manager

Senior Operating Executive recruited to transition this wireless cable television system from virtual start-up into a major player within the local region. Given full autonomy for establishing operating policies and procedures, spearheading marketing and business development initiatives, recruiting professional staff and building the organizational infrastructure. Full P&L responsibility.

- Established Sky Cable as a viable entertainment alternative, delivered 400% growth in subscriber base, and expanded coverage area throughout all of Omaha and parts of Western Iowa.

- Achieved a sustainable competitive position against major hardware operators (e.g., U.S. West, TCI, Cox Communications) throughout the regional market.

- Structured and negotiated agreement for the placement of a sophisticated transmitting facility atop of the highest building in Nebraska. Accelerated market penetration and regional expansion.

STORER COMMUNICATIONS, INC.   1979 to 1994

General Manager - Northwest New Jersey System, Port Murray, New Jersey (1984 to 1994)

Full P&L responsibility for the strategic planning, development, operation and management of 17 cable franchises throughout Northwestern New Jersey. Challenged to resolve long-standing employee and operating issues negatively impacting revenues, profits and growth.

- Built revenues from $3 million in 1984 to $9.6 million in 1994. Increased subscriber base from 15,000 to 28,000+ against major market competition. Expanded from 281 miles to 700 miles of hard line and 218 miles of fiber optic transmission lines.

- Transitioned average length of franchise contracts from 10 years to 17 years to further solidify market positioning. Negotiated five 15-year contracts with automatic 10-year renewal clauses.

STORER COMMUNICATIONS, INC. *(Continued)*:

- Directed over $15 million in capital improvement projects with average 24 to 36 month ROI.

- Negotiated exclusive regional broadcast coverage with major athletic conferences.

- Spearheaded the successful development of several innovative programming, local advertising, public relations, community outreach and customer service initiatives. Established Storer as a visible and contributing corporate citizen, and created several new profitable revenue channels.

- Successfully negotiated and decertified union.

General Manager - Central Minnesota System, St. Cloud, Minnesota (1981 to 1984)

Directed a 6-franchise cable television station during a period of rapid growth and regional expansion, from a small operation into a well-recognized, well-respected entertainment company. Accountable for P&L performance, sales/marketing, advertising, human resource affairs, budgeting, capital improvement and asset management.

- Built subscriber base from 7200 to 13,000 customers generating revenues of $1.2 million annually. Delivered a 51% annual operating profit.

- Pioneered Storer's entry into the direct response market and created a $25,000 annual revenue stream. Created model subsequently used by other Storer regions nationwide.

- Successfully penetrated the commercial market and built to 3000+ customers.

- Negotiated and won broadcast contract with the Minnesota Vikings and several other professional teams. Sold broadcast rights to other cable systems for sporting events and numerous other in-house produced broadcasts.

Customer Service Representative - Central Minnesota System, St. Cloud, Minnesota (1979 to 1981)

Recruited to one of Storer Communications' regional operating systems to build and direct a full-scale customer service organization. Given full autonomy for establishing policies and procedures for sales, marketing, service, credit and collections, accounting and internal audit.

- Successfully completed assignment and promoted to General Manager of the operating system.

PREVIOUS PROFESSIONAL EXPERIENCE (1972 to 1978) in Advertising Sales, Broadcasting and Broadcast Production. Employed with stations in Minnesota, North Dakota, Wisconsin and Illinois.

- Consistently ranked as a top revenue producer closing millions of dollars in sales with local, regional, national and multinational advertisers.

- Instrumental in restructuring and refocusing sales department of one station following acquisition by new ownership.

EDUCATION:

BROWN INSTITUTE, Minneapolis, Minnesota
Associate of Science Degree, 1973

DEPARTMENT OF THE ARMY
Leadership, Officer Development & Technology Training, 1969 to 1984

WILLIAM HUNTER
394 Surrey Place, Flat 2
Avon Von Stratton
London, England
011-34-5-646-8625

SENIOR OPERATING & MANAGEMENT EXECUTIVE
Pharmaceutical & Health Care Industries

Dynamic management career, building top-performing business units throughout the U.S. and abroad. Captured #1 market share in Europe against rapidly emerging competition through expertise in:

- Strategic & Business Planning
- Product Development & Market Launch
- Product & Market Positioning
- Management Training & Development
- Headquarters & Division Operations

- Profit Center Realignment & Reengineering
- Strategic Partnerships & Alliances
- Sales Team & Channel Development
- Cross-Cultural Business Development
- International Regulatory Affairs

Fellow, Royal Society of Medicine, England
Board Member, World Business Advisory Council, Thunderbird University
MBA Degree, Seton Hall University

PROFESSIONAL EXPERIENCE:

ALLERGAN, INC. 1989 to Present

Optical Director - North West Europe (Special Assignment), England (1994 to Present)

Challenged to lead a $50 million business unit through a traumatic transition from a stable optical-driven market with limited competition to a consumer/OTC-driven business with 10 new competitors in the first year. Given full strategic, operating and P&L responsibility for complete profit center reengineering and market realignment. Provide hands-on leadership to a talented team of 50 field sales/marketing professionals building market presence within seven European countries.

- Achieved 1995 YTD profit targets and #1 market share despite transition from ethical to OTC distribution and rapidly emerging competition (reduced the value of each patient by 50%).

- Realigned sales from product to customer/account focus and built grocery segment to 20% of total value. Concurrently, negotiated creative partnerships, alliances and marketing incentives to retain ethical customer base.

- Exploited the presence of private labelling to provide ethical market with a clear competitive advantage. Negotiated 100% private label partnerships with two of the three largest chains in the U.K. ($10 million in revenues in 1996). Currently creating European-wide program for late 1997 launch.

Senior Vice President of Marketing - Europe, England (1991 to 1994)

Senior Operating Executive with full responsibility for building a European Marketing Headquarters Organization. Integrated autonomous sales and marketing units with a centralized HQ function and provided the vision, strategy and action plans to achieve market positioning, improve new product flow, and achieve revenue growth and earnings objectives for the entire European continent. Member of the European Executive Management team.

Led team of 300+ field sales, marketing, and support personnel. Controlled a $105 million annual operating budget. Principal portfolio included optical, surgical, pharmaceutical and neurology products.

- Delivered strong and sustainable revenue growth. Closed 1993 with $328 million in sales and #1 in market share for optical and neurological segments. Established a strong voice for the international division within U.S. Headquarters.

WILLIAM HUNTER   *Page Two*

- Revitalized the entire European Marketing Organization. Reengineered strategic planning process, introduced market research and business development functions, realigned product portfolio and transitioned to multi-function marketing teams. Improved financial performance in all key operations.

- Advised Central European Management Team during development of initial strategic and market entry plans for Eastern Europe. Authored marketing plans, devised positioning strategies and developed distribution organization. Built revenues from $5 million to $15 million during initial thrust.

- Saved $7 million in potential lost revenues from international product diversion through modification to existing product packaging and labelling designs.

Vice President - International Marketing, Irvine, California (1989 to 1991)

Recruited as the Senior Marketing Executive accountable for rebuilding the entire international marketing organization. Challenged to provide vision, strategy and action to achieve international presence.

Scope of responsibility was diverse and directly impacted R&D, manufacturing, regulatory affairs, market positioning, product distribution and bottom-line financial performance. Supported a team of 300+ field sales and marketing executives in 100+ countries worldwide.

- Built a full-scale global marketing function. Recruited professional staff, developed new product planning function, introduced market research capabilities, and created the organization that now serves as the corporate prototype for marketing excellence.

- Delivered 10%+ annual sales growth while reconnecting the marketing function with R&D.

STERLING DRUG INTERNATIONAL, New York, New York   1983 to 1989

Director - International Marketing & Business Development (1984 to 1989)

High-profile, senior-level management position directing the strategic planning, development and implementation of international marketing and business development programs for all three core product lines (endocrine, diagnostic imaging, analgesic).

- Revitalized the international presence and financial performance of Sterling's principal product line. Doubled sales from $30 million to $60 million within two years.

- Spearheaded the development of an integrated marketing package, theme and corporate identity for key products in the entire worldwide market.

- Introduced state-of-the-art interactive video training programs for international sales team.

SCHERING-PLOUGH INTERNATIONAL, Kenilworth, New Jersey   1970 to 1982

Senior Product Manager / Product Manager (1978 to 1982)
Senior Market Research Associate (1976 to 1978)
Senior Health Scientist - International Regulatory Affairs (1974 to 1976)
Research Chemist / Group Leader (1970 to 1974)

Fast-track promotion through a series of increasingly responsible management positions working with a complete prescription/OTC pharmaceutical product line. Successfully transitioned from "hands-on" product research into global sales and marketing.

- Built Dermatology business unit from $200 million to $250 million (10%+ annual growth).

- Orchestrated development, licensing and international market launch of a new collagen product for plastic and dermatological surgery account base. Delivered $6 million in revenues within first year.

EDUCATION: **MBA / International Marketing**, Seton Hall University, 1979
                  MS / Chemistry, Rutgers University, 1974
                  BS / Chemistry, Augusta College, 1970

MICHAEL ALEXANDER
935 Avenida del Sol
San Juan, Puerto Rico 09832
(818) 313-3132

INTERNATIONAL BUSINESS EXECUTIVE - LATIN AMERICA

General Management / Sales & Marketing Management / Corporate Finance
Manufacturing & Operations / Multi-Channel Product Distribution
Union Negotiations / Executive Training & Development

Market-Driven Senior Executive with excellent qualifications in the strategic planning, development and leadership of high-growth international business opportunities.

- Delivered millions of dollars in profit growth through success in manufacturing process reengineering, new market development, cost reduction and profitability/quality improvement.
- Delivered outstanding achievements in sales, marketing and new business development.
- Acquired extensive experience in joint venture, strategic alliance and licensing negotiations.
- Demonstrated proficiency in cross-cultural communications and international liaison affairs.
- Fluency in English and Spanish. Conversational language skills in Portuguese.
- Member, American Society of International Executives.

PROFESSIONAL EXPERIENCE:

G.D. SEARLE & COMPANY   1978 to Present

President - Searle Caribbean, Inc., San Juan, Puerto Rico (1982 to Present)
General Manager - Searle Puerto Rico, San Juan, Puerto Rico (1980 to 1982)
General Manager - Searle Argentina, Buenos Aires, Argentina (1978 to 1979)

One of a select group of senior operating executives responsible for building Searle's presence throughout Latin America. Promoted through several high-profile management positions directing multi-site international manufacturing, sales and marketing organizations.

As the Senior Operating Executive, held full P&L responsibility for the strategic planning, development, financial and human resource affairs, operations and profitability of each business unit. Currently direct a 65-person organization generating $20 million in annual revenues. Previous staff responsibility up to 200.

- Led the successful turnaround and subsequent market growth of the Caribbean Operations. Established regional distribution network, opened critical new markets and launched several successful product introductions (including EQUAL). Increased net sales by 65.4% and operating profits by 75.3% within two years.

- Returned Argentine Operations to profitability. Revitalized and rationalized manufacturing operations, restructured finance department, reduced workforce 20% and reengineered business and production processes for a significant cost savings. Increased operating income by $1.1 million in first year.

- Identified opportunity and developed/negotiated joint venture in Uruguay to establish a licensed manufacturing operation.

- Created a portfolio of promotions, marketing communications and product training programs for distributors throughout Latin America.

MICHAEL ALEXANDER - *Page Two*

ABBOTT LABORATORIES, Lima, Peru   1974 to 1978

General Manager - Peru & Bolivia

Senior Operating Executive recruited to launch the turnaround and return to profitability of this 140-employee, $6 million manufacturing, sales and distribution organization. Company produced and marketed over 30 pharmaceutical, hospital and consumer products to an account base of 300. Given full P&L, ROI and operating management responsibility for the entire profit center.

Launched an aggressive reorganization of all operating and administrative departments throughout the company. Revitalized sales and marketing organization, implemented an aggressive asset management policy, innovated package designs and spearheaded dramatic cost improvements. **Achieved/surpassed all turnaround objectives.**

- Increased sales by 43.5% within first year through a combination of new product launch, key account development and regional expansion initiatives.

- Achieved aggressive growth throughout the Bolivian market. Increased sales by 185% and profits by 275% within three years. Recruited/trained distributor network and Country Manager.

- Negotiated favorable resolutions to critical labor union problems in a volatile economic and political environment.

- Transitioned company from #19 to #11 in the corporation (ranked on profitability).

- Controlled over $500,000 in annual capital plant and equipment improvements, resulting in a number of new and profitable business opportunities.

WYETH INTERNATIONAL, LTD., Radnor, Pennsylvania   1970 to 1974
(Division of American Home Products Corporation)

Area Sales Executive - Caribbean, Ecuador, Peru & Chile (1974)
Regional Sales Executive - Central America & Ecuador (1972 to 1974)
Coordinating Executive - Caribbean & Central America (1970 to 1972)

- Fast-track promotion through a series of increasingly responsible sales, marketing and business development management assignments to final position directing a 25-person regional sales organization with $18+ million in annual revenues.

- Delivered explosive growth within the Peruvian branch. Increased net sales 22% and operating profits 31% in one year.

MENLEY AND JAMES LABORATORIES, Philadelphia, Pennsylvania   1967 to 1970
(Division of Smith Kline & French Laboratories)

District Sales Manager - Central & Southern New Jersey

- Directed district sales, marketing and key account management efforts for a line of proprietary OTC drugs. Managed both commercial health care and military markets.

- Launched introduction of a new comestics line and closed 140 new accounts in three months.

EDUCATION:

MBA Candidate, Drexel University, Philadelphia, Pennsylvania, 1968 to 1970
BS, Business Administration, Saint Joseph's University, Philadelphia, Pennsylvania, 1967

Continuing Professional Development:

- Financial Management Policies & Practices, Wharton School, University of Pennsylvania, 1991
- Executive Effectiveness, American Management Association, 1978

DANIEL WARNER

932 Goose Run
Syracuse, New York 19821
(908) 231-5667

SENIOR OPERATING & MANAGEMENT EXECUTIVE

Complex Scientific Research, Testing, Product Development & Project Management

Unique management career leading the start-up, growth and profitable management of sophisticated scientific research and development facilities. Combines expertise in P&L management, organizational development, staffing and finance with equally strong scientific, technical and project management qualifications. Excellent record of performance in building and marketing profitable new business and product development ventures.

Extensive knowledge of OSHA, EPA, NIOSH, GLP, FDA and international regulatory requirements. Diverse industry experience in pharmaceutical, health care, chemical and metals industries. Strong PC qualifications. Diplomate of the American Board of Toxicology. Ph.D. (Toxicology), M.S. (Pharmacokinetics), M.S. (Genetics), B.S. (Biology).

PROFESSIONAL EXPERIENCE:

BRISTOL-MYERS SQUIBB, INC., Syracuse, New York   1992 to Present

Manager - Toxicology Department

Senior Business Manager responsible for the strategic planning, staffing and operating management of a large pre-clinical drug safety testing facility. Lead a staff of 22 scientists and professionals performing complex testing and evaluation of new drug candidates. Facilitate cross-functional project teams worldwide (e.g., discovery, clinical, analytical, pharmacokinetics, regulatory affairs).

- Negotiated complex drug registration agreements with the FDA and international regulatory agencies.

- Won the 1995 Presidential Award for outstanding achievement following successful drug registration with Japanese regulatory authorities.

NATIONAL TOXICOLOGY CONSULTANTS, Manlius, New York   1993 to Present

President

Founded consulting group providing scientific consultation and expert testimony related to hazardous materials assessment, handling and disposition. Established strategic alliances with other consulting groups to expand core competencies and areas of scientific knowledge.

- Authored a 2000+ page reference database (Toxicology Desk Reference) published by Taylor and Francis in 1996. Created the first-ever comprehensive information source on assessment of exposure to various hazardous compounds, now the authoritative resource for physicians, corporate medical directors, industrial hygienists and other safety/health care personnel.

CORNELL UNIVERSITY, Ithaca, New York   1993 to Present

Adjunct Assistant Professor - Institute for Comparative & Environmental Toxicology

Design and teach graduate-level courses in drug development and environmental toxicology. Pioneered R&D alliance between the Institute and Bristol-Myers Squibb to enable cooperative drug development projects.

DANIEL WARNER   **Page Two**

ROCHE BIOMEDICAL LABORATORIES, Burlington, North Carolina   1990 to 1992

Director of Environmental Toxicology

Recruited to launch start-up of corporation's Biological Monitoring Department, a for-profit venture providing biological testing services to corporate clients nationwide. Wrote business plan for new venture, designed business and operating infrastructure, recruited/trained 32 professionals, defined financial and budgetary requirements, and created portfolio of sales, marketing and business development programs. Held full P&L responsibility for daily laboratory and testing operations.

- Built business from concept through start-up to full-scale operation with revenues of more than $10 million within two years. Delivered 50%+ profit margins, positioning the operating unit as the #1 profit producer in Roche's niche business markets.

- Working in cooperation with Senior Sales Executive, created and taught a series of product and scientific training programs for 400+ person field sales organization. Launched start-up of nationwide customer service and technical support organization.

- Expanded 400 sq.ft. laboratory into state-of-the-art, 8000 sq.ft. testing facility. Acquired technology and instrumentation, guided methods development and designed reporting documentation.

- Provided expert consultation to physicians and other health care professionals in the design of medical surveillance and biological monitoring programs.

- Won the 1992 "Circle of Excellence Award for Top Managers," bestowed by the President on the top 1% of managers worldwide.

Previous Professional Experience:

Research Biologist, National Institute of Environmental Health Sciences	1986 to 1990
Research Technician, North Dakota State University Dept. of Food & Nutrition	1985 to 1986
Asst. Radiation Safety Officer, NDSU Radiation Safety Office	1983 to 1985
Chemist, State Toxicology Laboratory of North Dakota	1982 to 1983
Emergency Room Technician, St. Lukes Hospital	1977 to 1982

EDUCATION:

Ph.D., Toxicology, University of North Carolina at Chapel Hill, 1990
M.S., Pharmacokinetics, North Dakota State University, 1986
M.S., Genetics, North Dakota State University, 1986
B.S., Biology, North Dakota State University, 1982

PROFESSIONAL ACTIVITIES:

Publications	Published Author of more than 10 books, journal articles, abstracts and book chapters. Full listing upon request.
Editorial Boards	Associate Editor, In Vitro Toxicology journal and TOMES[R] Editorial Board.
Affiliations	Society of Toxicology, American College of Toxicology, American Industrial Hygiene Association (Biological Monitoring Committee)

BERNARD E. CLAYTON

5673 Oakwood Court
Aurora, CO 82151
Bclayton@attmail.net

Business   (303) 984-3816
Facsimile   (303) 984-4430
Residence   (303) 493-6217

SENIOR OPERATIONS & MANAGEMENT EXECUTIVE
Emerging Technology Industries

Vice President / General Manager with 16 years experience in building advanced technology organizations. Cross-functional expertise in systems/components design, development and engineering, and in all core general management, P&L management, sales and marketing management functions.

Published author in PC Times, Electronic Design, Digital Design, Mini-Micro Systems and IBM PC Fair. Wrote and published three books on emerging electronics and information technologies.

PROFESSIONAL EXPERIENCE:

Vice President - Worldwide Services   1993 to 1996
MICRO ELECTRONICS *($150 million leader in secondary materials management for electronics companies)*

Challenge: Transition from product-driven to service-driven organization to accelerate market growth and expansion.

Accountability: Full P&L and operating management responsibility for operating, sales and repair facilities in California, Texas, Tennessee, The Netherlands and the U.K. Lead a team of 11 project managers, both domestic and European sales teams, and a global network of independent sales representatives/distributors.

Lead development, implementation and sales of inventory management services for subsystem OEMs, PC manufacturers and PC service companies worldwide.

Results:
- Developed industry-leading technology and delivered strong sales results, including $12 million contract with Digital and $5.6 million contract with IBM.
- Reengineered newly-acquired repair facility for Micro and reduced breakeven by 50% within three months. Led facility to ISO 9002 certification.
- Appointed Interim Operations Director for another Micro facility and reduced WIP dollar value by 80% in just three months.
- Led multi-site facilities consolidation program following corporate acquisitions, and transferred critical people, processes and customers to other company sites. Resulted in a $3+ million savings in annual operating costs and significant improvement in facility/asset utilization.

Vice President - Sales & Marketing   1992 to 1993
EXECUDATA CORPORATION *(start-up venture in storage network market segment)*

Challenge: Lead new venture from R&D through market launch.

Accountability: Full P&L, engineering, technology, operating and marketing responsibility. Creation of new product, new applications and multiple versions for both OEM and VAR sales channels.

Results:
- Led company through complete product development cycle into untapped market niche for "storage safety" technology. Delivered first year revenues of $3 million with 75% gross margin. Company currently generates over $10 million annually.
- Negotiated joint development partnership with Novell and built nationwide network with 130 Novell VAR distributors.

BERNARD E. CLAYTON - *Page Two*

Vice President - Sales & Marketing   1990 to 1992
INTERNATIONAL DATA SYSTEMS *(venture-funded company in SQL database market)*

<u>Challenge</u>:	Lead an aggressive turnaround and return to profitability.
<u>Accountability</u>:	Complete responsibility for strategic planning, sales, marketing, business development and product/technology development. Competitively position company against major players (e.g., Oracle, Sybase).
<u>Results</u>:	• Transitioned company from $1 million in annual sales (at loss) to $5.5 million in annual sales (25% profit margin).
	• Released two major products for beta test within first six months and established two demonstration/technical evaluation sites.
	• Restructured and revitalized sales and marketing group, reduced operating expenses by 60% and significantly increased direct customer contact.
	• Negotiated profitable joint development contracts with two major customers.

Division General Manager   1988 to 1990
CHRISTA CORPORATION *($400 million manufacturer of high performance disk drives)*

<u>Challenge</u>:	Develop and implement a common technology plan across all divisions.
<u>Accountability</u>:	Full P&L responsibility for 150-person R&D, sales and marketing organization. Full operational responsibility for hardware, software and manufacturing for multiple product lines.
<u>Results</u>:	• Delivered strong performance gains: 30% improvement in productivity, 100% increase in first-time production yield, 80% reduction in capital equipment costs and 75% decrease in direct labor costs.
	• Created Supplier Quality Assurance program and "lifetime cost of ownership" program for vendor selection. Resulted in 50% reduction in vendor base and 30% decrease in component costs.
	• Built start-up disk drive division from concept to $30 million in annual sales. Developed control firmware for industry standard interface protocol (Small Computer Systems Interface - SCSI) and custom integrated circuits (ASICs).
	• Established profitable manufacturing facility in Singapore.

President   1986 to 1988
THE ITEL GROUP *(executive consultants to storage manufacturers nationwide)*

- Supervised definition and development of custom integrated circuits (ASICs) for assembly into numerous hardware and software development projects.
- Designed ASIC for disk drive control. Negotiated partnerships with ASIC vendors for ASIC design, library development and support.
- Developed SCSI Technical Seminar and presented to 50+ major computer/storage companies.

President   1980 to 1986
DATAWARE, INC. *(venture-funded company in storage controller market)*

- Founded and built new venture to $5 million in sales in the SCSI compatible storage controller market. Established national sales organization for OEM accounts.
- Closed major sales agreements and joint development contracts with Sperry, Concurrent Computer Corporation, 3-COM and others.
- Launched start-up of international technical conference program to promote and standardize SCSI, and spun off into separate business unit.

EDUCATION: **M.S.E.E.** (1980) / **B.S.E.E.** (1978) - Massachusetts Institute of Technology (MIT)

JAKE P. SMITH

UNC C - Seton Hall , Room 305   (910) 634-6413   Charlotte, North Carolina 26547

PROFESSIONAL QUALIFICATIONS:

Talented, resourceful and dedicated young professional offering a unique combination of professional skills. Creative and enthusiastic with proven success in building and managing relationships with peers, co-workers, team members, customers and the general public. Aggressive, decisive and committed to professional growth and opportunity. Experience includes:

- Public Relations & Promotions
- Team Building & Leadership
- Athletic Competition
- Project Planning & Coordination
- Office Administration & Reporting
- Public Speaking
- Group Dynamics & Motivation
- Oral & Written Communications
- Community Outreach
- Customer Service

Proficient in WordPerfect, Works and Microsoft Office (Word, Excel & PowerPoint).

EDUCATION:

Candidate for B.S. Degree in Communications, expected May 1997
Concentration in Public Relations / Minor in English
UNIVERSITY OF NORTH CAROLINA AT CHARLOTTE
    Pi Kappa Alpha Fraternity: Public Relations Chair, Master of Ceremonies, Executive Committee Member, Community Service Volunteer.

Graduate, St. Joseph's High School, Huntington, West Virginia, 1993
    Senior Class President. Member, Spanish Club & Chess Club.

HIGH SCHOOL & COLLEGIATE ATHLETICS:

- University of North Carolina - Charlotte Soccer Team (pre-season - ranked 10th in nation), 1994/95
- National High School All Region Team, 1992 & 1993
- West Virginia State High School Soccer Player of the Year, 1992
- West Virginia High School All State Team, 1991 & 1992
- West Virginia Olympic Development Team, 1992 to 1993
- St. Joseph's Varsity High School Soccer, 1990 to 1993

EMPLOYMENT EXPERIENCE:

Tutor - Downtown YMCA, Charlotte, North Carolina (January 1996 to Present)
    Participate in adult and child literacy programs.

Coach - St. Joseph's High School, Huntington, West Virginia (Summer 1995)
    Coached high school soccer team and facilitated group development.

Barback/Waiter - Southend Brewery, Charlotte, North Carolina (Summer 1995)
    High-volume, fast-paced food service position.

Barback/Waiter - Red Robin Restaurant, Charlotte, North Carolina (Summers 1993 and 1994)
    Expedited food and beverage preparation and guest services.

Landscaper - Lavalette Nursery, Huntington, West Virginia (Summers 1991 and 1992)
    Field landscaper with additional office/administrative responsibilities.

Assistant - Huntington Cubs Baseball Organization, Huntington, West Virginia (Summer 1990)
    Coordinated team equipment/resources.

GEORGE RICHARDSON
119 Old Stable Road
Lynchburg, Virginia 24503
(804) 384-4600

PROFESSIONAL QUALIFICATIONS:

- Investment Analysis & Reporting
- Stock & Mutual Fund Performance
- Mathematical & Statistical Analysis
- Project Planning & Administration

- Market Trends & Analysis
- Data Collection & Reporting
- Customer Sales & Service
- Oral & Written Communications

Proficient with WordPerfect, Excel and other PC database, spreadsheet and word processing applications. Experienced in Pascal and C++ programming. High aptitude for advanced mathematics and economic analysis.

EDUCATION:

B.A., Economics, University of Virginia, Charlottesville, Virginia, January 1996
Head Manager, UVA Varsity Women's Volleyball Team ... Chi Psi Fraternity ... Intramurals Chair

Honors Graduate, Jefferson Forest High School, Forest, Virginia, June 1992
GPA - 4.0 ... National Honor Society ... Graduated 7th in class of 167

PROFESSIONAL EXPERIENCE:

WHEAT FIRST BUTCHER SINGER, Lynchburg, Virginia   Summer 1996
SMITH BARNEY SHEARSON, Washington, D.C.   Spring 1996

<u>Broker Intern</u> selected from a competitive group of candidates for two professional internships. Worked cooperatively with brokers, financial planners and branch managers to research financial data, monitor market trends, analyze investment returns and maintain/update prospect databases. Conducted detailed analyses of stock and mutual fund performance.

PREVIOUS WORK EXPERIENCE:

J. CREW OUTFITTERS, Lynchburg, Virginia   Summers 1990 to 1991; 1993
Telemarketing Representative using an on-line, real time networked system for data entry, order processing and inventory control/verification. Extensive customer sales and service experience.

EASTERN ELECTRIC CORPORATION, Lynchburg, Virginia   1991 to 1993
Inventory System Coordinator working part-time to assist with inventory planning, control and distribution. Established item numbers and product descriptions/categories. Input and edited inventory data. Performed routine maintenance of computerized inventory system.

BERKLEY-HOWELL & ASSOCIATES, Lynchburg, Virginia   Summers 1992 to 1994
Survey Assistant working with field crews to conduct land surveys for residential and commercial property development.

REBECCA WRIGHT
945 North Wabash Street #904
Chicago, Illinois 60615
(301) 316-1655

OBJECTIVE: Professional position in the Health Care/Medical/Pharmaceutical Industries.

PROFESSIONAL QUALIFICATIONS:

- Strong academic training and two years of hands-on research experience in the Biological, Chemical and Health Sciences.
- Effective communications, interpersonal relations and public speaking skills.
- Extensive experience in project planning and management.
- Excellent leadership record throughout high school and college.
- Conversational French. PC proficient (spreadsheet, database, word processing).

EDUCATION:

B.S. Degree in Science (Pre-Med Major), to be awarded May 1997
(General & Cell Biology, Microbiology, Ecology, Genetics, Chemistry, Physics, Calculus)
UNIVERSITY OF ILLINOIS AT URBANA-CHAMPAIGN

- Summer Abroad in Aix-en-Provence, France, Institute for American University Program, 1994
- First Year Impact (Freshmen Orientation Team), Health Professions Society
- Habitat for Humanity, Special Olympics, Volunteer Illinois
- Kappa Kappa Gamma Sorority (Recommendations Chair)

Honors Graduate, Pontiac Township High School, Pontiac, Illinois, 1992

- 5 in Class of 183, Junior Women's Health Profession Scholarship, State Legislative Scholarship
- National Honor Society, Student Council, Leadership Group, All Conference Athlete

EMPLOYMENT EXPERIENCE:

Lab Assistant - Neurophysiology Research Laboratory   1993 to Present
BECKMAN INSTITUTE / UNIVERSITY OF ILLINOIS

Winner of a highly-competitive Howard Hughes Fellowship in the Fall of 1993. Assigned to a four-person laboratory research team determining the process of recovery from lesioning/operations by the ocular vestibular system. Acquired extensive histological experience including perfusion, embedding, cryostat sectioning, and slide preparation/processing. Hired directly by the University in January 1994 and continue to work an average of 15 hours per week.

Computer Processor   Summer 1993
STATES ATTORNEY OF LIVINGSTON COUNTY

Lifeguard/Swimming Instructor   Summers 1990 to 1992
PONTIAC HIGH SCHOOL NATATORIUM / PONTIAC ELKS CLUB

References Provided Upon Request

AMANDA R. BRIGHTEN
9344 River Road
Charleston, West Virginia 32145
(304) 354-3521

EDUCATION:

1992 to Present	**MARSHALL UNIVERSITY SCHOOL OF MEDICINE**, Huntington, West Virginia **Medical Doctor Degree**, expected May 1997 Electives for 1996/97 include Internal Medicine, Emergency Medicine, SICU, Surgical Research, Family Practice, Anesthesiology, Radiology and Cardiology.
1988	**UNIVERSITY OF LEXINGTON**, Lexington, Kentucky **Post Graduate Classwork**
1986 to 1988	**MARSHALL UNIVERSITY SCHOOL OF MEDICINE**, Huntington, West Virginia **Post Graduate Classwork**
1981 to 1985	**WEST VIRGINIA WESLEYAN COLLEGE**, Buckhannon, West Virginia **Bachelor of Science Degree in Chemistry & Biology**, 1985

MEDICAL ROTATIONS & INTERNSHIPS:

July 1996 to August 1996. Completed an elective 4-week sub-internship with the Department Chairman of Surgery, Marshall University.

July 1994 to July 1995. Completed 8-week rotations in Surgery, Internal Medicine, Family Practice, Pediatrics, Psychiatry and Obstetrics/Gynecology.

ACADEMIC HONORS, AWARDS & ACTIVITIES:

Medical School
- Alpha Omega Alpha, 1996
- Top 10% of 50+ Student Medical Class, 1996
- Committee Appointee, Student Liaison Committee on Medical Education (LCME), 1996
- Invited Presenter, Panel Discussion on Medical Student Transition from Classroom to Clinical Experience, 1996

Undergraduate School
- Cum Laude Graduate (GPA 3.65)
- Outstanding Senior of the Year Award, 1985
- Greek Woman of the Year Award, 1985
- Who's Who Among Students in American Universities & Colleges
- Member, National Dean's List
- Member, Mortar Board
- Member, Phi Kappa Phi (Junior/Senior Honorary)
- Member, Alpha Lambda Delta (Freshman/Sophomore Honorary)
- President/Member, Beta Beta Beta (Biology Honorary)
- Dean's List (seven semesters)

EXTRACURRICULAR ACTIVITIES & AFFILIATIONS:

Medical School
- Member, American Medical Student Association
- Member, American Academy of Family Practice (Student Chapter)
- Senior Medical Class Representative, Marshall University Yearbook Committee, 1995
- Senior Medical Class Representative, Marshall University Recruitment Video, 1995

AMANDA R. BRIGHTEN   *Page Two*

EXTRACURRICULAR ACTIVITIES & AFFILIATIONS *(Continued)*:

Undergraduate School
- Publicity Chairman & Purchasing Agent, Alpha Gamma Delta Sorority
- Judge, West Virginia Wesleyan Science Fair
- Member, Chapel Choir
- Member, College Republicans
- Orientation Leader & Tour Guide
- Volunteer Instructor, Shawnee State University Summer Science Program
- Secretary/Treasurer, Benzene Ring

RELATED EMPLOYMENT EXPERIENCE:

1990 to 1992   **DICKINSON COLLEGE**, Carlisle, Pennsylvania
                              Laboratory Technician

Assigned to the Chemistry Laboratory with responsibility for the preparation of student laboratories and laboratory instruction. Trained/supervised a staff of work study students. Coordinated all contracted work and refurbishment in the Chemistry Building.

Administered annual operating budget, controlled inventory, scheduled equipment maintenance and repair, and purchased supplies, equipment and chemistry/medical technology.

Appointed to campus-wide Safety Committee, working in cooperation with other departments to rewrite campus safety policy.

1990   **SHAWNEE STATE UNIVERSITY**, Portsmouth, Ohio
                    Laboratory Coordinator

Prepared scheduled laboratories for Chemistry and Biology Departments. Assisted in student instruction, prepared/presented lectures and coordinated laboratory materials and equipment.

Participated in Biology Department Research Study investigating the effects of cutting innervation to taste buds in the golden hamster. Responsible for laboratory testing, data collection, analysis and reporting. Assisted Principal Researcher in developing research protocols and study hypotheses.

1985 to 1986   **WEST VIRGINIA WESLEYAN COLLEGE**, Buckhannon, West Virginia
                              Laboratory Instructor

Assisted full-time undergraduate teaching staff in General Chemistry Laboratories. Responsible for pre-lab lectures and student instruction during laboratory sessions. Prepared midterm and final examinations, tutored students needing additional laboratory instruction, and assigned special projects. Awarded final laboratory grades.

OTHER EMPLOYMENT EXPERIENCE:

1991 to 1992   **THE BON TON**, Carlisle, Pennsylvania
                              Sales Associate

Full-time sales associate in a specialty retail store. Responsible for product sales, merchandising, promotions and customer service. Trained/oriented newly hired sales associates.

1989 to 1990   **LAZARUS**, Huntington, West Virginia
                              Sales Associate

Full-time sales associate in a high-volume retail department store.

AMY JONES
3959 Winterhaven   •   Rochester, New York 19463   •   (908) 654-3211

CHEMICAL ENGINEER
Design & Development / Process / Environmental

QUALIFICATIONS SUMMARY:

Recent graduate with three years related experience and 10 years prior experience. Strong skills in Applied Chemistry with hands-on analytical instrumentation knowledge with Perkin-Elmer DSC-4, HP 5890 Series II Gas Chromatograph with HP 5988A Mass Spectrometer, Lambda-9 Spectrophotometer, Hitachi HPLC and Nicolet FTIR.

Qualified in the use of leading edge information technologies for experimental data analysis, numerical problem solving, spreadsheets, graphic design and presentations. Software includes MathCAD, DEQ, CC, MS Word, WordPerfect, PowerPoint, EXCEL and QuattroPro. Proficient in FORTRAN and BASIC programming.

EDUCATION:

B.S., Chemical Engineering, May 1995
UNIVERSITY OF ROCHESTER, Rochester, New York

Additional Studies in Microelectronic Device Processing, Polymer Science & Technology, Environmental Science & Engineering and Environmental Geophysics.

PROFESSIONAL EXPERIENCE:

Research Technician   October 1994 to Present
LABORATORY FOR LASER ENERGETICS, Rochester, New York

Member of the Optical Materials Engineering Group working in cooperation with a team of senior researchers, scientists and engineers investigating the physical properties of polymers and related materials/components.

- Performed chemical characterization, optical analysis and thermal analysis of polymers using GC/MS, DSC, HPLC and FTIR.
- Formulated liquid crystal solutions for polarizers in Class 100 clean room environment.
- Implemented small scale separations to aid in the synthesis of optical polymers for use as optical waveplates.
- Maintained, troubleshot and calibrated electronic equipment and instrumentation.
- Procured chemicals/supplies from vendors nationwide. Managed vendor sourcing and price negotiations.
- Documented experimental results, findings and recommendations.

Pharmacy Technician   April 1992 to December 1993
STRONG MEMORIAL HOSPITAL, Rochester, New York

Formulated prescriptions for intravenous additives and assisted pharmacists in preparing injectable medications. Specialized in sterile preparation and custom formulations. Documented distribution of controlled substances.

Technician   January 1992 to April 1992
CANTISANO FOODS, INC., Rochester, New York

Conducted and documented on-line product testing to determine pH and NaCl levels. Compiled data for USDA inspections and reports to verify regulatory compliance. Inspected product packaging and labeling to ensure adherence to corporate specifications. (Temporary position in affiliation with undergraduate studies at Monroe Community College in Rochester.)

Previous Experience (1980 to 1992) as an Administrative Assistant, Customer Service Representative, Telemarketing Representative and Recreational Program Assistant in New York City and Rochester.

PROFESSIONAL AFFILIATIONS:

American Institute of Chemical Engineers (Member), American Chemical Society (Member), Society of Women Engineers (Member), University of Rochester Chapter of The Materials Research Society (Volunteer)

NEWMAN W. GRANT

234 Cross Point
Katonah, New York 15615
(516) 654-6427

CORPORATE TAX EXECUTIVE
Domestic & International Taxation

Comprehensive and substantive knowledge of all facets of corporate tax planning, compliance and audit management. Consistently successful in identifying and capturing advantageous tax positions through combined expertise in strategic business planning, transactions management, corporate finance and corporate legal affairs. Guided senior management and financial executives through complex corporate development and financing projects.

TAX EXPERTISE:

Federal Tax — Consolidated returns (investment accounts, earnings and profits, net operating loss allocations, SRLY's, allocation of tax benefits), corporate development (mergers, acquisitions, reorganizations, liquidations, partnerships, joint ventures), loss limitations, related party interest deductions, earnings stripping and intercompany pricing.

State & Federal Audits — Complete audit engagements, from pre-audit conferences through audits, protests, rulings, requests and appeals to Claims and Tax Courts.

State Tax — Income, franchise, property, severance, sales and use.

PROFESSIONAL EXPERIENCE:

ELF AQUITAINE, INC., New York, New York   1979 to Present
($3 billion specialty chemical & natural resource company)

> **Director of Taxes / Corporate Officer** (1993 to Present)
> **Manager - Federal Tax Audits & Planning** (1984 to 1993)
> **Senior Tax Accountant** (1981 to 1984)
> **Intermediate Tax Accountant** (1979 to 1981)

Fast-track promotion through a series of increasingly responsible management assignments to current position as **Director of Taxes** for all U.S. operations. Scope of responsibility includes all tax issues impacting Elf Aquitaine, three other principal subsidiaries, business operations in 40 states and a total workforce of more than 4000 employees. Manage a direct reporting staff of 20 at three locations.

Establish all tax policies and procedures for the company, direct all compliance and audit functions, and facilitate long-term tax planning for company and individual operating units. Advise senior level operating executives in the U.S. and Paris (parent company) regarding domestic and foreign tax matters relative to operations, proposed acquisitions and divestitures, asset management and disposition, strategic planning and a diversity of other corporate initiatives. Manage all IRS audit engagements.

Currently directing litigation proceedings in Claims Court, Tax Court and IRS Appeals Office. Issues involve foreign tax structures, allocations and regulatory interpretation.

NEWMAN W. GRANT   **Page Two**

ELF AQUITAINE, INC. *(Continued)*:

Significant Projects & Achievements:

- Managed five major IRS audit engagements including a complex Tax Benefit Transfer Audit resulting from Elf's acquisition of Texasgulf Inc. Prepared appraisal and allocation of purchase price for $3.2 billion transaction. Negotiated proposed $30 million of disallowed deductions down to only $1.5 million.

- Restructured land transfer tax agreement to "form over substance" for a $600,000 net savings.

- Converted $700 million of equity to debt, reducing withholding tax liability to parent company by $34 million.

- Consulted directly with the Joint Committee on Taxation related to proposed energy tax affecting the cogeneration industry and on Section 382 (limitations of net operating losses for privatization transactions).

- Provided tax expertise in preparation of 1995 IPO, subsequently discontinued by company in favor of acquisition.

- Directed planning, compliance, audit and appeals engagements for Federal and Provincial Canadian taxes.

- Spearheaded the introduction of sophisticated PC LAN, client/server, CD-ROM, OCR and software technologies to automate the entire tax planning and reporting functions. Designed complex financial and tax modeling spreadsheets.

> ***NOTE:***   Originally recruited to Texasgulf Inc. in 1979. Acquired by Elf Acquitaine in 1981, retained by new management team and promoted.

PRICE WATERHOUSE & CO., Bridgeport, Connecticut   1977 to 1979

Tax & Audit Staff Accountant

Tax Advisor to corporations, partnerships, trusts and individuals. Audit experience in industrial manufacturing, apparel manufacturing, health care, brokerage/investment services and commercial banking.

EDUCATION:

MS Degree - Corporate Finance, Fairfield University, Fairfield, Connecticut, 1990
JD Degree, Vermont Law School, South Royalton, Vermont, 1977
BBA Degree - Accounting, St. Edward's University, Austin, Texas, 1974

PROFESSIONAL AFFILIATIONS:

- Treasurer, Organization for International Investment
- Member, Tax Executive Institute
- Member, International Fiscal Association
- Member, The Corporate Bar
- Member, Committee on State Taxation

GARY BLOCK

3154 Desert Sands
Reno, Nevada 64512
(644) 365-4321

TRANSPORTATION / LOGISTICS / DISTRIBUTION
Start-Up, Turnaround & Management of
Profitable, Multi-Site Dedicated Logistics Operations

Over 15 years experience in the Transportation Industry. Strong record of cost reduction, revenue improvement and quality/performance management. Excellent qualifications in operations planning/management, customer management, union negotiations and fleet management.

PROFESSIONAL EXPERIENCE:

RYDER DEDICATED LOGISTICS   1988 to Present
(Contracted Logistics, Distribution & Transportation Operations)

OPERATIONS MANAGER (1991 to Present)
OPERATIONS SUPERVISOR (1989 to 1990)
DISPATCHER (1988 to 1989)

Operations Manager responsible for the start-up, development, growth and management of RDL's contract services to Montgomery Ward throughout California and Nevada. Scope of responsibility includes the entire operation of each facility, including staffing, budgeting, financial reporting, cost control, dispatching, routing, scheduling, union relations/negotiations, DOT regulatory affairs, safety, training and customer management.

Transferred between three Ward logistics operations to coordinate the start-up of each and the subsequent turnaround following unsuccessful transition to other management teams. Assigned full P&L responsibility in 1994 for all three locations and a staff of 87.

- Built Montgomery Ward account from start-up to $5.5 million in annual revenues.

- Directed start-up of Las Vegas Home Delivery, San Diego Home Delivery and Garden Grove shuttle operations. Built each into a fully-staffed, full-service logistics facility operating at profitability within three months.

- Troubleshot and turned around poorly-performing operations. Delivered significant and sustainable financial gains through efforts in cost reduction, productivity improvement, service improvement and staff consolidation.

- Maintained competitive position against other dedicated logistics service contractors. RDL guaranteed a 20% reduction in operating costs to Ward following its take-over of Las Vegas facility. Delivered an actual 33% reduction in their costs while continuing to exceed RDL's profit objectives.

- Consulted with upper level management personnel to negotiate and resolve labor union problems.

GARY BLOCK - Page Two

RYDER DEDICATED LOGISTICS *(Continued)*:

Since March 1995 have provided start-up expertise to numerous operations. Hold full responsibility for all logistics, distribution and transportation functions (e.g., budgeting, financial reporting, staffing, union relations, safety, training, dispatching, routing). Highlights include:

- Currently directing the turnaround of logistics and distribution operations for the Fletcher Challenge warehousing center in Los Angeles, California. Given full autonomy for this fast-paced, union operation managing incoming sea freight, warehousing and distribution to *The Los Angeles Times* and other major publishers, print shops and advertising agencies throughout the region. Supervise team of 25.

- Completed two-month special project as Operations Manager for the start-up of the Standard Brand Paints shuttle service facility in Torrance, California. Brought operation to profitability within two months with $1.1 million projected in first year revenues (10%-12% profit).

- Orchestrated the start-up of a complete logistics operation to service Homestead Home Delivery's customer base throughout the Western U.S. Held full P&L and operating management responsibility for this operation.

- Consulted with RDL management team in Toronto for the start-up of Canadian logistics operations for Consumer Gas and Sears Home Delivery.

Early career positions as a Dispatcher for RDL's fully-integrated logistics operations at Howard's Home Delivery, Circuit City Home Delivery and General Electric. Assisted in the shutdown of all three facilities, reassignment of personnel and reallocation of equipment.

EARLY LOGISTICS & TRANSPORTATION INDUSTRY EXPERIENCE as a Dispatcher and Driver with Wallace Transport and several other warehousing/distribution companies in the Western U.S.

EDUCATION:

RYDER DEDICATED LOGISTICS
Frontline Leadership Training
Logistics Management Training
Supervisory & Leadership Training

References Provided Upon Request

JOHN SPENCER
93489 Old Salem House
Boston, Massachusetts 65441
(697) 653-1654

DISTRIBUTION OPERATIONS / WAREHOUSING / TRANSPORTATION EXECUTIVE
Building Profitable, Efficient & Quality-Driven National Logistics Operations

Well-qualified executive with 20+ years experience in the strategic planning, development, staffing, budgeting and management of large-scale distribution operations. Expertise includes:

- Multi-Site Operations Management
- Transportation Planning/Operations
- Carrier Selection/Negotiations
- Equipment Acquisition/Asset Management
- Human Resource Affairs/Labor Relations
- EDI/Supplier Partnerships

- Materials Planning/Management
- Capital Project Management
- Facility Design/Specification
- Budgeting/Financial Affairs
- JIT/Quick Response Inventory
- OSHA/DOT Regulatory Affairs

Managed up to 22 distribution sites supplying 130 sites nationwide with an inventory valued at $140+ million and a 140-vehicle fleet. Captured multi-million dollar cost savings through efficiency, productivity, quality and safety improvements.

PROFESSIONAL EXPERIENCE:

Senior Partner   1992 to Present
OUTSOURCE, INC., Boston, Massachusetts

Recruited by executive team of this full-service transportation management firm to provide strategic and tactical leadership for an aggressive business growth and diversification program. Company specializes in the design and delivery of customized logistics operations to reduce costs of product acquisition, transportation and warehousing for client companies.

Manage client projects from initial consultation, through a comprehensive service improvement, cost reduction and analysis program for design, development, and oversight of logistics operations. Evaluate existing logistics operations and integrate within newly-established programs. Analyze efficiencies of existing warehousing, fleet and traffic management processes to determine alternative paths of supply management. Provide on-site training to company personnel and personally negotiate carrier price and service contracts.

- Won nine major traffic management contracts which generated over $1 million in revenues to Outsource.

- Spearheaded three major logistics projects with full responsibility for design of turnkey warehousing, distribution, fleet and logistics operations.

Vice President of Distribution   1978 to 1991
CHANNEL HOME CENTERS, INC., Whippany, New Jersey

Senior Operating Executive responsible for the strategic planning, development and management of a regional distribution program servicing 167 home centers in 10 states throughout the Eastern U.S. Total revenue volume exceeded $650 million. Total SKUs of approximately 20,000 items.

Scope of responsibility included five distribution centers, a 100-tractor private fleet, 400 personnel, a $31 million inventory and the entire domestic/import traffic management program. Managed a $17 million annual operating budget, administered all DOT and OSHA regulatory compliance programs, and introduced a complete safety, health, quality and productivity improvement plan. Directed distribution operations purchasing and vendor management programs.

Conducted ongoing operational analyses to maximize operational efficiencies through redesign of warehousing facilities and realignment of regional distribution network. Negotiated contracts with common carriers to reduce transportation costs and administered union contract agreements for Channel employees.

CHANNEL HOME CENTERS, INC. (*Continued*):

- Created an innovative cross-docking program in cooperation with major suppliers that reduced Channel's annual product acquisition costs by more than $15 million.

- Introduced a proactive program for inventory control that reduced shrinkage from $1.4 million to only $250,000 within two years.

- Consulted with A.D. Little to design and implement leading edge computer technology for the optimal replenishment method for each SKU category.

- Implemented JIT/quick response inventory and stock replenishment programs that resolved previous problems with merchandise distribution and provided adequate inventory at all 165 retail locations.

Assistant Vice President of Corporate Distribution   1970 to 1977
TWO GUYS DEPARTMENT STORES (Vornado, Inc.), Garfield, New Jersey

Promoted from Director of Distribution to Assistant Vice President within one year of hire with responsibility for 22 distribution centers (3 million square feet), 1100 employees, 140-vehicle fleet, $140 million inventory and $23 million annual operating budget. Directed stock replenishment and merchandise distribution (87,000 hard and soft goods) to 130 stores in nine states. Total revenues exceeded $1 billion.

- Launched a series of aggressive cost reduction initiatives that saved over $9 million in annual expenses. Realized savings through redesign of existing warehousing and transportation programs, negotiation of discounted purchasing and service agreements, realignment of staff requirements, and improved operating policies and procedures.

- Initiated and secured ICC approval for a wholly-owned subsidiary contract carrier. Reduced annual costs to the corporation by $2.5 million through savings in payroll and equipment costs concurrent with a significant decrease in union exposure.

- Restructured the entire distribution network, consolidated operations and eliminated four distribution centers for a net annual savings of more than $6.5 million.

- Negotiated favorable collective bargaining agreements with three Teamsters local unions and the International Ladies Garment Workers Union.

EDUCATION: **BS / Business / Summa Cum Laude**, Bloomfield College, Bloomfield, New Jersey, 1994
                      BA / Psychology, Rutgers University, Newark, New Jersey, 1970

                      Highlights of Continuing Professional Education:

- Traffic Management, Rutgers University
- General Transportation Management, Rutgers University
- Computer Applications in Distribution, American Management Association
- Warehouse Layout, American Management Association
- Materials Handling Management, International Materials Management Society

PROFESSIONAL AFFILIATIONS:

American Management Association   Council of Logistics Management
International Materials Handling Society   Warehouse Education & Research Council
Private Carrier Council   American Trucking Association

MICHAEL De LEON
9834 Avenida de Peces   Buenos Aires 6416, Argentina
011-64-4-713-8977

GLOBAL TRAVEL & TOURISM INDUSTRY EXECUTIVE

Sales & Marketing Management / Key Account Management / Customer Relationship Management
Travel Agency Operations / P&L Management / Information Technology / Professional Staffing
Public Relations & Promotions / Strategic Business Partnerships / Revenue & Income Growth

Well-respected Industry Executive with more than 15 years professional and managerial experience. Pioneer in the introduction of travel, tour and expedition programs throughout new regions worldwide. Established relationships with leading corporate, industry and embassy officials that have resulted in millions of dollars in travel revenues and a distinctive positioning within the highly competitive global market.

Fluent in English, Spanish, French and German. Dual citizenship in Argentina and France.

PROFESSIONAL EXPERIENCE:

Owner / Managing Director   1979 to Present
ASTRA TRAVEL, S.R.L., Buenos Aires, Argentina

Senior Operating Executive with full P&L responsibility for an exclusive travel agency specializing in adventure tours and expeditions worldwide (e.g., Antarctica, China, Easter Island, Galapagos, Tibet, Greenland, Vietnam). Hold full accountability for annual business/market planning, sales management, public relations and promotions, travel/tour design, corporate client development and management, supervision of accounting and finance functions, professional and support staffing, training, information technology and all administrative affairs. Negotiate and manage strategic partnerships with travel agencies and airlines (e.g., British Airways, Canadian Airlines) worldwide.

- Built revenues from **US$1.8 million to US$3 million**. Delivered consistent increases in sales performance with growth of up to 100% annually.

- Established global business relationships with embassies, companies, banks, international news agencies and other corporate accounts to plan and direct their travel and tour programs. Key accounts include Bank of America, Lloyds Bank, ICI Pharmaceutical and the British Embassy.

- Ranked as the **#1 agency in Argentina** for airline ticket sales between Argentina and Canada and the only travel agency in Argentina to exceed Canadian Airlines' sales quotas in 1993 and 1994. Earned the Airline's prestigious **"Sales Quota Achievement Award"** in 1994.

- Orchestrated the introduction of PC-based technologies to automate all reservation systems, accounting, reporting, database management and administration (Amadeus, Sabre, Galileo).

- Managed a key strategic partnership with Lindblad Travel, U.S.A. as their exclusive South American representative. Significantly expanded account revenues to the agency.

- Recognized worldwide by leading travel authorities and publications for innovative, upscale and high-quality tours and expeditions. Recommended in major travel guides including <u>South American Handbook - The Travellers World Guide</u> and Rand McNally's <u>South American Handbook</u>.

- Guest speaker at the University of El Salvador (Buenos Aires), American University Club, Argentine Travel Association, and other industry groups and symposia.

Agency won the German "Medal for Professional Tourism" for technical tours designed and sponsored in cooperation with Lufthansa, and the "Gold Medal" from the Argentine Association of Travel Agencies and Travel Agents as the first travel agency to open the Antarctic continent for tourism.

MICHAEL De LEON

Page Two

Manager - Cruise Department   1978
LINDBLAD TRAVEL, New York, New York

Recruited to join this prestigious travel operator catering to an exclusive clientele (e.g., Prince Bernard of Holland, President of Shell International). Responsible for the sale/marketing of cruises and adventure expeditions to "new" destinations including Antarctica, Galapagos, South Pacific and the Arctic Region. Trained and supervised three travel agents.

Early Experience aboard the M.S. Lindblad travelling throughout the Antarctic region. Attended on-board lectures presented by Jacques-Yves Costeau, Roger Tory Peterson and Sir Peter Scott. Played a critical role in emergency rescue following the vessel's grounding and transfer of passengers to a Chilean Navy vessel.

EDUCATION:

ARGENTINE CATHOLIC UNIVERSITY, Buenos Aires, Argentina
Major in Political Science (1977)

UNIVERSITE DE SCIENCES POLITIQUES, Paris, France
Major in Political Science (1975)

LONDON UNIVERSITY, London, England
Certificate in Spanish Literature (1973)

UNIVERSITY OF CAMBRIDGE, Cambridge, England
Certificates in English, Spanish, Geography and Economics (1972)

Highlights of Management Training & Development:

- Management Training & Development, Lufthansa (1980 to 1981)
- Developing Management Skills, Pan American Airways (1979)
- Sales Dynamics, Pan American Airways (1978)
- Rates & Tariffs, Pan American Airways (1977)

PROFESSIONAL AFFILIATIONS:

Association of Tourism Industrial Professionals (SKaL)

- Appointed as the youngest member ever. Elected to the Board of Directors in 1982. Served as the Club Secretary in 1984 (honored as "Club of the Year" by the international association).

International Air Transport Association
American Society of Travel Agents
Argentine Association of Travel Agents
Association of Travel Agents of Buenos Aires
Argentine Chamber of Commerce for Tourism

PATRICIA BRADFORD
731 Northwind Drive
Greenwich, Conneticut 65464
(203) 413-47389

CORPORATE TREASURY MANAGER
Cash Management & Investment / Debt Management & Recapitalization / Pension Plan Administration

Fifteen years of progressively responsible experience in the planning, development and management of complex treasury operations worldwide. Combines expert financial, analytical, negotiations and executive presentation experience with excellent qualifications in MIS technology, investment planning and capital structure/capital investment. Thunderbird Masters Degree.

PROFESSIONAL EXPERIENCE:

THE COCA-COLA BOTTLING COMPANY OF NEW YORK, Greenwich, CT   1989 to Present
(Fortune 400 company with $700 million in annual revenues)

Assistant Treasurer (1994 to Present)
Manager of Treasury Operations (1991 to 1994)
Manager of Cash & Debt (1989 to 1991)

Fast-track promotion to current position as **Principal Treasury Officer** for all domestic operations. Responsible for structuring $650 million in debt, managing $65 million in pension assets, negotiating $220 million in letters of credit and directing accounting operations for $700 million in annual sales. Hold full strategic planning, operating and management responsibility for:

- **Debt Management** — capital structure, rating agency presentations and negotiation of loan covenant amendments.
- **Pension Management** — financial management of defined benefit and contribution plans.
- **Cash Management** — short term investments, automated treasury systems, and treasury policy/procedures.

Concurrent management responsibility for cash flow forecasting, financial reporting, bank relationships management, interest rate risk exposure and professional staffing/training. Administer $700,000 annual operating budget.

- Recapitalized the company, transitioning from a highly-leveraged and below investment grade position to liquidity with capability of meeting all future cash requirements. Restructuring included $160 million in preferred stock, $315 million in senior debt and $175 million in subordinated debt. Negotiated amendments to loan agreements to restructure capital base and lowered cost of debt by $15+ million annually.
- Launched a complete reengineering of cash management function, introduced leading edge technologies (e.g., lockbox, control disbursement, direct deposit of payroll, general ledger software), and reduced annual operating costs by 25%.
- Defined organizational requirements and successfully introduced an enhanced 401(k) plan.
- Analyzed and executed a successful interest rate hedging strategy.
- Orchestrated annual three-year strategic planning process for the entire company.

TRIANGLE INDUSTRIES, INC., New York, NY   1987 to 1989
(Fortune 200 company with $1.8 billion in annual revenues)

Cash Manager

Dual management responsibility for all cash and treasury operations of holding company and its seven subsidiary manufacturing operations (e.g., American Can, National Can, Uniroyal Chemical). Scope of responsibility included design/implementation of cash management systems, cash forecasting and investment of $100 million, high-yield, short-term portfolio.

* Spearheaded the selection and implementation of cash management systems to automate all treasury operations. Managed project from concept through development and implementation, creating a fully-integrated, state-of-the-art technology function.

* Demonstrated expertise in short-term investment management, outperforming Donaghue Index by an average of 300 basis points.

* Authored policies and directed implementation of the corporation's first formal cash forecasting and cash control procedures.

JOSEPH E. SEAGRAM AND SONS, INC., New York, NY   1982 to 1987

Assistant Cash Manager (1985 to 1987)
Senior Cash Analyst (1983 to 1985)
Cash Analyst (1982 to 1983)

Promoted through a series of increasingly responsible assignments to final position as second-in-command of this multinational corporation's global cash management program. Defined short-term investment objectives and executed investment transactions and spot purchases of foreign exchange.

* Planned strategy and directed investment of $100 million short-term portfolio.

* Designed and implemented a foreign exchange netting system which reduced the cost of foreign exchange by more than 40%.

* Automated and subsequently managed a $300 million commercial paper program.

* Recruited to Seagram following year-long banking relationship at Manufacturers Hanover.

MANUFACTURERS HANOVER TRUST CO., New York, NY   1981 to 1982

Operations Specialist

Direct liaison between the bank and several major corporate clients (e.g., Texaco, Seagram, Continental Grain) to facilitate banking, cash management and short-term credit/lending transactions.

CENTRAL NATIONAL BANK, Berkley, CA   1979 to 1980

Operations Trainee

Completed an intensive 12-month professional training program.

EDUCATION:

MASTERS DEGREE IN INTERNATIONAL MANAGEMENT, 1978
American Graduate School of International Management (Thunderbird), Phoenix, Arizona

BACHELOR OF ARTS DEGREE / BUSINESS MINOR, 1976
College of Santa Fe, Santa Fe, New Mexico

CHAPTER THREE

KEYWORDS

You talk to a resume professional, and they mention **KeyWords**.

You read about the Internet and job search technology, and the emphasis is on **KeyWords**.

You listen to a news brief about employment trends, and they mention **KeyWords**.

You go to a job search training and networking seminar, and the focus is on **KeyWords**.

What Are KeyWords and Where Do They Come From?

Keywords are buzz words — "action" verbs and nouns you can use in your resume to sharpen the text and enhance the presentation. There are virtually hundreds and hundreds of KeyWords — some that are general and everyone can use; others that are specific to your industry and your profession.

> ### Incorporate words from the following list to make your resume "buzz"!

BE CAREFUL! Use these words wisely to highlight your skills, experiences, qualifications, competencies, achievements and success — NOT IN EXCHANGE FOR THEM! Your career is the core of the resume. KeyWords are used to "surround" and "sell" it.

Look on the bookshelves this fall for "100 Words for $100,000+ Jobs" (written by Wendy S. Enelow and published by Impact Publications). This book contains hundreds of KeyWord nouns and action verbs for use in resume and cover letter writing.

Accelerated	Cataloged	Corrected	Dramatized
Accomplished	Charted	Counseled	Drew
Achieved	Checked	Created	Drove
Acquired	Clarified	Critiqued	Earned
Acted	Classified	Dealt	Edited
Adapted	Closed	Decided	Educated
Addressed	Coached	Defined	Effected
Administered	Collected	Delegated	Eliminated
Advised	Commanded	Demonstrated	Emphasized
Analyzed	Communicated	Depended	Enacted
Anticipated	Compared	Designed	Encouraged
Applied	Compiled	Detailed	Endured
Appointed	Completed	Detected	Enforced
Appraised	Composed	Determined	Engineered
Approved	Computed	Developed	Enhanced
Arbitrated	Conceived	Devised	Enlisted
Arranged	Conceptualized	Diagnosed	Ensured
Ascertained	Concluded	Directed	Entertained
Assembled	Conducted	Discovered	Established
Assessed	Confronted	Dispensed	Estimated
Assisted	Conserved	Displayed	Evaluated
Assured	Consolidated	Disproved	Examined
Attained	Constructed	Dissected	Exceeded
Briefed	Continued	Distributed	Executed
Budgeted	Contracted	Diverted	Exhibited
Built	Converted	Doubled	Expanded
Calculated	Coordinated	Drafted	Expedited

Explained	Imagined	Launched	Observed
Experimented	Implemented	Lectured	Obtained
Expressed	Improved	Led	Offered
Extracted	Improvised	Learned	Officiated
Facilitated	Increased	Licensed	Operated
Filed	Induced	Listened	Ordered
Finalized	Influenced	Located	Organized
Financed	Informed	Logged	Oriented
Fixed	Initiated	Maintained	Originated
Followed	Innovated	Managed	Overcame
Formalized	Inspected	Manipulated	Oversaw
Formed	Inspired	Manufactured	Painted
Formulated	Installed	Mapped	Participated
Found	Instituted	Marketed	Perceived
Founded	Instructed	Measured	Perfected
Gathered	Insured	Mediated	Performed
Generated	Integrated	Mentored	Persuaded
Governed	Intensified	Modeled	Photographed
Graduated	Interpreted	Modified	Piloted
Guided	Interviewed	Monitored	Pinpointed
Handled	Introduced	Motivated	Pioneered
Headed	Invented	Named	Placed
Helped	Inventoried	Navigated	Planned
Hired	Investigated	Negotiated	Played
Hypothesized	Judged	Nominated	Praised
Identified	Justified	Normalized	Predicted
Illustrated	Kept	Noted	Prepared

Prescribed	Recorded	Served	Targeted
Presented	Recruited	Serviced	Taught
Presided	Reduced	Set-up	Tested
Printed	Referred	Shaped	Trained
Processed	Regulated	Shared	Transcribed
Procured	Rehabilitated	Showed	Transferred
Professed	Reinforced	Sketched	Transformed
Programmed	Related	Simplified	Translated
Progressed	Rendered	Sold	Treated
Projected	Reorganized	Solved	Traveled
Promoted	Repaired	Sorted	Troubleshot
Proofread	Reported	Specified	Tutored
Proposed	Represented	Spoke	Typed
Protected	Researched	Stimulated	Understudied
Proved	Resolved	Streamlined	Undertook
Provided	Responded	Structured	Unified
Publicized	Restored	Studied	United
Purchased	Retrieved	Succeeded	Updated
Qualified	Restructured	Suggested	Upgraded
Questioned	Reviewed	Summarized	Used
Raised	Revised	Supervised	Utilized
Rated	Risked	Supplied	Verbalized
Realigned	Satisfied	Supported	Verified
Reasoned	Scheduled	Symbolized	Weighed
Received	Secured	Synthesized	Won
Recognized	Selected	Systematized	Worked
Recommended	Sensed	Tabulated	Wrote
Reconciled	Separated	Talked	

RESUME & JOB SEARCH RESOURCES

THE ADVANTAGE INC.

Executive Resume & Career Management Center

The Advantage, Inc., one of the nation's foremost resume and job search centers, was founded by Wendy S. Enelow in August 1986. The firm specializes in resume development, job search and career coaching for professional, management, senior management and executive job search candidates. To date, The Advantage has worked with more than 5000 professionals worldwide to plan and manage their successful job search campaigns!

Professional writers and coaches work one-on-one with you to explore your professional goals, develop career strategies, create winning resumes and implement action plans that competitively position you to:

> ## Win in Today's Competitive Job Search Market!

Executive Resume Development   Targeted Direct Mail Campaigns
Cover Letter Writing Services   Internet Online Services
Executive Career Planning & Coaching   Interview Counseling
Executive Job Lead Publications   KeyWord Presentations

Consultations with Wendy Enelow are by scheduled appointment. If you are interested in executive resume, career coaching or job search management services, fax the form below with your resume to (804) 384-4700 or phone (804) 384-4600.

- -

❑ **YES!**   Please contact me regarding your services and pricing.
              My resume is attached.

NAME: _____

ADDRESS: _____

PHONE: _____

FAX: _____ *Is this a private fax?* **YES   NO**

211

Career Resources

C ontact Impact Publications to receive a free annotated listing of career resources or visit their World Wide Web (Internet) site for a complete listing of career resources: *http://www.impactpublications.com.*

The following career resources are available directly from Impact Publications. Complete this form or list the titles, include postage (see formula at the end), enclose payment, and send your order to:

IMPACT PUBLICATIONS
9104-N Manassas Drive
Manassas Park, VA 20111-2366
Tel. 1-800-361-1055, 703/361-7300 or Fax 703/335-9486
E-mail: impactp@impactpublications.com

Orders from individuals must be prepaid by check, moneyorder, Visa, MasterCard, or American Express. We accept telephone, fax, and e-mail orders.

Qty.	TITLES	Price	TOTAL
Author's Books and Audios			
__	100 Winning Resumes For $100,000+ Jobs	$24.95	_____
__	201 Winning Cover Letters For $100,000+ Jobs	$24.95	_____
__	301 Key Words for $100,000+ Jobs	$14.95	_____
__	Resume Explosion (audio program)	$29.95	_____
Resume Books			
__	101 Best Resumes	$10.95	_____
__	101 Great Resumes	$9.99	_____
__	101 Resumes For Sure-Hire Results	$10.95	_____
__	175 High-Impact Resumes	$10.95	_____
__	Adams Resume Almanac	$10.95	_____
__	Asher's Bible of Executive Resumes	$29.95	_____
__	Best Resumes For $75,000+ Executive Jobs	$14.95	_____
__	Building a Great Resume	$15.00	_____
__	Complete Idiot's Guide to Crafting the Perfect Resume	$16.95	_____
__	Designing the Perfect Resume	$12.95	_____
__	Dynamite Resumes	$14.95	_____
__	Electronic Resume Revolution	$12.95	_____
__	Electronic Resumes: Putting Your Resume On-Line	$19.95	_____
__	Electronic Resumes For the New Job Market	$11.95	_____
__	Encyclopedia of Job-Winning Resumes	$16.95	_____
__	Gallery of Best Resumes	$16.95	_____
__	Gallery of Best Resumes For Two-Year Degree Graduates	$14.95	_____
__	High Impact Resumes and Letters	$19.95	_____
__	How to Prepare Your Curriculum Vitae	$14.95	_____
__	Just Resumes	$11.95	_____
__	NBEW's Resumes	$11.95	_____
__	New Perfect Resume	$10.95	_____

__ Portfolio Power	$14.95	_____
__ Power Resumes	$12.95	_____
__ Quick Resume and Cover Letter Book	$12.95	_____
__ Real-Life Resumes That Work!	$12.95	_____
__ Resume Catalog	$15.95	_____
__ Resume Pro	$24.95	_____
__ Resume Shortcuts	$14.95	_____
__ Resume Solution	$12.95	_____
__ Resume Writing Made Easy	$10.95	_____
__ Resumes and Cover Letters For Transitioning Military Personnel	$17.95	_____
__ Resumes For Advertising Careers	$9.95	_____
__ Resumes For Architecture and Related Careers	$9.95	_____
__ Resumes For Banking and Financial Careers	$9.95	_____
__ Resumes For Business Management Careers	$9.95	_____
__ Resumes For Communications Careers	$9.95	_____
__ Resumes For Dummies	$12.99	_____
__ Resumes For Education Careers	$9.95	_____
__ Resumes For Engineering Careers	$9.95	_____
__ Resumes For Environmental Careers	$9.95	_____
__ Resumes For Ex-Military Personnel	$9.95	_____
__ Resumes For 50+ Job Hunters	$9.95	_____
__ Resumes For the Healthcare Professional	$12.95	_____
__ Resumes For High Tech Careers	$9.95	_____
__ Resumes For Midcareer Job Changers	$9.95	_____
__ Resumes For the Over 50 Job Hunter	$14.95	_____
__ Resumes For People Who Hate to Write Resumes	$12.95	_____
__ Resumes For Re-Entry: A Woman's Handbook	$10.95	_____
__ Resumes For Sales and Marketing Careers	$9.95	_____
__ Resumes For Scientific and Technical Careers	$9.95	_____
__ Resumes That Knock 'Em Dead	$10.95	_____
__ Resumes, Resumes, Resumes	$9.99	_____
__ Sure-Hire Resumes	$14.95	_____

Resume Books With Computer Disk

__ Adams Resume Almanac With Disk	$19.95	_____
__ New 90-Minute Resume	$15.95	_____
__ Ready-to-Go Resumes	$16.95	_____

Resume Software (specify disk size and system)

__ Perfect Resume Kit (Individual Version)	$49.95	_____
__ Perfect Resume Kit (Counselor Version)	$259.95	_____
__ Perfect Resume Kit (Lab Pack Version)	$639.95	_____
__ Perfect Resume Kit (Network Version)	$999.95	_____

Resume CD-ROMs

__ Adams Resumes and Cover Letters	$49.95	_____
__ ResumeMaker CD Deluxe	$49.95	_____
__ Resume Express	$129.95	_____
__ Top Secret Resumes and Cover Letters	$39.95	_____
__ Win Way Resume 4.0	$69.95	_____
__ The Ultimate Job Source (individual version)	$49.95	_____

Resume Videos

__ Does Your Resume Wear Blue Jeans Resume Writing Workshop	$99.95	_____
__ Effective Resumes	$98.00	_____
__ The Miracle Resume	$129.95	_____
__ Resume Remedy	$119.00	_____
__ Video Resume Writer	$102.95	_____
__ Your Resume	$98.00	_____

Cover Letters

__ 175 High-Impact Cover Letters	$10.95	_____
__ 200 Letters For Job Hunters	$19.95	_____
__ 201 Dynamite Job Search Letters	$19.95	_____
__ 201 Killer Cover Letters (with Disk)	$16.95	_____
__ Adams Cover Letter Almanac and Disk	$19.95	_____
__ Cover Letters For Dummies	$12.99	_____
__ Cover Letters That Knock 'Em Dead	$10.95	_____
__ Dynamite Cover Letters	$14.95	_____
__ Perfect Cover Letter	$10.95	_____
__ Sure-Hire Cover Letters	$10.95	_____

Interviews, Networking, and Salary Negotiations

__ 101 Dynamite Answers to Interview Questions	$12.95	_____
__ 101 Dynamite Questions to Ask At Your Job Interview	$14.95	_____
__ 111 Dynamite Ways to Ace Your Job Interview	$13.95	_____
__ 201 Answers to the Toughest Job Interview Questions	$10.95	_____
__ Dynamite Networking For Dynamite Jobs	$15.95	_____
__ Dynamite Salary Negotiation	$15.95	_____
__ Great Connections	$24.95	_____
__ How to Work a Room	$9.95	_____
__ Interview For Success	$15.95	_____
__ Job Interviews For Dummies	$12.99	_____
__ Power Schmoozing	$12.95	_____
__ Power to Get In	$24.95	_____
__ The Secrets of Savvy Networking	$11.99	_____

SUBTOTAL   _____

Virginia residents add 4½% sales tax   _____

POSTAGE/HANDLING ($5.00 for first
title and 8% of SUBTOTAL over $30)   _____

TOTAL ENCLOSED ---------------------------- _____

SHIP TO:

NAME _____

ADDRESS _____

_____

❑   I enclose check/moneyorder for $ _____ made payable to
     IMPACT PUBLICATIONS.

❑   Please charge $ _____ to my credit card:

     ❑ Visa   ❑ MasterCard   ❑ American Express

     Card # _____

     Expiration date: _____/_____

     Signature _____